Dr. Patel presents a wi[...] American society. The thought-provoking topics offer a basis for discussions and in-depth analysis of modern culture.

- Judith Toscano RN. MSN Clinical System Analyst

I much appreciate how Dr. Patel unpacks her insightful, multinational approach and how it helps her reader gain a bigger picture view on the issues plaguing our collective society today. These are important topics that everyone needs to gain perspective on and to truly think about; I find this work to be timely, educational, and thought provoking.

- Jenifer M Brand, CMRP,
Engineering Development Laboratory Manager

Dr. Patel takes you on a journey exploring the problems exhibited in American families today while offering a historical perspective and positive solutions for change. Her analysis of the workplace provides a look back at the widespread awakening of sexual abuse, discrimination, and the associated legal ramifications. Dr. Patel's sincere interest in analyzing the current, most severe sociological problems in the United States is to bring about change for a more compassionate, intelligent, and forward-thinking society. She attacked every problem with rigorous analysis, and most notably, offered recommendations. Dr. Patel is challenging all of us to reach for a higher standard of civility, morality, and responsibility to ourselves, our families, and our fellow citizens.

- Arthur D. Gottlieb, Retired Queensbury Middle School
Principal, Queensbury, New York

US Unhinged delves into relevant challenges facing society today. Instead of turning to fear tactics, Dr. Patel turns to pragmatism and provides a language for important conversations; understanding how we got here and how we get out. Dr. Patel offers a dialogue rich in research and clinical experience.

- Catherine Kozen, Director Marketing & mom of 2

Dr. Patel's autobiography and perspective of our current American society illustrates and embodies the New American Dream. She is an immigrant from the third world; a woman of color who has faced and overcome immense challenges. Yet has maintained her levelheaded and fair-minded approach to life. For both the young and old, her ideas are a roadmap to acquire skills and achieve a mindset to face and overcome the challenges of our society.

- Paul Miller, Retired teacher

This book is wonderfully insightful, enlightening, frightening, and very sad in places. It has relevance today as it addresses many subjects from a professional, rather than a politically biased, individual's viewpoints. Everyone would benefit from reading it but especially parents. As a grandmother, all parts relating to children resonated with me. As I read the book, I found myself wishing my son and his wife were reading along with me. I gained insight and knowledge with a better understanding of what is happening in our country today. This is a very good book that hopefully, will reach many, many readers.

- Nancy Bray

I found US Unhinged engrossing. This book has so much relevance today. It doesn't matter how talented or rich you believe you are. It's how you treat people. Integrity is everything. I have benefitted greatly from reading this book. I am hoping to be more tolerant and respectful with my daughter and 17-year-old granddaughter, who was adopted from China at the age of 18 months and has a lot of problems. The book made me realize that your life is shaped by the decisions you make and have made, not by the ones you didn't. We all need to adopt a better understanding of people and their problems and appreciate our differences.

- Angela Paporello

I loved it! This is a book I would keep in my night table by my bed. The chapters are self-contained, and it is not necessary to read them in order. I was definitely challenged but felt I agree or have a similar belief system as the author, Dr. Patel. I felt the section on loneliness is very appropriate at this time with social distancing and self-quarantine during the pandemic.

- Gloria Ragonetti

US UNHINGED

Book-2

Understanding the chaos and navigating the turbulence in our society, while learning how to thrive within our family and community today.

An analysis of cultural issues, societal problems, and recommendations for change in America 2020.

Dr. Shila Patel, M.D.

Paperback ISBN: 978-1-7377849-5-1
Ebook ISBN: 978-1-7377849-6-8

Printed on acid-free paper.

US Unhinged Book 2 is printed in Times New Roman.

Library of Congress Cataloguing in Publication Data
Patel, M.D., Dr. Shila
US Unhinged: Book-2 by Dr. Shila Patel, M.D.
Library of Congress Control Number: 2021919793

Dedicated to my Parents

They set a wonderful example and instilled within me
to have compassion for others and improve their lives.

Disclaimer

This book details the author's personal experiences with and opinions about societal problems, relationships, and parenting. The author is not currently a healthcare provider.

The author and publisher are providing this book and its contents on an "as is" basis and make no representations or warranties of any kind with respect to this book or its contents. The author and publisher disclaim all such representations and warranties, including for example warranties of healthcare for a particular purpose. In addition, the author and publisher do not represent or warrant that the information accessible via this book is accurate, complete or current.

The statements made about services have not been evaluated. They are not intended to diagnose, treat, cure, or prevent any condition or disease. Please consult with your own physician or healthcare specialist regarding the suggestions and recommendations made in this book.

Except as specifically stated in this book, neither the author or publisher, nor any authors, contributors, or other representatives will be liable for damages arising out of or in connection with the use of this book. This is a comprehensive limitation of liability that applies to all damages of any kind, including (without limitation) compensatory; direct, indirect, or consequential damages; loss of data, income, or profit; loss of or damage to property and claims of third parties.

You understand that this book is not intended as a substitute for consultation with a licensed healthcare practitioner, such as your physician. Before you begin any healthcare program, or change your lifestyle in any way, you will consult your physician or other licensed healthcare practitioner to ensure that you are in good health and that the examples contained in this book will not harm you.

This book provides content related to topics of physical and/or mental health issues. As such, use of this book implies your acceptance of this disclaimer.

Chapter Summaries

Part 1 –Professional Journey

Introduction
Can we, as Americans, examine the ills that exist today and work together to create a healthier, more compassionate society for tomorrow's citizens? This analysis refers to all people, from the youngest to the oldest, promoting discipline, education, work ethic, family support, physical and mental health care for all, and respect for all human rights. This book is a sociological study of our American society today. It presents a discussion in understanding what has happened in our culture. Why have these beliefs and events transpired? How do we move forward to a more informed, compassionate, and disciplined society?

A Professional Journey
How did I end up practicing as a child, adolescent, and adult psychiatrist? A review of these professional insights is presented. This knowledge has inspired me to examine and offer solutions to the ills of American society that plague us today.

Part 2 – Human Emotions

The Biochemistry of Emotions
Lust, Love, and Attachment

An Emotional Spectrum

A review of how the body functions in response to human emotions is presented. Human behavior revolving around sexual and non-sexual relationships helps us form healthy and productive life partnerships and friendships. There are significant differences between male and female brains that affect our thoughts and experiences. Both physical and psychological studies of the human condition are explored. Topics discussed include:

> Heartbreak
> Loneliness
> How to Deal with Loneliness
> For a Better Marriage, Act Like a Single Person
> Happiness
> Laughter
> Negative Emotions

Part 3 - Enough is Enough - Get Over It

Changing the Culture

What will it take for future generations to change from being self-centered with unrealistic expectations and minimal skills, while experiencing unhealthy emotions, to learn how to acquire the ethics of loyalty, character, and American sacrifice? The focus is on changing our future generations' personal attitudes to transform the inner and outer aspects of their lives. Why did the Black Lives Matter Movement cause so much chaos?

The "Do-Gooders"

Many well-meaning people want to "do the right thing." They propose changes but inflict and propagate their agendas without fully understanding the consequences or ramifications on society. The range of issues includes parenting, the education system, dealing with mental health, gun violence, corporate greed, student debt, climate change, corruption in the government, allocation of funds, religion, end of life decisions, pro-life issues and abortion, marriage, overpopulation, and resource allocation.

Part 4 - Moving Forward

Child Development and Parenting
An understanding of the biological differences in the brains of males and females is presented.

The Raising of Girls and Boys
Historical aspects regarding raising girls and boys are reviewed. Different parenting skills are explored and analyzed, in addition to suggestions on how to bring up an emotionally healthy child.

Last Thoughts to Ponder
It is a challenge to move forward positively, rather than focus on negative aspects of life that leave humans feeling hopeless and pessimistic.

Epilogue: February 2020 in the United States –

The Arrival of a Foreign Visitor, Coronavirus COVID-19

All the cultural issues and problems in American society discussed in the preceding chapters of this book may or may not exist any longer. Our world, as we once knew it, has completely shut down due to the deadly virus, COVID-19.

During the Coronavirus Pandemic of 2020
A comparison of this pandemic to past pandemics: How did this one start? How did the US government and Americans deal with this disaster? How did other countries perform in comparison to the US? What were our shortfalls? How did Americans feel while being challenged by the pandemic? What did people do to assist others?

After the Coronavirus Pandemic of 2020
Lessons learned from other countries dealing with the pandemic are reviewed. Why did the countries with female leaders do better? Why is America #1 in the greatest number of infections and deaths? What is the emotional toll of the pandemic? What do we have to do better as a society? What happened in America due to poor leadership dealing with the pandemic? How should government officials prepare us for such future disasters? How will life change after the pandemic? What were the benefits in climate change due to the pandemic? What will people remember, and who will be affected the most from the pandemic? What will change within us and the US after the pandemic?

Acknowledgements

US UNHINGED
Book-2

Table of Contents

Part 1

Professional Journey

Introduction

Professionally, I understand human behavior, not just because of my training as a psychiatrist, but also from my twenty plus years of experience treating numerous patients (children, men, and women). It is essential to understand my background. I was brought up in a very conservative Indian household until the age of sixteen years old. Then I moved with my family to the United Kingdom and eventually, to the United States. By that time, I was fully indoctrinated into western culture. I had exposure to psychiatric patients during medical school rotations in the United Kingdom, four years of psychiatric training in the United States, followed by private practice, which allowed me the opportunity to understand human behaviors in a variety of dysfunctional situations.

I have always preferred the one-on-one approach to address life issues. However, many current topics are too important to reach solely one individual at a time. It is essential to reach as many people as I can through the written word. I am fearful, as are others in this country that we are losing the principled values upon which this country was established. Children need to learn discipline.

The anger and racial divide, fueled by politicians who cannot agree on anything and continue to tear at the fabric of American society has unhinged the US. It has made us appear weak, undisciplined, and a laughingstock for others around the globe. Culture refers to the shared attitudes and actions of a particular social group. Social media has created a "Cancel Culture," in the form of group shaming. It refers to the popular practice of withdrawing support for (canceling) public figures and companies after they have done or said something considered objectionable or offensive.[1] People must be held accountable for their actions and behavior, and receive the consequences when they break the rules of society and decency. However, many young people have no knowledge of the history of this country or what their predecessors had to endure to make America the country it is today. They want to rewrite history without even knowing what it is, other than the headlines or few words spread on social media as the gospel truth. When did Facebook and Twitter and other social media outlets become judge and jury, causing many individuals to lose their careers, reputations, or work opportunities after being outed?

Other figures were getting canceled for past racist and anti-LGBTQ remarks.[2]Students were trying to get a professor from the University of Chicago fired because of the remarks he made, but after an investigation by the staff at the University, he was reinstated. Some staff members at Hachette Publishing refused to work on J.K. Rowling's next book after she was smeared as being a "transphobic." She had made a comment about women and her publisher spoke up for her stating "Freedom of speech is the cornerstone of publishing." Social media allows all sorts of freedom of speech, but the cancel culture has gone too far. Critics of canceling feel that people are too quick to judge and ruin lives over mistakes made recently or from many years ago, without knowing all the facts. It has become a way of rejecting anyone you disagree with or someone who did something you did not like. People do not get a second chance. Former President Barack Obama argued that rash social media judgments do not amount to true social activism. The solution is to challenge these people, and those of us who can, must speak up.

I believe in being tolerant and forgiving to individuals who have hurt me. Remaining angry and unforgiving only hurts yourself. You have to take full responsibility for your mistakes, accept the consequences, and learn from those experiences. You must accept disappointments and not dwell on them. You have to focus on working hard in order to succeed. Do not be complacent with mediocre work. It is important to always show appreciation to those individuals who have assisted you in your personal and professional life. You must take care of yourself, including your physical, mental, and spiritual well-being. You should remember often to reach out to your parents and elders who sacrificed throughout their lifetime to enrich your life. Most parents do their best to meet the needs of their children but obviously some fall short. Sadly, these may turn out to be the children that become society's problems. Most of all, be happy with your family and what you have accomplished in life. Surround yourself with positive people to enjoy and celebrate the various milestones and rewards in your life. Work on being an excellent role model with integrity to influence others. Be strong enough to deal with negative peer pressure and stand up to bullies. Become involved in your community to assist others. Take charge of your own life and destiny!

The ideas put forth in this book are my beliefs, in addition to the views of other individuals, results from documented studies and academic articles. I hope my presentation challenges you to look at human behavior from a different perspective. I want to provoke discussions about the issues of gun violence, parenting, childrearing, the damage that social media is inflicting, and other societal vows. My hope is that this book will provide you with an understanding of human behavior and tolerance. It expresses different viewpoints about stressful situations in our society. I am asking you to be open-minded and to believe in forgiveness. It is time to contemplate the direction our country is taking. It is up to all of us to make our world a better place.

A Professional Journey

Recently, when I sat down and thought about why I became a psychiatrist, memories from my childhood while living in Africa came back to me. I remember my father carrying me out of the movie theater; I was crying and disturbing the audience. The movie included fight scenes where people were getting hurt. Traditional Indian Bollywood movies always depicted brawling. There were also news clips before the main feature. At that time, there was news about the war between India and China. "The two countries were fighting over the Aksai-Chin region at the northernmost section of India, part of the Kashmir region covering almost fifteen thousand square miles. The Chinese had built a military road through the territory. The Indian government had discovered this road and strongly objected to its presence. This incident led to extreme border clashes between the two countries."[3] Ironically 65 years later, since May 5, 2020, Chinese and Indian troops have engaged in aggressive, face-offs and skirmishes at locations along the Sino-Indian border, including near the disputed Pangong Lake in Ladakh and the Tibet Autonomous Region, and near the border between Sikkim and the Tibet Autonomous Region.[4] I was too young to understand the concept of war, but I recall those frightening images even today. I was a sensitive child. From a young age, watching someone being injured, was very upsetting to me.

During my teenage years, I was quiet and melancholy. I always listened to 'The Carpenters' and 'Simon and Garfunkel's Greatest Hits.' 'Bridge Over Troubled Waters' was one of my favorite songs. And Karen Carpenter had one of the saddest voices in the pop industry in the 1970s. She died in 1983 after losing a battle with anorexia nervosa.[5] Their music reflected my mood at the time.

While in high school, Indian movies were the main form of entertainment. Indian fathers ruled their families, and their subservient daughters had to obey or face severe consequences. When coming of age, they were not allowed to date or interact with males in any capacity. Most movies depicted a couple falling in love, and both sets of their parents would strongly object and forbid them to marry. Either their parents had already formalized a marital arrangement for their children, or the parents considered the partner to be unacceptable due to association with the wrong social class. After a lot of drama and crying, the young woman would get married in a traditional Indian wedding, only to be poorly treated by her in-laws. The young couple lived with the husband's family. The woman rarely spoke up, tolerated the injustice, and was expected to accept this role in Indian society. Looking back, I wonder if subconsciously, I felt that this was also my future destiny. These thoughts may have contributed to my sadness. Even then, I had a deep-rooted desire to change the way Indian society treated women. Sixty years later, many television shows depict the same scenarios. My overly sensitive nature from childhood may have contributed to take on social injustices as an adult. In my profession, I assisted both women and children in building resilience and going against the norm. I taught them a skillset to learn how to think for themselves, and not be heavily influenced by any unjust rules of society.

Personality is formed at a young age, but situations in life can assist in molding you into the person you become. I did not want to be a weak, dependent woman. As a teenager and until I attended medical school, I responded to situations in a very subservient way. I was exploited and abused; I did not stand up for myself. My best friend in high school experienced similar issues. She tried to commit suicide by jumping off our tall condominium building. Her father had discovered that she was dating a Muslim boy; she was Hindu. There has always been an intense rivalry between the two religious sects. Hindus and Muslims believe in two different religious philosophies with social customs and literary traditions. They neither intermarry nor eat together, and indeed they belong to two different civilizations which are based mainly on conflicting ideas and conceptions.[6] I do not know how my girlfriend survived. I decided to pursue a career to heal individuals with destructive behaviors. My parents wanted all three of us to be educated and obtain a college degree. Most Indian families wanted their daughters married at a young age.

Before starting medical school, I became friends with a coworker during the summer holidays. He attended the same medical school in St. Andrews. Unfortunately, during our last year, he started showing symptoms of major depression. He was unable to get out of bed or attend classes. He had a family history of bipolar disorder. He did not graduate with our class. When our class continued our clinical rotations in Manchester, England, he joined us a year later. However, he continued to suffer from depression, and eventually, dropped out of medical school. He moved back to London to live with his family. It has been a challenging road for him, but with medications, he was able to become an accountant. Throughout the years, we have remained close friends. His mental health struggles influenced me greatly in my medical profession as a psychiatrist. He inspired me and helped me realize that a significant illness does not have to destroy your life. The right treatment and support can lead to a productive life and career. During my practice, I reminded myself often of his battle to survive and find normalcy. I found myself working more diligently with my patients to reach an optimal level of functioning to achieve their life goals.

In England, doctors tend to use more counseling and social services rather than medications for psychiatric patients. In the United States, we use more medicines for depression, anxiety, sleep disorders, and attention deficit disorders with or without hyperactivity in children. In my second year of rotations in Manchester, we had a three-month elective and could choose to practice outside of England. I decided to go to Florida where my family was living. I trained with an excellent pediatrician. This experience was an eye-opener. Out-patient pediatrics involved a lot of crying babies, health check-ups, immunizations, colds, and sometimes, challenging parents. In England, the pediatric rotation was in a hospital setting where there is more control over the patients and parents. Babies get sick quickly and can become extremely ill. Treating dying babies is traumatic enough but learning how to console a grieving family over the death of their child is overwhelming. I knew that this field of medicine would be tough for me even though I had planned on pursuing a career as a pediatrician.

Fortunately, I had an opportunity to work with a child psychiatrist for a few weeks during this elective period. He was very enthusiastic about his work. I began to drift toward this specialty. After the elective term, I returned to England to finish my last year of medical school before graduating. The following year, I completed a one-year internship to register as a doctor in the United Kingdom. Following that period, Bipin and I moved to the United States. Bipin received an offer for a residency slot in neurology at the Medical College of Georgia. I interviewed with the psychiatric department at the same college and was presented with an opportunity to start a residency program the following year.

For the first six months, I trained at Georgia Regional Hospital where we treated the indigent and most psychotic patients. These experiences taught me to become very efficient with paperwork, how to manage a heavy workload, and how to treat acutely psychotic patients with proper medication. In the United States, we had access to newer medicines in comparison to the older ones used in the United Kingdom. The next several rotations were at the VA hospital working with PTSD patients, evaluating disabilities, and treating patients in the outpatient clinic. I also worked in the hospital setting where we treated patients with severe psychiatric conditions. The most interesting cases that required treatment were patients with multiple personality disorders. *"Sybil, The True Story of a Woman Possessed by 16 Separate Personalities"* is the most famous case of an individual with this severe condition.[7] We learned how to use ECT, electroconvulsive therapy. This practice may seem primitive, but the catatonic patient is physically frozen, unable to eat or drink. Usually, after treatment, the patient can function again. One has to believe that these measures are necessary for the patient's survival. Severely depressed and suicidal patients, and others, who were unresponsive to prescribed medications, also received ECT.

Training was comprehensive and included treatment modalities like psychoanalysis used by Freud and Jung to help patients understand their behaviors, and the use of behavior and cognitive therapy with individuals, couples, and families. Psychopharmacology was taught to learn how medications could help stabilize the patients' chemical imbalances. We also received instruction on how to conduct and interpret psychological testing and analyze studies. The residents were expected to participate in group therapy with others in training. We were required to work through some of our personal issues, so they would not interfere with the treatment of our future patients.

The next two years of my medical training were dedicated to child and adolescent psychiatry fellowship. I again started my training at Georgia Regional Hospital where court-mandated children and adolescents were evaluated, pending their court hearings. We learned how to treat these children, earn their trust, and make recommendations for the court system. Most of the children in this facility were from poor socio-economic backgrounds. The different conditions that brought them into the hospital were depression, being suicidal, aggressive, unwilling to attend school, or addicted to drugs. The last six months of my training was the most exciting. I had the opportunity to work at a new Charter Hospital in Georgia, which offered in- patient treatment for only children and adolescents. Together with several of my peers, nurses, and counseling staff, we established policies and procedures for patient treatment, with the approval of our supervising physicians. Within three months of opening, the new hospital was close to full capacity.

Upon completion of my training, I moved to Valdosta, Georgia, the location of my husband's medical practice. I joined a psychiatric office with attending rights at a near-by private psychiatric hospital. By the time I retired twenty years later, many of the hospitals, including the Charter Hospital, had closed due to financial issues. Insurance companies were not providing sufficient reimbursement for services rendered by medical facilities. It became challenging to treat children in a hospital setting. In most areas of the country, the only option for children and adolescents to receive psychiatric care was on an out-patient basis.

In the early years of my practice, I had a most challenging patient, a five-year-old from an active-duty Air Force family. She was extremely oppositional; she acted out at home and in school. After receiving individual and family therapy, medications, even short periods of hospitalization to gain insight into her behavior of extreme rage, she did not improve. Finally, I sent her for long-term residential treatment. She was at the center for several months, and then, was treated in our out-patient care. Within a month of returning from the residential treatment program, she killed her younger brother. It was truly shocking. To this day, I cannot state the cause of her extreme hostility. She was sent to a juvenile facility, and I never heard of what became of her. This case highlighted the fact that we never know whether it is nature versus nurture when young children commit a horrendous crime.

In our society, we are used to instant gratification. We use more medications than are required for treatment. Many psychiatric patients have been suffering emotional turmoil for years. The moment they seek help, they want to start feeling better instantly. It takes time for the medication to provide relief, and to gain insight through therapy to change thought processes and individual behavior. Young girls would come to my office for therapy and lay down on my couch in the office. They were imitating what they saw on television or in the movies where patients visited their psychiatrists for psychoanalysis. I learned that the right medications and behavior therapy moved a case along more rapidly. Most children and their parents did not have the luxury of waiting months for behaviors to improve. Insurance companies had a limit on how much they paid for therapy and psychiatric care. Mental health reimbursement costs have always been a low priority for most insurance companies. With all the evidence that many psychiatric conditions require help from professionals, insurance companies limit coverage or do not offer any at all.

There are numerous studies that quote figures on lost income and revenues for individuals and businesses due to mental health problems of their employees. Rather than putting pressure on insurance companies to provide coverage, Americans have been passive and do not get the help when they need it. The mental health toll from the pandemic is going to be horrendous. Without appropriate resources, and adequate help, there will be major fall out and unnecessary suffering.

I found providing therapy rewarding when treating patients. It helped them understand the source of their turmoil or dysfunction. I evaluated a young girl who was psychotic. She presented with symptoms of schizophrenia. After establishing a trusting relationship with her, she was able to verbalize that her issues stemmed from her stepfather sexually abusing her. Once she started talking about these problems, her psychotic symptoms cleared up, and she was hopeful about her future. Her mother divorced the stepfather. Hopefully, the young girl would never be sexually abused again. This is a classic case of someone remaining dysfunctional without getting the appropriate care.

In 2018, Sally Field wrote about the sexual abuse she received from her stepfather. She felt so alone, and it left deep psychological scars in her.[8] She became a very successful actress. The challenge, as always, is not to be controlled by the traumatic events in your life. In time, working with a therapist and developing a bond of trust, a patient can take charge, recover from the abuse, and move forward to lead a productive life. It is essential to understand that psychiatric treatment requires time for healing to begin. It is not like surgery or curing an illness with antibiotics. Often, medications are administered, in addition to one-on-one therapy with a psychiatrist or therapist. As physicians, we hope that the interventions we administer result in long-term wellness.

In the office where I practiced as a psychiatrist, two social workers also acted as staff administrators. During one weekend on a Saturday, I went to the office to pick up some paperwork. One of the male administrators was in his office with an adult female patient. The office rules mandated that no doctor or therapist should be alone with a patient of the opposite sex to protect the staff from any legal ramifications. When the therapist and the female patient came out of his office, they both appeared uncomfortable. The next day I posted an article on the office bulletin board addressing the illegality for therapists to be sexually involved with their patients. Shortly after that event, several other women in the clinic reported their involvement with this therapist. I encouraged the women to report him. An investigation ensued; he was arrested and sent to jail. He also lost his license to practice as a social worker.

During my last year working in that practice, one of my patients was murdered. At the time, she had been an in-patient at the hospital but was permitted a therapeutic leave. She never returned to the hospital. The next morning, I received a call from her therapist, to inform me that this patient had been found dead in her car. Her murder was never solved.

At this time, our clinic had five physicians and five therapists. Instead of expenses decreasing, they kept increasing. Eventually, we figured out that the administrator had been embezzling our funds for his own expenses before he went to jail. Medical training does not include courses in business management. As physicians, we know how to care for patients, but are not skilled in accounting. With all the bad decisions within the practice, I decided to leave and open my own office. It involved finding an office, hiring staff, and setting up a new billing system with the insurance companies. I was fortunate to find an office manager who had experience. Three other professionals from the other office joined me. Within six months of our departure from the former medical practice, that office closed. They were not able to meet the office expenses. Fortunately, all our patients followed us to our new location. By the time I retired eleven years later, I was able to sell my share in the practice and receive a return on my investment. Looking back, I wish I had the confidence to venture out on my own much earlier in my career.

For fifteen years, I worked long hours, seven days a week when I was in town. I made rounds daily to see my-patients in the hospital. After five years, I was the only child and adolescent psychiatrist in the hospital. As the only female psychiatrist, often, even when I was not on call, the staff called me to take patients who requested a female doctor. During my last two years of practice, I decided that I could not continue working at that pace. I gave up working in the hospital and focused on treating out-patients. Many low-income women were bringing their children into the office, insisting that I diagnose them with a mental health illness. With a diagnosis, they would be eligible to receive additional disability income. The mothers were extremely irresponsible, having multiple children with different men, and trying to increase their family income through fraudulent medical claims. In most cases, it was a grandmother who cared for the children full-time, not their mother. My tolerance was low, and it was difficult for me to be empathetic with these women. I understood what they were trying to do. Sadly, they involved their children, and consequently, they suffered emotionally. After twenty years in psychiatry, I was ready to retire. It was a dilemma for me because there was not another child and adolescent psychiatrist practicing in our community. There were also, many changes occurring in the medical industry regarding insurance reimbursements, record management, and financial compensation from Medicare and Medicaid.

A report on NBC news questioned why physicians were leaving medical practices to pursue other careers.[9] Becoming a doctor remains one of the most challenging career paths that you can choose. It requires years of education, which is expensive. After medical school, a future doctor must obtain a residency before earning an income. Generally, all this hard work should pay off, not only financially, but also, in terms of job satisfaction and a work-life balance. There are personal benefits from helping people and saving lives. So, the question is why is there a decreased interest in pursuing a career in medicine? The Association of American Medical Colleges projected a shortage of 42,600 to 121,300 physicians by 2030.[10] There appear to be two main reasons why individuals are not entering into the field of medicine. Young people today are less interested in pursuing medical careers with the rise of STEM (science, technology, engineering, and mathematics) professions. Millennials are more interested in living in urban areas. Straight out of medical school, it is doubtful that the residency program will be in a city. Another concerning issue is the lack of available residency programs for recent medical school graduates. My nephew had to wait two years before he was accepted into a residency program. He worked for free an entire year shadowing other doctors and demonstrating that he was worthy of a residency slot. He was just about ready to give up, but his parents and grandmother kept him afloat financially.

You cannot practice medicine unless you have completed a residency program. There should be a reallocation of funds to residency programs that are now being used to train Physician Assistants (PAs) and Nurse Practitioners (NPs). Although they perform like physicians, they do not have a formal medical school or residency training. During annual physicals at a doctor's office, physician assistants and nurse practitioners are performing these examinations and even evaluating new patients. Unfortunately, the lay public is unaware of this vast difference in medical training.

Many doctors are retiring earlier than expected due to the requirement of electronic health records (EHRs). Old school doctors have not kept up with computer technology. Stanford Medicine Research found that 59% think EHRs "need a complete overhaul," while 40% see "more challenges with EHRs than benefits."[11] Doctors are overwhelmed by the paperwork, reporting to insurance companies for verification of treatment, and the denial of treatment for patients. Individuals are making decisions without any medical training. It is a disheartening situation. Today, thousands of doctors have closed their practices to join community-based health networks of medical professionals under one organization. The company administers and negotiates all business operating expenses and patient billing services.

There has always been a shortage of child and adolescent psychiatrists. It requires two more years of training after four years of adult psychiatric training.[12] Monetary issues, such as medical school debt and low resident salaries prevent many future psychiatrists from completing this specialty. Much to the surprise of many of my colleagues, I retired at an earlier age than most doctors. My work was challenging. I never regretted my career choice. We spend a third of our lives working. Hopefully you can enjoy what you do. Unfortunately, with the help of lawyers in this country, doctors are seen as 'deep pockets'. I was never sued and wanted to leave with a clean slate when I was financially set for my retirement. I also wanted to focus on my health and wellness and provide care for my aging parents, who were becoming frail.

When I look back on my career, I hope to have made a difference in the lives of at least one out of ten patients whom I treated. In knowing that, I feel I have succeeded in my profession. Working with children, they needed someone to listen and give them the courage to heal and lead a productive life, no matter what their family circumstances were. We cannot choose our parents who gave birth to us. However, we can find a great source of strength from other individuals who reach out to us and provide us the support needed.

Lastly, here are the profound thoughts of an unknown 24-year-old young man dying of cancer before he passed away.

- I would not waste your time on work that you do not enjoy. *It is obvious that you cannot succeed in something that you do not like.* Patience, passion, and dedication come easily only when you love what you do.

- Take control of your life. Take full responsibility for the things that happen to you.

- Limit bad habits and try to lead a healthier life. Find a sport that makes you happy. Most of all, do not procrastinate. *Let your life be shaped by the decisions you made, not by the ones you did not.*

- We care so much about the health and integrity of our body that until death, we don't notice that the body is nothing more than a box, a parcel for delivering our personality, thoughts, beliefs, and intentions to this world. If there is nothing in this box that can change the world, then it does not matter if it disappears. I believe that we all have potential, but it also takes a lot of courage to realize it.

- You can float through a life created by circumstances, missing day after day, hour after hour, *or you can fight for what you believe in and write the great story of your life.* I hope you will make the right choice.

- Appreciate the people around you. Your friends and relatives will always be an infinite source of strength and love. That is why you shouldn't take them for granted."[13]

> *"Your work is going to fill a large part of your life, and the only way to be truly satisfied is to do what you believe is great work. And the only way to do great work is to love what you do."*[14]
>
> *Steve Jobs*

Part 2

Human Emotions

The Biochemistry of Emotions
Lust, Love, and Attachment

Read this chapter if you are interested in understanding how the body works. We are a machine with an amazing capacity to function and create, but it also has flaws. We all have an expiration date, but how we use this machine in our lifespan is up to each individual.

Numerous studies have been performed to understand the sexual response in human beings. We are, after all, sophisticated machines with brains wired differently and plumbing systems that function at a personal rate. We have automatic responses in our bodies whether we like it or not. Pupils dilate, our mouth goes dry, male sexual organs engorge, women experience lubrication even when they are not expecting to have sex. Men experience erections without any sexual thoughts which are entirely beyond their control.

A "normal male" thinks of sex nineteen times a day. Women have similar thoughts ten times a day, according to a study done by Terri Fisher & her research team at Ohio State University.[15] This study was conducted in November 2011 and published in *The Journal of Sex Research*. These thought patterns vary wildly between people, and within the same person, depending on circumstances. There are myths that males think about sex every seven seconds. We can dismiss this idea. Men would never be able to get any work done with that constant distraction. Thoughts cannot be measured like distance. "They are responses to stimuli that are either intrinsic (arising from within), or extrinsic (arising from the environment). Thought or thinking is considered to mediate between inner activity and external stimuli."[16]

Throughout the ages, men and women have been attracted to each other physically, which sets off chemical reactions in the body and the brain. Love is the most exhilarating of all human emotions and is nature's way of keeping the human species alive and reproducing. Love is said to be the master key which opens the gate to happiness. Our brains entice us to fall in love. It is a very primitive emotion. We smile in private moments, thinking about the ones we have loved. Do we fall out of love, or do our feelings change? If you genuinely loved someone, you want what is best for them, and want them to be happy. You want to cherish your special memories and make peace with the individual who chose to end the relationship.

"Remember that the best relationship is one in which your love for each other exceeds your need for each other."[17]

Dalai Lama

New York Psychologist, Professor Arthur Arun has been studying the dynamics of what happens when people fall in love. "He has shown that it takes between ninety seconds and four minutes to decide if you fancy someone. Fifty-five percent of the decision is arrived at through body language, thirty-eight percent is the tone and speed of the voice, and only seven percent is from what is said. Falling in love can hit you hard in mind and body."[18] You feel irresistibly attracted to the person of your choice. You may feel a rush of euphoria. You feel you have met a unique individual, "your soulmate." Excitement wanes over time. However, if you retain the good feelings, once the novelty wears off, a warm, nurturing feeling takes effect. Your brain chemistry explains all these emotions. Neurotransmitters are set in motion when you are attracted to another person. Helen Fisher, an anthropology professor from Rutgers University, has proposed three stages of love: lust, attraction, and attachment.[19] Dr. Melanie Greenberg discussed how different hormones and chemicals within our bodies drive these various stages.[20]

In Stage 1, lust is driven by the sex hormones testosterone and estrogen in both men and women. This strong sexual desire could be the reason why stress, sex, and rape are so interconnected. It is the body's automatic response to get relief when highly aroused from life events. They can be war experiences, fear of dying, or even an incredibly stressful day at work. Historically, pillaging a village and raping women were part of the "bounty" when the victors won the battle and the enemies suffered defeat. This strong sexual desire can bring serious, ethical problems when acted upon inappropriately. Most people do not act on these feelings without considering the serious consequences. Apparently, in the past, many men did not consider the results of their sexual actions seriously. Today, most people do not act on these feelings without considering the consequences. The #MeTooMovement has awakened society's consciousness to stand up against sexual abuse, harassment, and assault.[21]

In Stage 2, an attraction for another individual is extraordinarily strong. It is as if you are "love- struck." Anyone who has fallen in love understands the changes that the body experiences: lack of sleep, constant thoughts of the person, lack of appetite, and the inability to concentrate on anything else. Scientists believe that the three main neurotransmitters in this stage of attraction are adrenalin, dopamine, and serotonin.[22] The initial phase of "falling in love with someone" activates the stress response by increasing the blood levels of adrenalin and cortisol. You will experience increased sweating, a racing heart, and a dry mouth. Dopamine stimulates "desire and reward" by triggering an intense rush of pleasure. By the way, taking the drug cocaine produces the same effect. This chemical in your body heightens your energy level, also decreases your appetite, and need for sleep.

Serotonin regulates your mood, social behavior, memory, and sexual desire, in addition to your appetite and sleep. When you are in love, you are constantly thinking of your partner. In most cases, individuals who are in love are not depressed. One of the reasons why people become depressed is a lack of serotonin. Love changes the way you think. "The person's virtues are magnified while his or her flaws are explained away," noted Ellen Berscheid, a leading researcher on the psychology of love.[23] This compulsion to view our beloved through rose-colored glasses compels us to stay together and enter the next phase of falling in-love, attachment.

In Stage 3, couples develop a strong bond that unites them and encourages them to have a family and raise children together. Scientists think that there are two major hormones influencing couples during this stage: oxytocin and vasopressin. "Oxytocin is a hormone that acts on the organs in the body, including the breast and the uterus, and as a chemical messenger in the brain, controlling key aspects of the reproductive system, including childbirth and lactation, and aspects of human behavior."[24] Vasopressin is a peptide hormone formed in the hypothalamus. It maintains the fluid volume by regulating the renal handling of water, leading to an increase of blood volume, cardiac output, and arterial pressure.[25] These hormones play a role in sexual behaviors, social recognition, and stress response. Men and women release oxytocin during orgasm. It deepens the feelings of attachment. The more sex a couple has, the deeper their bond becomes. Vasopressin is also released after sex and increases the commitment stage. Professor Arthur Arun has been studying why people fall in love. "He asks his subjects to carry out three simple steps to fall in love:

1.) Find a complete stranger.

2.) Reveal to each other intimate details about your lives for half an hour.

3.) Then, stare deeply into each other's eyes while talking for four minutes."[26]

At the end of this experiment, many of the individuals felt deeply attracted to their partner. Starring into each other's eyes and talking intimately to one another creates a deep connection.

"Time decides who you meet in life. Your heart decides who you want in your life. Your behavior decides who stays in your life."[27]

Ziad K. Abdelnour

An Emotional Spectrum
Heartbreak

"It is a dull sensation, your heart breaking, like the sound of a pebble dropping on the sand. Not a shattering, not a tearing apart, there is nothing grandiose about the sensation. It is merely an internal realization that something treasured, you never knew you had, is leaving forever."[28]
Samantha Bruce-Benjamin, The Art of Devotion

People change for two main reasons. New experiences and relationships have opened their minds, or their hearts have been broken. Let us look at the biochemistry of how heartbreak hurts your physical and mental health. What causes the pounding headache, fatigue, dark circles under the eyes, sleeplessness, weight gain or loss, and overall ability to think clearly? The natural, feel- good chemicals of dopamine and oxytocin decrease in the body. They are replaced by a steady release of the stress hormones, cortisol, and epinephrine.

In small doses, the stress hormones are needed, ensuring that we respond quickly and effectively to any threat or danger. In terms of long-term distress, these hormones accumulate and cause physical symptoms. Too much cortisol in the brain sends blood to the major muscle groups. They tense up, ready to respond to the threat (the fight or flight syndrome). However, without a real need for a physical response, the muscles have no opportunity to expend this energy. Muscles swell, causing headaches, a stiff neck, and you feel like your chest is being squeezed. Cortisol diverts blood away from the digestive system to ensure that the rest of the muscles in the body have enough blood. This effect can cause stomach trouble such as cramps, diarrhea, or appetite loss. When there is an excess of stress hormones, the immune system is compromised and increase your vulnerability to infection. Other physical changes that can occur include skin breakouts like acne and hair loss.

A steady release of cortisol might cause sleep problems and interfere with the capacity to make sound judgments. Emotional breakups activate the area of your brain that processes cravings and addictions. Suffering the loss of a relationship can cause you to experience withdrawal symptoms, which is why it is so difficult to function. With a partner, your mind and body adjust to being intimately connected to someone. When you separate from one another, the brain must readjust. The pain can be relentless, but eventually, the body chemistry will change back to normal, and the hurt feelings will diminish.

Recovering from a breakup can be as much a physical process as an emotional one. A study by Helen Fisher and her research team found activity in the part of the brain that also registers physical pain during emotional breakups. "While no one has yet studied what exactly goes on in the chest during moments of heartbreak, that might account for the physical pain, results from fMRI (functional Magnetic Resonance Imaging) study of heartbroken individuals indicate that when the subjects looked at and discussed their rejecter, they trembled, cried, sighed, and got angry, and in their brains these emotions triggered activity in the same area associated with physical pain. So, when you say you're 'hurt' as a result of being rejected by someone close to you, as far as your brain is concerned, the pain you feel is no different from a stab wound."[29] Tylenol has been shown to reduce emotional pain.

The American Heart Association explains that your blood pressure may increase temporarily with stress. An individual who already has high blood pressure could suffer a hypertensive crisis. "When your blood pressure is too high for too long, it damages your blood vessels. LDL (bad) cholesterol begins to accumulate along with tears in your artery walls. The workload of your circulatory system increases while its efficiency decreases."[30] "In broken heart syndrome, there is a temporary disruption of your heart's normal pumping function in one area of the heart. The remainder of the heart functions normally or with even more forceful contractions due to a surge of stress hormones."[31] The heart changes shape as the left ventricle weakens, causing it to balloon out. These symptoms can mimic a heart attack, but an electrocardiogram could confirm if you suffered an actual heart attack. These symptoms can be treated. Generally, the condition usually reverses itself within days or weeks. This condition is rare.

Loneliness

"It is not what we have in life, but who we have in our life that matters."[32]

J.M. Lawrence

Since human beings are not meant to be islands to themselves, let us look at what loneliness does to the human body. Researchers define loneliness as "the perceived discrepancy between one's desired level and their actual level of social connection."[33] Some people who are socially isolated don't necessarily feel lonely. Some lonely people are surrounded by people who make them feel more alienated, not less.

Daniel Russell and his colleagues at UCLA created a standardized test to measure people's loneliness.[34] For forty years, the UCLA Loneliness Scale has become a valuable tool in studying what is now being called an epidemic in some western countries. The United Kingdom announced a new government position in 2018, the Minister for Loneliness.[35] Last year, there was a report released declaring over nine million British adults who reported being "often or always lonely."[36]

Research is scarce in the United States. A 2012 study in the Social Science and Medicine Journal by Ye Luo, Ph.D., Louise Hawkley, Ph.D. and John Cacioppo, Ph.D. reported that between twenty and forty-three percent of American adults over the age of fifty years old experienced "frequent or intense" loneliness.[37] Lonely workers take twice as many sick days and demonstrate less commitment and weaker performance. Their emotions can spread to others, as well, causing a ripple effect throughout an organization. "Technology has created the illusion that workers are connected, when in reality they feel isolated, lonely, disengaged, and less committed to their organizations"[38] This high percentage of lonely people is likely to put a strain on national productivity and the health care systems. Depression is estimated to cause 200 million lost workdays each year at a cost to employers of $17 to $44 billion.[39] Prolonged loneliness can put a person at risk for chronic health care conditions, exacerbate various health conditions and ultimately, increase the risk for premature death.

Some of the health conditions that lonely people are most likely to have:

1.) High blood pressure and cardiovascular disease – These effects are frequently attributed to cortisol, the stress hormone. Chronic high blood pressure leads to hypertension, a risk factor for heart disease.

2.) Reduced immunity – Lonely people can be more susceptible to illness. Their bodies do not produce the same amount of antibodies as compared to non-lonely people. Stress hormones with other peptides secreted from the brain may affect the distribution and function of the white blood cells. These cells protect the body from infection and disease. The Covid-19 pandemic may have put these individuals more at risk, especially people in nursing homes.

3.) Inflammation – People experiencing loneliness are especially susceptible to chronic inflammation which is involved in a wide array of health issues, like Alzheimer's, certain cancers, rheumatoid arthritis, clogged arteries, heart disease, and periodontitis.

4.) Poor sleep – Lonely people take longer to fall asleep, sleep for a shorter amount of time, and suffer from daytime dysfunction. Sleep-deprived people are more likely to have a lower glucose tolerance which sometimes leads to Type 2 diabetes. Impaired sleep also diminishes nightly restorative processes. A build-up of brain toxins is removed nightly during REM (Rapid Eye Movement - dream stage) sleep.

How to Deal with Loneliness

*"The tragedy of life is not the deathbed but
what we let die inside of us while we live."* [40]

Norman Cousins

Risk factors leading to loneliness should be identified. For example, hearing loss causes social isolation. If you cannot hear, it is hard to be part of a conversation and there is a tendency to feel more alienated. Insurance companies or makers of these hearing aids need to offer them at a more affordable price, especially for the elderly. Assessing the risk of loneliness and loneliness-related issues should be part of medical training. All doctors need to communicate to patients how to prevent self-imposed isolation and encourage them to take it seriously as part of a healthy lifestyle. Unfortunately, doctors cannot help their patients if they are too ashamed or embarrassed to admit that they are lonely. Many people have issues with social problems, or even worse, suffer from social anxiety and phobia. Schools need to develop a curriculum in social education, like teachers and coaches instruct physical education. Children need to receive instruction about good relationships and why social interactions are so crucial to your health. It is essential to learn how to be a good friend. They need to learn to respect everyone whether they like them or not. Just like being physically active, we need to be socially active.

*"Good friends help you find important things
when you have lost them – your smile, your
hope, your courage."*[41]

Doe Zantamata

Professor Claude Fisher, a sociology professor at UCLA Berkeley reported in a five-year study, "Understanding How Personal Networks Change," that even though adults between the ages of twenty-one and thirty had more extensive social networks, they felt lonely or socially isolated twice as many days in comparison to adults between the ages of fifty and seventy years old.[42]

During an interview, Dr. Sanjay Gupta, a neurosurgeon, stated that even a simple gesture like saying 'hello' to a stranger or cashier when checking out in a store is like CPR for the brain.[43] Sending an email or text is not enough. Speaking directly to someone helps to decrease the trauma of loneliness. Pick up the phone and call someone whom you can talk to if you are suffering from the symptoms of loneliness.

Many dating and meeting sites are available on the Internet. A website exists for almost every ethnicity, religious background, and sexual orientation. If someone is seeking to have an arranged marriage within a particular ethnicity, there are marriage online websites. The Internet provides an excellent way to communicate with other individuals without going to a bar or a club to seek companionship. With any dating website, you must be aware of fake online profiles. Most sites receive a rating for the accuracy and validity of the information provided. Single, wealthy men tend to use sites like "sugardaddie.com" to find a companion. Women often receive financial compensation and career assistance. Staff members carefully examine every submitted profile. "Not only does Sugardaddie.com get recognized as a millionaire dating site, but they also give sound dating advice to people looking to hook up. The company has a quality staff to ensure that the experience remains top notch."[44]

Joining book clubs and reading circles at your local library offer an excellent opportunity to meet people. At many condominium complexes, game nights are scheduled. You will find bridge and canasta groups. You would be surprised at the number of individuals who attend these events. If you have a religious affiliation with a church, synagogue, or mosque, many opportunities are available to meet and interact with people. Volunteering for various community organizations is another way to meet people, and at the same time, you can truly make a difference by offering your professional service.

"An invisible red thread connects those who are destined to meet, regardless of time, place and circumstances. The thread may stretch or tangle, but it will never break."[45]

Ancient Chinese Proverb

For a Better Marriage, Act Like a Single Person

"Don't depend too much on anyone in this world because even your own shadow leaves you when you are in darkness."[46]

Ibn Taymiyyah

Stephanie Coontz is the Director of Research and Public Education for the Council on Contemporary Families and Emeritus Faculty of History and Family Studies at The Evergreen State College in Olympia, Washington, in addition to an author of five books on gender, family and marriage. She was quoted in a New York Times article that your soulmate is no substitute for a social life. In a marital or couple relationship, it is vital for both spouses or partners also to have their own social life.[47] "Maintaining social networks and self-reliance after marriage does far more than protect you against depression and ensures against the worst outcomes of divorce or widowhood. It can also enhance and even revitalize your marriage."[48]

In this era, when both partners in a relationship are working outside the home, they are spending more time apart. It is essential to acquire skills as individuals to be successful. Whether you are single, with a partner, or married, there are significant personal rewards to be gained by fostering independence. "The reality is, 110.6 million Americans ages 18 or older (or 45.2 percent) are single, according to data from the U.S. Census Bureau—a number that's been rising since 2015. People are staying single longer than ever before. In 2018, the highest median ages ever for a first marriage were reported: 30 years for men and 28 years for women."[49] This statistic lowers the risk of getting a divorce. Most divorces occur in individuals between the ages of 20 and 24 years old. 24.6 percent get divorced between the age of 25 and 39. Couples are getting married later in life. Individuals have reached their educational goals, achieved career and financial stability, have developed life skills such as managing a budget, learning to cook, and acquiring some skills at completing household repairs.

Single people have more extensive social networks than married couples, who tend to rely on each other for companionship. They interact more with friends, neighbors, co-workers, and extended family. As individuals, they participate more in clubs, political organizations, teams, unions, churches, and cultural events. This aspect of participation protects them against early mortality. It has been proven that your risk factor for dying young increases with fewer social networks, as compared to the risks of obesity and leading a sedentary life.[50]

Having a vast network of friends is most beneficial, in addition to family socialization. Today, many families live far apart. It is not always possible or affordable to travel and be together for all the holidays and family celebrations. Unresolved disagreements with family members may be the reason to disassociate from destructive family relationships. Close friends are your extended family; life events can be just as joyful with this network of individuals around you. Harper Lee in *"To Kill a Mockingbird"* wrote: "You can choose your friends, but not your family."[51] She expounded on the value of "your kin," but close friendships are invaluable when family relationships are not positive or available.

> *"Family is not about blood. It is about who is willing to hold your hand when you need it most or who can you depend on to stand by you in the middle of the night when called upon to do so."*[52]
>
> Author Unknown

A long-term study in the United Kingdom of more than six thousand five hundred people found that people having ten or more friendships at age forty-five years old, had significantly higher levels of psychological well-being at age fifty, regardless of their partnership status, as compared to people with fewer friends.[53]

William Chopik from Michigan State University completed two other recent studies of nearly two hundred and eighty thousand people in almost one hundred countries. He found that friendships become increasingly vital to well-being at older ages.[54] Relationships with friends are a better predictor of good health and happiness among older adults than relationships with family.

The institution of marriage can provide emotional, financial, and practical support. Having a perfect mate should not be a substitute for pursuing relationships with friends and enjoying interests separate from one another. Partners in marriage can be encouraging and helpful with careers, childrearing, and household chores. They can also be uncooperative in sharing family responsibilities, depending on their different personalities and assumed roles. Some marriages break up; one partner changes and becomes more self-sufficient and fulfilled. The other partner feels he or she has been left behind. Divorces often occur with older couples after the children have left home to pursue their own lives. The wife may attend college to pursue a profession for a new career. The husband feels that his wife is no longer the woman he married. This could cause stress in the relationship. The couple is no longer compatible. Divorces also occur when complacency, routine and boredom set in. Neither one in the relationship feels any excitement or looks forward to sharing events together.

Successful singles make excellent marriage partners and usually end up in happy marriages. On average, studies show that married people are more satisfied with life and live longer than single people. The most distressed single people are the ones who are newly divorced or widowed. This anxiety and pain may stem from an over reliance on one's spouse before the divorce or death of the spouse. The surviving partner appears unable to cope and seems lost without a partner. Only time and maybe therapy will heal the pain. Single individuals with a low income report the most psychological problems. Low income married couples have more resources to draw from their partners. Single people, who become more affluent, foster more relationships and interests compared to married individuals. Those individuals who have remained single with the highest incomes tend to be happier than married couples.

Most marriage counselors tend to focus on improving marital relationships, when in fact, the focus should be on fostering individuality and responsibility for one's happiness.

Partners are happier when their spouses are content and have strong social networks. When problems in the relationship arise, talking with a close friend outside of the marriage can be greatly beneficial. "You are my everything" is not the best recipe for a happy marriage. However, there are a few exceptions. Some couples prefer to do all their socialization with each other. They enjoy the company of their partner to the extent that they may not need other people. This relationship must be acceptable to both partners. However, this arrangement limits the opportunities to meet different people. Socialization with others enhances our daily life experiences.

> *"One smile can start a friendship, one word can end a fight, one look can save a relationship, and one person can change your life."* [55]
>
> *Author Unknown*

Happiness

"Happiness is a choice, not a result. Nothing will make you happy until you choose to be happy. No person will make you happy unless you decide to be happy. Your happiness will not come to you. It can only come from you."[56]

Ralph Marston

Happiness should not be a fleeting experience, here one moment, and gone the next. These days, people seem to look for experiences rather than contentment and peace that you can get from daily living. Happiness is the frequency of positive experiences, not intensity. Path to happiness is not fame or fortune. It is living an honest and authentic life. This can be something simple or be potentially more difficult. Mahatma Gandhi preached that happiness was experienced when what you think, say and do are in harmony.

Stephanie Schriock, president of EMILY'S List, America's largest resource for women in politics, says reframing the discussion from "work/life balance" to "happiness and fulfillment," would make a big difference.[57] Life isn't about balance. It is about finding the right mix of things that make you happy, whether it is work, going to the gym, spending time with your children, or kicking back with a good book. It is not a perfect science. You must find the power within yourself to change the things in your life that make you unhappy. Also, it may mean that you will have to increase your financial assets. Whoever you are and wherever you are in life, it is important to remember that there is more than one path in life. Only you can figure out what ignites your passion. Do not let society dictate what that should be for you. It is up to you, and it is your choice.

Half the battle of enjoying life is to be passionate about your work and leisure activities. Nothing becomes a chore if you put a dose of passion into it. Cooking a meal, making a dessert, reading a book, taking a walk on the beach, spending an evening laughing with friends, taking your mother shopping, talking to your father, watching sunsets, watching a movie and eating popcorn, swimming, listening to music, dancing, all of these activities can become most pleasurable by actively and fully engaging in each one of them. If you have the financial resources, traveling, exploring different cultures, eating different foods, and meeting new people from other countries, offer exciting adventures of a lifetime. You may also develop new friendships with people from around the world. The list is endless. Just find out what motivates you. You have the power to increase the dopamine and serotonin in your brain and fend off depression.

> *"The happiest people don't have the best of everything; they just make the best of everything they have."*[58]
>
> *Author Unknown*

David Shimer wrote an article about Yale University's Psych157 class, entitled "Psychology and the Good Life." Within three days of the class offering, one thousand and two hundred undergraduate students had signed up for the class.[59]

Professor Laurie Santos teaches the course. She said "students want to change, to be happier themselves, and to change the culture on campus. If one in four students at the university took the course and developed better habits, like showing gratitude, procrastinating less and increasing social connections, the seeds for change would be planted on the campus."[60] The course is now available for free online via Coursera or pay a fee of forty-five dollars for a certificate of completion.[61]

The students reported being anxious, stressed, unhappy, and tired of numbing their emotions, both positive and negative. However, it is not only these students who feel this way. Any individuals who are not allowed to express themselves, to explore their desires and fears without being judged or criticized, can become anxiety-ridden, depressed, and melancholy. People misunderstand what truly brings them happiness. Getting a good grade, winning the lottery, graduating from school, getting a job, being reunited with family and friends are temporary fixes for contentedness. Longstanding happiness must come from within one's self.

> *"One thing I have learned in my life is that the grass is not always greener on the other side."*[62]
>
> *Ricky Gervais*

Many people think that moving away and starting a new life will bring happiness. If you leave with a broken heart or troubled mind, you will be taking these problems with you to your new destination. Happiness is not a new city, new home, or new backyard, with hopes of greener grass. Satisfaction is something that you must find in your own heart. Eventually, you may find happiness if you leave intending to fix your "heart and mind" and with the know-how to work on it.

Even Albert Einstein had a theory for happiness. "A calm and modest life brings more happiness than the pursuit of success combined with constant restlessness."[63] Back in 1922, Einstein was on a lecturing tour, and he was staying in the Imperial Hotel in Tokyo, Japan. He had just learned that he had received the Nobel Prize for theoretical physics, his discovery of the law of the photoelectric effect.[64] When the bellboy came to give him a message, he did not have any change in his pocket for a tip; instead, he gave him "his tip" on how to have a happy life. He told the bellboy that perhaps his missive would become more valuable than a tip someday. In 2017, at Winner's Auction House and Exhibition in Jerusalem, Israel, the written message sold for $1.56 million. Einstein became the largest tipper in the world.[65]

The Western world prescribes to the personal belief of "*Know Yourself*," while the Eastern world advises "*Become Yourself*." The world may now be ready for a synthesis of both points of view. The healthiest people are in touch with their inner motivations, values, and attitudes. At the same time, they are also in tune with their passions and life purposes. They continue to follow their path with steadfast and conscious self-direction.

In the article "The Power of Positive People," Tara Parker-Pope questioned whether friendships you have, give you a boost or bring you down.[66] She advocated you need to spend time with the right people for your health and happiness. Many people focus on diet and exercise to achieve better health. However, researchers have found that social networks, whether in person or online, can have positive or negative influences, such as happiness, or depression and anxiety. Cyberbullying has been known to be toxic causing the recipients to suffer depression, anxiety, and even committing suicide. It would be beneficial to be cognizant of your relationships and be aware of who encourages and inspires you or makes you feel joyful. If you do not have many positive people in your life, it is time to reach out and meet new people.

Dan Buettner, a National Geographic fellow, and author has studied the health habits of people who live in regions of the world known as Blue Zones. "These projects focus on initiatives to make changes in local environments, public policies, and social networks. The main objective is to improve the health and well-being of the individuals who live in these areas. People are living much longer lives and thriving."[67] He noted that positive friendships are a common theme in these Blue Zones. "Friends can exert a measurable and ongoing influence on your health behaviors in a way that a diet never can."[68]

In Okinawa, Japan, the average life expectancy for women is around ninety years old, the oldest in the world.[69] From a very young age, the elders here have formed social networks called "moais."[70] They offer social, emotional, logistical, and even financial support for a lifetime. Traditionally, parents place their children into moais when they are born. They begin a lifelong journey with these individuals together. In a moai, the group benefits when things go well, such as sharing a bountiful crop. The group's families support one another through illnesses and deaths. They also foster and promote healthy behaviors throughout their lifetimes together.[71]

Buettner is working with federal and state officials to create moais in two dozen cities around the United States. The key to building a successful moai is to start with people of similar interests, passions, and values. Several residents have formed walking moais - groups of people who meet regularly to walk and socialize. Initially, the Blue Zone team tries to group people based on geography, work, and family schedules, and then they ask the individuals a series of questions to discover their common interests. They have created a quiz to help people assess the positive impact of their social network. The subjects include an assessment of their friends' health: how much they drink, eat, exercise, as well as their outlook on life. The answers identify the people in their life who score the highest about wellness and encourage them to spend more time with this group of people.

"You stack the deck in favor of a long-term relationship. I argue that the most powerful thing you can do to add healthy years is to curate your immediate social network,"[72] said Buettner. He also advises people to focus on three to five real-world friends rather than a multitude of distant Facebook friends. In general, you want friends with whom you can have a meaningful conversation. You should be able to call them when you are having a bad day, and they, in turn, will care. "Your group of friends is better than any drugs or anti-aging supplements and will do more for you than just about anything."[73]

My parents were born in India, traveled, and settled in Africa, then to the United Kingdom. For the last forty years, they have been living in the United States. Their moai consists of friends who have stayed connected for over sixty years, despite living on different continents. These relationships transpired over an era without the Internet, cell phones, Facebook, or other social media. I find it extremely rewarding to hear my mother talk regularly with friends who are either in the UK or India. She has known these individuals since her school days and as a young adult. She is now eighty-five years old. She still discusses ongoing issues in her life, as well as their concerns. There is a fantastic bond that exists between them. Today, with all the modern technology, you do not have to live close by to have a successful moai.

As for myself, my moai has been changing over the years. My ex-husband is still part of it. We share many of the same values since we have known one another since the age of sixteen. We can discuss problems and look for solutions together, although we live in different states. With technology, it is effortless to stay connected. My partner of thirty years is an essential part of my moai. We share a common interest in exercising regularly and keeping each other healthy, both mentally, physically, and emotionally. The oldest person in my moai is my mother. She taught me how to cook, clean, sew, and how to be responsible as a woman and partner within a family. Every day, we talk to one another. Her wisdom, faith, and generosity toward others for the right reasons, have kept me grounded. After the death of my father, I have become her caretaker with the help of my sister. The roles are reversed now as my mother has aged.

New friends can also become part of your moai. A new friend has inspired me to write this book. We have had in-depth discussions about the issues that need to be addressed in our society today. We both agree that our culture needs to change for the better. Another new friend is also a child and adolescent psychiatrist. We spend a lot of time discussing women's issues and thinking about how to analyze people's behaviors. A young male friend, who is like an adopted son, offers insights on the world's events and problems. It is an exciting mix of people and professions in my moai. They play different roles in my life and keep me energized and fulfilled.

I have always believed that if you can count the number of true friends on one hand, you have been most fortunate. The best of times for me have been to spend evenings around a dinner table with a few close friends, eating, laughing, listening to music, and sharing special occasions. Sadly, we know people who suck the energy out of you, and at the end of the day, you feel drained from their company. Negative people, who always see the glass as half empty, have a destructive effect on everyone around them. They thrive on creating chaos and enjoy creating stressful situations. They need to drag others down to their level "to feel like they belong." They are not able to be happy and have difficulty seeing other people happy or content. My advice is to limit your time with these people, or remove them from your social circle, if possible.

"Toxic people defy logic. Some are blissfully unaware of the negative impact that they have on those around them, and others seem to derive satisfaction from creating chaos and pushing other people's buttons."[74]

Travis Bradberry

When you spend time with positive, energetic people, you feel so much better even after a short time together. Optimistic individuals have a can-do attitude in comparison to pessimistic people. The challenge in your life is to recognize who energizes you and who makes you feel anxious and depressed. Often, it is difficult to disassociate with family members. You can choose your friends, but not your family. Around the holidays, it can be an incredibly stressful time for family members. Most parents buy expensive toys or technology for their children for presents. Too often, you observe children playing with the box that contained the toy. Do not educate your children to be rich. Educate them to be happy, so they know the value of things and not the price. Life should be simple. As humans, we tend to complicate things and create problems.

"Happiness comes from spiritual wealth, not material wealth, happiness comes from giving, not getting. If we try hard to bring happiness to others, we cannot stop it from coming to us also. To get joy, we must give it, and to keep joy, we must scatter it."[75]

John Templeton

Laughter

"There is nothing in the world, so irresistibly contagious as laughter and good humor."[76]

Charles Dickens

In the last decade, a lot of attention has been focused on the benefits of laughter. The proverb "laughter is the best medicine" helps you recover from a busy, stressful life. In conservative countries like India, groups assemble in parks and other places, to laugh out loud and receive the therapeutic benefits. Today, there are over two hundred Laughter Clubs in Bangalore, India alone, making it the country's best Laughter City. Every day, between 6 am and 7 am, and 5:30 pm and 6:30 pm, residents from a cross-section of professions, classes and creeds get together for an hour-long laughter therapy session which also combines simple flexibility exercises, yoga, and pranayama.[77]

It always feels good to share a good laugh, but it can also improve your health. It triggers positive physical and emotional changes in your body. It strengthens the immune system, boosts mood, diminishes pain, and protects you from the damaging effects of stress. Children tend to laugh a lot more than adults, who become somber as they grow older. Humor and laughter can also improve your relationships, help you find greater happiness, and even add years to your life.

Humor lightens your burdens, inspires hopes, connects you to others, keeps you grounded, focused, and alert. It also helps you to release anger and to be more forgiving. With so much power to heal and renew, the ability to laugh easily and frequently is a tremendous resource for surmounting problems. Best of all, this medicine is fun, free, and easy to use, and available on-demand.

Laughter relaxes the whole body. A good hearty laugh relieves physical tension and stress, leaving the muscles relaxed for up to forty-five minutes.[78]

Laughter decreases stress hormones and increases immune cells and infection-fighting antibodies, improving resistance to infections.

Laughter triggers a release of endorphins which promote an overall sense of well-being and even temporarily relieves pain.

Laughter protects the heart by increasing blood flow and function of the blood vessels, which in turn, can help protect against a heart attack and other cardiovascular problems.

Laughter burns calories, but it is not a replacement for going to the gym!

Laughter lightens the tension due to anger. Nothing diffuses hostility and conflict faster than a shared laugh. Looking at the funny side of problems can put them into perspective. It can enable you to move on from confrontations without holding onto bitterness and resentment.

Laughter can help you live longer.

A fifteen-year study in Norway found that people with a strong sense of humor outlived those individuals who didn't laugh as much.[79] Individuals who battled cancer experienced this effect. Their life expectancy improved. The team assessed the cognitive, social, and affective components of humor using a validated questionnaire completed by 53,556 men and women. It traced the mortality rate for cardiovascular diseases, infections, cancer, and chronic obstructive pulmonary diseases.

Negative Emotions

"Forget the things that make you sad.
Remember the moments that make you glad.
Forget the troubles that passed away. Accept
the blessings that come your way."[80]

Author Unknown

Not only are the teenage students struggling with negative emotions, but now they have to deal with the physical, psychological, and emotional trauma of school shootings. They are experiencing more mental health issues as compared to adolescents from the Great Depression era, 1929–1939. "Suicide is now the second leading cause of death for adolescents, surpassing homicide deaths."[81]

Suicide is the leading cause of death for men under the age of thirty-five. Men report being significantly less satisfied with life than women. According to statistics compiled by the Men's Health Forum, "men make up seventy-six percent of all suicides, ninety-five percent of the prison population, and seventy-three percent of adults who are reported as missing."[82] They are very reluctant to seek help. The Jo Cox Commission described male loneliness as a "silent epidemic. More than one in ten say that they are lonely but won't usually admit it."[83] Suicide becomes an easy option when there is no one to whom you can turn for guidance or support. Many lives are lost when people feel lonely and are incapable of seeking alternate coping techniques. Sometimes, all you need is a supportive parent, friend, neighbor, teacher, coach, pastor, or roommate. The list is endless if you are willing to reach out and trust someone to help you look for ways of dealing with your inner turmoil. A depressed person spirals downward with negative emotions, while a helpful individual throws them a lifeline to end the destructive spiral. Without support or professional assistance, the negative behavior can lead to severe illness and death.

A mentoring program can be beneficial and offer a lifeline to a depressed individual. Mentoring is a relationship between two people. "Mentoring, at its core, guarantees young people that there is someone who cares about them, assures them that they are not alone in dealing with day-to-day challenges, and makes them feel that they matter. Research confirms that quality mentoring relationships have powerful effects on young people in a variety of personal, academic, and professional situations. Ultimately, mentoring connects a young person to personal growth and development, and social and economic opportunity."[84] Mentorship happens with people, both young and old, when they share a common interest or background. Men often mentor other men because of their similar social and business interests. There is a shortage of professional mentors for women. It is more difficult for women because senior men executives may feel uncomfortable due to improper sexual connotations. This situation has been made worse by the #MeToo Movement. Mentoring has a lifelong, positive impact on both the recipient and the mentor.

Today, young people spend most of their time using technology, especially text messaging, twitter, chat rooms, and game rooms. They also log onto Facebook, Instagram, or Snapchat to update their daily personal status. These social media platforms are impersonal and can lead to confrontation and bullying. It is impossible to express genuine emotions without face-to-face connections. When dealing with difficult life situations, teens and young adults will not receive the best advice from acquaintances or friends who are of the same age. They are struggling with the same issues themselves.

Communication skills are necessary to function in any setting whether in school, at work, or with family and friends. Learning to communicate effectively and appropriately is both a challenge and a need. When an individual is speaking, there is a risk that it may cause a negative reaction with others. It is essential to learn how to communicate in a non-threatening manner. Very quickly, negative comments can become highly offensive and spread like wildfire on the Internet. One's reputation can be destroyed in seconds, whether the comment was true or false. In-person active listening is an essential life skill. It requires your full attention in reference to what is being said. You must understand the meaning of the communication. It is not equal to a quick text message or an emoji. Problems can be resolved because there is participation from both sides and consideration of each other's opinions. Miscommunication can be minimized because you are face-to-face with the individual.

> *"It doesn't matter how educated, talented, rich, or cool you believe you are, how you treat people, ultimately tells all. Integrity is everything."*[85]
>
> *Author Unknown*

Drug overdoses have been increasing. Number of deaths was four times higher in 2018 than in 1999. Nearly 70% of the 67,367 deaths in 2018 involved an opioid. The number of drug overdose deaths was projected to be 70,980 according to the CDC for 2019, an increase of 4.8%.[86] It is not surprising since drugs provide a temporary escape from negative emotions and reality. Why do so many people need this release? Suffering from loneliness and loss of social contacts causes many individuals to turn to drug use. The question remains: why are so many young people suffering from negative emotions?

According to a CNN report on May 21, 2018, there have been two hundred and eighty-eight school shootings since 2009. The US has had 57 times as many school shootings as the other major industrialized nations combined. Recent research studies have indicated that many high school students feel anxiety or depression. Dr. Mike Ronsisvalle addressed this issue after the Parkland High School shooting on February 14, 2018, where seventeen people lost their lives.[87] He wanted to understand what has happened in our culture. How do young people become motivated to walk into a high school and carry out this heinous act? This tragic event has occurred repeatedly throughout our country, and we are still looking for answers.

The questions are endless about how we control gun sales. How to we keep children safe in our schools? How do we influence the National Rifle Association and politicians to enact laws in our country to protect all citizens? After the Parkland High School massacre, the students asked Senator Marco Rubio of Florida, whether he could make a commitment not to accept funding for his campaign from the NRA.[88] The Senator defended accepting contributions from the NRA, stating "the influence of these groups comes not from money, it comes from the millions of people that agree with the agenda, the millions of Americans that support the NRA." The problem of gun violence does not reside solely with the NRA. It is an organization founded in 1871, which protects our Second Amendment of the United States Constitution, guaranteeing a citizen's right to keep and bear arms.

Individuals have had access to guns for hundreds of years. When the baby boomer generation was growing up, some students even had shotguns in their cars on their way to school. They still do in some parts of the country. No one carried out random school shootings. Back then, students settled their differences with fistfights, not mass murders. This tragedy is happening way too often in the United States. It indicates severe family dysfunction, lack of family supervision, mental illnesses, bullying, and an extreme means to receive recognition.

> *"Sociologists well understand that chaos at home causes violent behavior, educational failure and social alienation among children. Yet, many of us in America stay far, far away from this topic. That in itself is a national scandal. Bad parenting is gravely harming the nation."*[89]
>
> *Bill O' Reilly*

Evil has been with us for an eternity, but this savage reaction is a relatively, new phenomenon. As a society, we must try and understand why these young, disturbed individuals have chosen to carry out such extreme violence. What has led them to this outcome? What actions can be taken to prevent future occurrences? Dr. Ronsisvalle has suggested that young people may be reflecting the culture of violence around them. "Much has changed in the last generation. There was an overemphasis on materialism in the '80s and '90s. And with the explosion of technology and push to succeed at any cost at the turn of the century, we have created a culture promoting a self-focused, entitled world view."[90] So today, we have a generation of young people who have unrealistic expectations about what their lives should be, and the way other individuals should treat them. They cannot cope with their extreme disappointments and anger. Instead, they resort to feeling powerful; they obtain a gun and plan an attack on innocent victims.[91]

Most of the young people and millennials have grown up playing video games. Most of the games are exceptionally violent. Points are awarded for killing by shooting, slashing, stabbing, or mutilating another individual. Many teenagers spend hundreds and hundreds of hours playing these types of video games. At this age, they are easily influenced and can become numb, desensitized to the idea of killing and mass murder. It is just a game, or is it? Are these school shooters picking up a fully loaded weapon, realizing that they are doing something wrong? Are these innocent victims only points in the game of life, or is this their way to finally be noticed, to be infamous forever, another teenage serial mass murderer in the record books?

Recently, a study entitled *"Increases in Social Media and Television Viewing Associated with Increases in Teen*

Depression," was published in JAMA (Journal of the American Medical Association) July 15, 2019. Four thousand Canadian teens between the ages of twelve and sixteen years old provided information about the amounts of screen time they use. The study included their use of social media, television, video gaming, and computers. Conclusions drawn from this analysis of the data showed that higher than average use of social media and time in front of the television were associated with more severe symptoms of depression. And with even greater participation, they fell deeper into depression.[92] Media exposes teenagers to unrealistic images of wealth, exciting lifestyles, and perfect bodies. At this young age, they do not have the mental acuity or emotional maturity to realize that what they see and read is not reality. It is a fantasy world promoting consumerism and self-gratification.

Media thrives on chaos. Advertisement revenues increase when people are tuning in to reports on mass tragedies. The teenage and young adult shooters are aware that they will receive 24/7 coverage of their mass murder and finally have their "five minutes of fame." "Dr. Jennifer Johnston and her coauthor, Andrew Joy, BS, also of Western New Mexico University, reviewed data on mass shootings by media outlets, the FBI and advocacy organizations, as well as scholarly articles. They concluded "media contagion" is largely responsible for the increase in these often-deadly outbursts. They defined mass shootings as either attempts to kill multiple people who are not relatives or those resulting in injuries or fatalities in public places. The prevalence of these crimes has risen with the mass media coverage of them and the proliferation of social media sites. They tend to glorify the shooters and downplay the victims. The frightening homicides are their No.1 ratings and advertising boosters."[93]

On August 26, 2018, a mass shooting took place at a virtual football video-gaming tournament where the winners would continue to compete at an advanced tournament in October in Las Vegas, Nevada. Huge cash prizes would be awarded. One of the participants, David Katz, a twenty-four-year-old gamer from Baltimore, Maryland, became a disgruntled competitor after he lost. He brought a gun into the venue, opened fire, and proceeded to kill two people and injure eleven other individuals. He then turned the gun on himself and committed suicide.[94]

During the past three decades, the recurring message is that video games are a toxic pursuit and a teenage preoccupation. This association has led to questions in the media about whether the games themselves deserve scrutiny for their roles in these kinds of mass shooting tragedies. Apart from the fact that e-sports tournaments are increasingly staged at high profile venues and predominantly attended by young men, mark these events as especially high-risk targets for a mass shooting. The Columbine shooters, Eric Harris and Dylan Klebold were avid gamers.[95] In 2011, Anders Breivik, killed more than seventy teenagers on a Norwegian island retreat. He wrote in his diary that he played "Call of Duty" and "Modern Warfare 2," as part of his training before the mass shooting of his victims.[96] Adam Lanza, who killed twenty elementary school children, six adults, and his mother in Connecticut in December 2012 played video games as well. He favored non-violent games.[97]

On June 6, 2018, a new video game entitled "Active Shooter" was scheduled to be released. Gaming participants would take part in a simulated school shooting scenario. Parkland high school parents, who were in the process of recovering from the mass shooting at their local high school, were outraged. After facing harsh criticism for their absolute insensitivity to horrendous school shootings, the game developer and the digital distribution company announced that they would pull the game off the market.[98]

On the opposite side of the spectrum, in relationship to video games being the cause of extreme violence among young men, psychologists Patrick Market and Christopher Ferguson wrote a book, entitled *Moral Combat.* They note that millions of children across America are playing video games, roaming violent virtual worlds with virtual guns in their hands. They suggest that the concern about the effects of this visual violence is misplaced. The fears voiced by the media and politicians after each mass shooting do not support the evidence. They further enumerate that scholars are finding that violent video games are not one of society's greatest evils. The games may even be a force for good. They can have a positive impact on relieving stress and even make us more morally sensitive.[99]

It is unclear how they researched and reported what kind of short- or long-term consequences these violent video games can have on young, developing brains. With every event in life, we attach our own meaning and interpretation.

Part 3

Enough is Enough – Get Over It

Changing the Culture

"The world will not be destroyed by those who do evil, but by those who watch them without doing anything."[100]

Albert Einstein

"We as a nation must foster individuals to return to the ethics of loyalty, character, and sacrifice that this country was built upon, instead of an identity based on the accumulation of material things, self-centeredness, and having an unbridled belief that we all deserve special privileges."[101] We have raised a generation of individuals who have unrealistic expectations about how others should treat them. They do not have the coping skills to deal with the negative emotions that are part of a dysfunctional world. Adolescents have a natural tendency to feel invincible and to be narcissistic. They maintain a deep sense of entitlement and lament being cheated out of a life they were promised. These thoughts and behaviors have fostered the self-centered 'selfie culture'. They lack empathy for those who are struggling or different. They make fun of peers who dress differently or even those who are excelling due to being self-motivated. They bully the weak and only associate with like-minded peers.

"Children; they have bad manners, contempt for authority; they show disrespect for elders and love chatter in place of exercise. They no longer rise when elders enter the room, they contradict their parents and tyrannize their teachers. Children are now tyrants."[102]

Socrates, circa 470BC.

The result of this imagined entitlement leads to feelings of hopelessness, desperation, and unhealthy behaviors. Desperation fosters hatred of oneself and towards others. The individual directs his anger on society and carries out heinous violent acts. Evidence of extreme anguish and distress are the crimes of mass murder, sexual and physical abuse.

Recently, Fareed Zakaria recommended a book, "The Coddling of the American Mind."[103] It addresses the issue that something has been occurring on college campuses within the past few years, which is shockingly wrong. Professors and students in the classroom are afraid to speak honestly. The teachers are shouted at and are rudely interrupted. They feel like they are walking into a minefield of rage. The authors, Greg Lukianoff, a First Amendment expert, and Jonathan Haidt, a social psychologist, are referencing the children of the post-millennial era. They are discussing how these problems on college campuses are rooted in three terrible ideas, which are woven into American childhood and education: what doesn't kill you, makes you weaker; always trust your feelings, and life is a battle between good and evil.[104] "These three great untruths contradict basic psychological principles about well-being and ancient wisdom from many cultures. Embracing these untruths and the culture of safetyism, interferes with young people's social, emotional, and intellectual development. It makes it more difficult for them to become autonomous adults who can navigate the bumpy road of life."[105]

Safetyism is a culture whereby parents have overprotected their children. They have created a fragile generation who has not had any experience with unstructured or unsupervised playtime. Every moment of the day, the children were monitored to prevent them from being harmed in any way. Parents felt that they had to protect them from danger, both inside and outside of the house. The extreme fear experienced by parents, alternating with trying to constantly protect their children led to this unrealistic philosophy of parenting. As a result of this upbringing, the young people are physically, mentally, and emotionally unprepared for the rigors of everyday life, away from their home fortress and their 24/7 vigilant parents.[106]

Lukianoff and Haidt investigated the many social trends that have intersected to promote the spread of these untruths. They explored the changes in childhood, such as the rise of fearful parenting, the decline of unsupervised child-directed play, and the new world of social media that has engulfed teenagers this past decade. They examined the changes on college campuses, including the corporatization of universities and the emergence of new ideas about identity and justice. They placed the campus conflicts within the context of America's rising political polarization and dysfunction. They advocated that this book "The Coddling of the American Mind," should be read by anyone who is confused about what is happening on college campuses today. And they also advised parents of children to read this book. "Parents should be thinking seriously about preparing their children for the road, not the road for the child. Their children need to learn how to respond to everyday irritations and provocations, and that risk-deprivation breeds risk aversion. Young children need to engage in unsupervised play and solitary walks in their neighborhood. Parents need to limit their screen time and encourage face-to-face contact and productive disagreements with peers and adults."[107]

Chief Justice John Roberts of the United States Supreme Court was presenting a speech at his son's middle school graduation in June 2017. He emphasized: "Whether I wish these things or not, the graduates would experience betrayal, loneliness, bad luck, and pain. Those willing to learn from messages in misfortune would be far more likely to be better citizens and better people."[108]

The Academy of Pediatrics suggests that there is a link between aggressive behavior and the amount of time the child plays violent video games.[109] The children have more nightmares, sleep problems, and behavior problems. It is challenging to research and understand how constant violent and sexual images affect the psyche. We need to examine what chemicals are triggered in the brain, and what are the long-term effects in susceptible individuals, especially children. Why do some veterans suffer from PTSD (Post Traumatic Stress Disorder)? Exposure to difficult, life-threatening situations leaves some individuals with significant mental problems, while others can compartmentalize these feelings and function effectively after the trauma. Some individuals decide to address their issues directly and attempt to find solutions to help them cope with or justify their beliefs.

How do we understand what happened to these school shooters in their lifetime? Were they more sensitive to the violent material of video games? Are they just bad seeds? Or along the way of parenting, no one showed them alternative ways of dealing with frustration, anger, and disappointment. Some lessons need to be learned early in childhood and through adulthood: applying coping skills, taking responsibility for your actions, and being accountable for your behavior. As adults, we need to take responsibility in recognizing mental health issues, signs of drug and alcohol use and not permitting young people to have access to firearms. How difficult is that for us to accomplish? It is only common sense.

Being aggressive seems to go hand in hand with young boys and men. It gets out of control when they get together in gangs or with like-minded peers. Bullying weaker individuals comes naturally to those who experience anger and hostility in their homes and community. Some of these young men are insecure, and they need to pick on weaker individuals to feel better about themselves. They would benefit tremendously from positive role models who would teach them alternate ways to deal with their anger and frustrations. Participation in boys' and girls' clubs would help foster appropriate behaviors. They need lessons in tolerance to improve their self-esteem. As they begin to realize their self-worth, the need to bully other people should diminish.

We can also blame parents for being too lax and providing violent video games for their children's entertainment.

Sometimes, they do not want to deprive their children of the electronic gadgets that many of their friends have or what the parents did not have growing up. Even though games are rated, parents buy inappropriate games for their children. Cris Rowan, an occupational therapist in British Columbia, Canada, outlined ten reasons why exposure to violent video games by young children is dangerous to their health.[110] While playing these games, their blood pressure and heart rate increase, and over time, can cause physical bodily harm. Brain damage, such as frontal lobe atrophy, has been reported when children spend four to five hours a day gaming. Many children have computers in their bedroom and are staying up late to play these games. They become sleep-deprived, exhausted, and unable to function in school. Their academic performance is poor while demonstrating little initiative to succeed. Hours spent looking at violence on a video screen only increases aggressive behavior in children. They are too young to make the correlation between what they are watching and their behavior. They are also limiting their social interactions greatly with their peers by spending hundreds of hours per month in front of a computer screen. Doctors and therapists are now reporting game transfer phenomena where children are retaining the violent imagery even after they have finished playing the game. They close their eyes and can still see the violence that appeared on the screen. Children have become addicted to technology and are unable to be disconnected for any period. The rate of mental illness has increased among children and teenagers. Young people are living in these virtual worlds. They have great difficulty communicating and solving problems in the real world. Extreme gamers have committed many of the mass shootings in the United States. They were young men who simulated their crimes by mimicking one of the violent games they had been playing.[111]

We often complain about people being too attached to their smartphones. They are obsessively checking to see if they have received text messages, emails, or if someone is trying to connect with them. A typical teenager and adult check their phones between fifty-one and one hundred times a day, which is double the predicted amount estimated in a study released by Deloitte in 2019. Americans collectively check their smartphones fourteen billion times a day. Deloitte also found that eighty-one percent of Americans spend time looking at their phones while dining out in restaurants.[112]

Billions of text messages are sent to individuals in the United States every day. In the past, people talked and paid attention to the person with whom they were speaking. Today, the text message system involves rapid responses with no emphasis on having a meaningful conversation. They are short, curt messages, sometimes with just emojis, small digital images used to express an emotion or an idea. With the increase of technology, we have lost our humanness, the ability to communicate on a deep level with another human being. We are missing the real story behind the angry emoji. Do not get me wrong. Technology has connected the world and opened opportunities that were unimaginable fifty years ago. It has made millions of advances and contributions in every field today, but along the way, we have lost something in the process. Innovation has enslaved us. What seems to connect us has also separated us from one another, from our shared experiences.

Unfortunately, parents do not have to go through parenting classes to learn how to be good parents. We must learn to read and write. We take time to study and master a trade or profession. We even have to pass a test to drive a car. And for the most critical job in the world, raising children, individuals are left to fend for themselves and can only hope that they will make the right parental decisions. In the past, generations of families lived together. Grandparents, aunts, and uncles coached their children in childrearing and offered tremendous psychological and emotional support. Today, the co-habitation of multi-generational families is just about non- existent. Children with their own families have moved away geographically from their neighborhoods, even across the country. They are not in close contact with their family and often feel isolated away from their support. They no longer stay in touch with their families. Children do need to learn how to become independent, and sometimes, physical distance is necessary to foster independence. Many parents suffer from the "empty nest syndrome" when their children move away from home or graduate from college and find employment in another city. Some parents can be overly protective and want their children to touch base with them every day. They fear that something will happen to their children unless they can speak to them. This parental behavior is not helpful for the growth and development of their child. It fosters dependence and does not allow the child to make their own mistakes. Children must stumble and correct their errors. This rite of passage is the only one leading to responsible adulthood.

New terms about parenting have been coined, such as "helicopter parenting." It refers to parents who hover over their children, like helicopters, overseeing every aspect of their children's lives. They pay awfully close attention to their child's experiences and problems, particularly at educational institutions. At the first sign of a problem, they swoop in to advocate and try to protect their child. This overindulgent behavior is not exclusive to American parents. In China, parents of freshmen students are also invited to spend the first few days at the college with their children. The college gyms are turned into campsites with "love tents," so the parents can help their children settle into college life.[113]

"Snowplow parenting" is the latest controversial technique in which a parent is constantly removing obstacles out of their child's path. They are focused solely on the future success of their children. These parents have no sense of boundaries. They will even call their children's employers if they are having an issue at work. During 2019, there were several cases of celebrity parents in the news who falsified their children's college applications and entrance exams. They also paid exorbitant sums of money to college coaches for admission to ivy league colleges and universities.[114] Some parents even spent time incarcerated for these actions.

Some parents allow their children to make major decisions without appropriate guidance. Children learn what is socially appropriate from their parents. The way they behave in society is the way they are brought up in the home. Growing up with neglectful parents leads to poor social behaviors. Children become isolated in school for their inappropriate actions. As young adults, their maturity is delayed, which can affect both their professional and financial future.

During the 1950s and 60s, the baby boomer generation played outside without supervision. They would leave the house early in the morning after completing their chores. They would not return home until dinner time, except maybe to eat a sandwich for lunch, and run out again to be with their neighborhood friends. They were expected to fend for themselves and settle their arguments on the playground without any parental involvement. When they had a bad fight or experience with another child, they were expected to accept the results or consequences, and "move-on." Nowadays, any crisis in a child's life seems to require weeks of counseling with a therapist, or the parent interferes to handle the conflict.

Unfortunately, due to a lack of funding for mental health services for children, who are in dire need of counseling, they are unable to receive help. This health crisis leaves many children without adequate support to recover from psychological trauma and illnesses. Children are less resilient today. Parents are worried that someone will abduct their children without constant supervision. Young people are relying heavily on their parents for all their financial needs and wants. They have not been taught self-reliance, to rely on their abilities and resources. They do not see it as their responsibility to reciprocate financially to the family's income. There is an unrealistic expectation to be compensated for all the chores they perform around the house. Children expect to receive an allowance without earning it. They feel that they are entitled to this financial support. In past generations, children had to work hard and start saving for anything they wanted. Nothing was just given to them. People tend to appreciate things more when they must work for it by earning their own money. In the end, they take better care of their belongings; they realize the effort they had to put forth to acquire these possessions.

When I was seeing patients as a psychiatrist, children's parents would often comment that their children expected them to pay for everything, even as adults. Young people have no problem accepting presents, even extravagant ones, without any thoughts of reciprocating gifts to their parents. This lack of understanding and mutual respect stem from the days when parents did everything for their children to make them happy. Perhaps this process of becoming financially independent from your parents is not that simple. Many parents are uncertain as to when to cut those ties, particularly following periods when their children struggle with young adulthood and transitioning into professional life. For children, the desire to be independent is sometimes in conflict with other desires, like the security of having easy financial backing and the perceived emotional needs of their parents and themselves.[115]

These days, young girls and boys do not seem interested in learning how to cook, sew, clean, and perform other chores associated with household management. Parents make excuses for their children, who are too busy with schoolwork, or they are participating in sports activities. They need to spend time with their friends and have time to relax. Within most families, both parents are working full-time to provide for the family. Why aren't all family members sharing the household responsibilities? Parents must realize that they are sending the wrong message to their children, especially when they also give them an allowance for doing nothing around the house. They are encouraging them to be dependent, instead of becoming self-sufficient individuals. Besides, they are not teaching them to respect the contributions of all family members. Incentives are extrinsic motivators. They do not create an enduring commitment to any value or action.[116]

Growing up, it never occurred to me not to help around the house. That was not an option. There was not any extra money for an allowance. My sisters and I enjoyed spending time with my mother and her friends learning how to participate in household activities. We learned how to bond with other females and respect our elders. Sometimes, it is as simple as deciding what expectations you have for your children from an early age. They will experience different family dynamics within other families. Talking and communicating with your children about what your expectations are will assist them greatly in their personal development.

The entertainment industry has invested millions of dollars in violent and sexual media because it sells. Whether it is a television program, movie, or computer game, both adults and children are watching and buying these products. What people do not realize is that what they see is fantasy. Real-life has complications, issues, and relationships to navigate. Today, nothing is left to the imagination when we watch television or a movie or play with video games. Blood is seen spewing from all parts of the body; brains are battered; heads and limbs are cut off; throats are slashed. Violence has always existed throughout history, but the way it is now depicted makes it all too real and even exciting in young minds. Parents must monitor more closely what programs their children are watching and supervise their computer time. Most of all, they should take the time to read reviews of video games before purchasing them for family entertainment. With recent worry about mass shootings and gun violence in the United States, one of the questions that always comes up is whether violent media promotes violent or aggressive behavior. Various studies were conducted with children watching an aggressive video and even being exposed to film clips with guns, and with the guns edited out. Not surprisingly, the children who watched the clips with guns played more aggressively after seeing the film than those children who did not have exposure to the guns.[117]

Sexuality has also become a prominent theme in media. Nothing is left to the imagination. Steamy sex scenes and intercourse are shown on evening television and in the movies. It is embarrassing and uncomfortable watching many of these programs with children or older adults. One wonders how much reality is necessary. A study of sexually active teenagers concluded "those who watched the most sexual media were less likely to protect themselves and use a condom when having sex. Also, from their increased exposure, they reported having more sex than their peers who did not participate in excessive media exposure to sexuality."[118] Parents need to monitor their teenagers' phones and computers carefully to assure that they are not spending time on pornography sites or in chat rooms with strangers.

It is now politically correct to introduce LGBTQ (lesbian, gay, bisexual, transgender, and queer) relationships in most shows. The couples are also shown performing sexual activities. Whether we are heterosexual or LBGTQ, is it necessary to portray our sexual lives so intimately across the screen? The producers must feel that these sexual scenes will keep our interest and are relevant to the story. It would be interesting to know what the actors and actresses think of their performances. They are doing what most couples only do in the privacy of their homes without a whole camera crew and a director calling the shot to order. More research needs to be done to assess the effects of sexuality and the media on our culture and youth. Sex and violence are closely related.

> *"The greatest revolution in our generations, the discovery that human beings, can change the outer aspects of their lives, by changing the inner attitudes of their minds."*[119]
>
> *William James*

Problems in Society Today: Do-gooders, Parenting & Discipline

Do-gooders are well-meaning individuals who think that they are helping others but fail to realize that people do not find their actions beneficial at times. They want to do the "right things" according to their own beliefs. Some want to change old established patterns of discipline to hold people accountable for their behaviors. They try to impose their values and beliefs onto others without a thorough understanding of what is involved, especially if they do not have any experience in these matters.

For many years, parents have not been allowed to discipline their children using their own methods. The parents are under the threat of DFCS (Department of Family & Children's Services). The social workers will descend upon them if they punish their children in any manner unacceptable to their standards. Any unusual form of discipline is seen as outrageous, and the media portrays it as horrific. Parents still have rights to discipline their children, but they have become restricted. Today, it is challenging to discipline a child who is acting out in public. There is a strong possibility that someone who is watching the parent discipline the child will take offense and interfere with the rights of the parent. Strangers observing the incident will take out their phone and video tape the interaction. They think nothing of sending the video clips to the police, other authorities or posting it on social media outlets. The DFCS must intervene if a child is starved, physically or sexually abused, beaten, and left with bruises and broken bones, emotionally abused, or neglected. They must step in when children are not receiving basic needs such as food, clothing, and shelter. Parents must care for their children. They should also have some freedom to decide how they want to discipline their children.

The current sentiment is against spanking your child. As of November 2018, The American Academy of Pediatrics has updated its stance on spanking. "Do not do it. Adverse discipline strategies, including all forms of corporal punishment, yelling at or shaming children, are minimally effective. Researchers link corporal punishment to an increased risk of negative behavioral, cognitive, psychosocial, and emotional outcomes for children."[120] Parents are responsible for shaping their children's behavior in a positive direction. Parenting is a hard job. Children do not come with an instructional manual. Spanking can be an effective tool to steer children's negative behavior and guide them towards becoming responsible young adults. Properly administered, spanking is effective as a deterrent to undesirable behaviors for younger preschoolers, but never with infants. Toddlers do not respond to reasoning or taking away privileges.

As children age, spanking should become less frequent and completely phased out by adolescence. Parents should use spanking in case of willful disobedience or defiance of authority, not for being irresponsible. It should never be administered harshly, impulsively, or cause physical harm. There is a difference between discipline and punishment. The latter demonstrates anger and may result in compliance due to fear. The child could also become rebellious and have feelings of shame, guilt, and hostility. Discipline is motivated by love for the child. It focuses on the future. Parents hope to instill obedience and feelings of security within their children. They need to understand that the sting of a spanking is from making bad choices. Prevention is easier than the cure. The child should know why they are receiving this disciplinary action. If he or she disobeys, the parent should inform the child of the upcoming spanking within a private area. Afterward, the parent can remind the child of the lesson, so he or she understands and learns from this experience.

I advised parents to use spanking on younger children if their behavior was out of control. Sometimes, children just do not respond to consequences like time out, standing in a corner, or sitting in a safe place. Out of control, children tend to escalate their misbehavior when they do not understand appropriate boundaries. Children need to be a little fearful of parents and respect them enough to realize that they cannot get away with breaking the rules of the household or society. The only stipulation for parents when administering punishment is that they should not be angry. They should also not use implements that would hurt the child excessively or leave marks on the child. A child's body should not have any welts, red swollen marks left by a blow or pressure on any part of the body. A misbehaved child can receive a paddle on their buttocks, but not a slap on their face, arms, or legs. The whole idea of corporal punishment is to get the attention of the child, not to abuse them.

Today, many parents perceive themselves as their child's friend. They do not want to be their child's disciplinarian. Children need their parents' love and affirmation, as well as their authoritative guidance, concern, and correction. Discipline is part of the tough work of parenting. As a child psychiatrist, several children said to me during their treatment or incarceration that they felt their parents did not care for them. Their parents did not discipline them when they did something wrong. They also did not offer any guidance. "My parents did not care enough to stop me. I could get away with anything." Children need parents to be loving and gentle, but also firm and consistent.

Teachers & Student Discipline

School teachers are trying to discipline unruly children, who can be angry, rude, disrespectful, and unwilling to follow classroom procedures. Educators have very few resources to care for these children. Follow-up procedures include recommended evaluations by school psychologists. There are many school budget restrictions today. Usually, the school psychologist is spread very thin throughout the school district, covering the elementary, middle, and high schools. The school psychologist is unable to effectively serve such an extensive community of students. In the classroom, when children are disruptive, they will often cry foul and complain to their parents that the teacher was picking on them. It was not their fault. Parents will usually side with their children and are unwilling to accept the responsibility to correct their behavior. It is a vicious cycle where classroom management becomes an issue, and the other students witness negative behavior and disruptions by a few students. Instructional time is lost forever with classroom disciplinary problems. The ones that suffer are the students who want to learn.

Teachers need to have authority to remove the disruptive children from the classroom. Allowing children with problems to attend regular classes has not been a good mandate. There are alternative classes and schools for disruptive children and for ones who are mentally challenged. It is a disservice to regular students when everyone is kept together so that the mentally or physically handicapped children do not feel ostracized. If parents complain about their children being disciplined in school, the parents need to be responsible to get help and come up with appropriate consequences when their child acts up.

Disruptive College Campuses

In the previously mentioned book, "The Coddling of the American Mind," studies have shown that even college students have become highly disruptive. They have become vocal and outspoken when they do not agree with a professor or the dean of the college.[121] They will misinterpret messages, comments, and use social media to spread their anger across the campus. They will invite other students to march, protest, destroy offices, and even take over buildings to demonstrate their beliefs. Sadly, many academic professionals have resigned or lost their jobs due to the students' demands for social justice, whether they were right or wrong. Within society, we have lost the ability to have an honest face-to-face discourse and be open to listening to both points of view.

In 2017, Berkeley students protested over the invitation of the right-wing commentator Milo Yiannopoulos to speak on the campus. They caused over one hundred thousand dollars' worth of damage on the campus. Black-clad protesters threw fireworks and rocks at the police, and even Molotov cocktails, which started fires. They smashed windows and injured people. As a result of the violence, the administrators canceled the event.[122] Ironically, Berkeley was the bastion of democracy in the 1960s during the protests of the Vietnam War.

College students need to understand that they attend college to get an education and can voice their opinions in an appropriate manner. They are not in college to be disruptive, argumentative, or destructive. These behaviors should not be tolerated, and parents need to be informed and billed for any damages their child causes. Unfortunately, in the name of freedom of speech, our young people have lost their sense of respect for authority and the institution of education.

Difficult Working Conditions
& Teacher Shortages

The problems in education continue. By the year 2025, there will be a shortage of two hundred thousand teachers in elementary and secondary schools in the United States. That number may rise due to the problems created by the COVID-19 pandemic. Teachers feel tremendous stress about performance reviews based on student performance and testing. Since 2002, as a result of the "No Child Left Behind Act" and the 2015 "Every Student Succeeds Act," students are tested consistently from third grade through eighth grade in math and literacy.[123] The effect has resulted in a thirty-five percent decrease in enrollment in teacher training programs at colleges and universities.[124] There is a lack of qualified teachers in special education, math, science, and bilingual education. Teaching conditions are at a low point in the United States due to poor salaries, working conditions, and the available access to strong preparation and mentoring.[125] Even experienced teachers are leaving the profession. Their significant complaints are insufficient resources, poor school leadership, and vision. Sixty percent of teachers have reported that they cannot make ends meet on their salaries alone. Our educational system needs improvement, beginning with offering a substantial wage to teachers, in addition to supporting them and giving them the authority to discipline unruly and disrespectful students.[126]

School Discipline & No-tolerance Policy

When I was working as a child psychiatrist in Georgia, there was a no-tolerance policy in the school system. If a child acted up or even brought a pill to school that the school nurse was not aware of, the child received a suspension. The school district contacted the parents immediately. Parents would have to seek a psychiatric evaluation for their children's adverse behavior.

However, in August of 2017, the Georgia Supreme Court addressed the issue of zero tolerance in schools. They stated that there is an issue of a student using self-defense and the school district using disciplinary action against this student. All school districts' legal authority was put on notice.[127] In April 2019, a comprehensive booklet was published by the U.S. Department of Education, entitled "Georgia Compilation of School Discipline Laws and Regulations." It describes explicitly in-school discipline, out-of-school and exclusionary discipline: suspension, expulsion, restraint and seclusion, and alternative placements, disciplinary approaches addressing specific infractions and guidelines, prevention and behavioral interventions (non-punitive), monitoring and accountability, school resource and safety officers, truant and attendance officers, and state education agency and support.[128] School discipline policies and their legal ramifications have required school districts to hire numerous legal and professional personnel. It has become a major line item within a school district's annual financial budget. In the end, disruptive students endanger the welfare of other students and teachers. Valuable teaching time is diminished since the teacher must stop and try to discipline the student. The administrative staff and school psychologists have to step in to treat the child with the parent's permission and consent. All these resources cost the school districts across America thousands and thousands of taxpayer dollars. We must ask ourselves the question why the vast majority of well-behaved students have to suffer and lose valuable instruction time due to the continual misbehavior of a few. These students are being robbed of the education that they so well deserve. And good teachers are leaving the profession because the classroom stress can be overwhelming. According to the U.S. Department of Education, a "zero tolerance" or "no tolerance" policy is "a school or district policy that mandates specific predetermined consequences for specific offenses."[129]

Nikolas Cruz, the High School Shooter from Parkland, Florida

On Valentine's Day 2018 in Marjory Stoneman Douglas High School in Parkland, Florida, Nikolas Cruz, a nineteen-year-old, entered the school and shot and killed seventeen individuals, including students and employees. He also wounded seventeen others. Initially, Cruz had been seen by a Henderson Behavioral Health counselor in January 2013. He had thrown his mother against the wall because she had taken away his video games. On several occasions the police were called, Mrs. Cruz told the police that her son suffered from ADHD (Attention Deficit Hyperactivity Disorder), OCD (Obsessive-Compulsive Disorder), and anger issues. The counselor who treated Nikolas Cruz determined that a mental health evaluation was not warranted at the time. However, in 2014, he was transferred from Westglades Middle School to Cross Creek School, an alternative school for developmentally disabled children and students with behavioral problems. In January 2016, he transferred to Marjory Stoneman Douglas High School, where he was eased back into regular classes. He began attending half-day classes, then became a full-time student. Early in February 2016, a neighbor called the police after seeing an alarming Instagram post stating that Cruz may be planning "to shoot up the school." A police deputy responded and entered the home. He found knives and a BB gun. The officer passed the information onto the school resource officer. It is unclear what the school resource officer did with the information or why this young man was not referred for any psychological or psychiatric evaluation.[130]

Also, one wonders why the school officer or other family relatives did not act on the resources available through the Baker Act. It is a Florida law, which "enables family members and loved ones to provide emergency mental care services and temporary detention for people who are impaired because of their mental illness, and who are unable to determine their needs for treatment. It also allows law enforcement, school counselors, and medical personnel to petition for someone to be institutionalized for seventy-two hours when the individual is perceived as a danger to themselves or others, without their permission, or, in the case of children, without their parents' permission."[131]

In September 2016, the administrators suspended Cruz and referred him to social services after he got into a fight following the breakup with his girlfriend. At the end of the month, a friend reported to the school resource officer that Cruz was depressed and cutting himself. He had also attempted to kill himself by ingesting gasoline. Talk about a cry for help! Counselors from Henderson Behavioral Health again determined that Cruz was not a risk to harm himself or others and advised the police of this decision. Cruz was on a treatment plan at the time for ADHD, depression, and autism. It is not known if the school resource officer shared any information with the social worker about what the student had told him in reference to Cruz's self-mutilation and suicide attempt.

Teachers and counselors at the high school hoped that a transfer to an alternative school would provide the mental health services that Cruz needed after his aggressive behavior and increased number of discipline problems. In January 2017, Cruz was suspended from school for "low assault" by an assistant principal and there was a request for a threat assessment. In 2017, Cruz refused to return to Cross Creek School. Broward County School Superintendent Robert Runcie stated that Nikolas Cruz had turned eighteen, and it was impossible to force an adult to receive these services.[132] School officials in Parkland, Florida, had considered enacting the Baker Act for an involuntary mental health examination of Nikolas Cruz in 2016. However, more than a year before the massacre in 2018, a mental health counselor told the school district that Cruz did not need to be detained. When one reviews the interview of Cruz after his arrest, it was obvious that he had serious mental health issues and should never have been allowed anywhere near firearms.

Mental Health Issues & Young Adults

Young adults were a challenging age group to treat in my professional practice as a psychiatrist. Unless they were an immediate threat to themselves or others, you could not force them into treatment, get them to take their medications, or force them to attend school or vocational training. Dysfunctional adult children are indeed a nightmare for parents and a real burden on society. "In 2018, parents living in upstate New York went to court to remove their thirty-year-old son from their home. The judge in the case sided with the parents declaring that they were no longer responsible for an able-bodied son who did not work or contribute to the household."[133] In previous generations, like the baby boomer generation, young people knew that by the time they reached eighteen to twenty-one years of age, they would be financially responsible for themselves. They left home, went to college, enlisted in the armed forces, or found full-time employment.

It is important to note, as a child and adolescent psychiatrist, there were times when our recommendations clashed with the court decisions or assigned caseworkers from the DFCS (Department of Family and Children's Services). Unfortunately, neither group had the education and training to determine "what was in the best interest of the child." As psychiatrists, we were only asked to provide recommendations. The courts made the final decisions. With the shortage of child and adolescent psychiatrists, and not enough well-trained mental health personnel to assess and treat young people, cases like the Nikolas Cruz case will continue to fall through the cracks.

There has always been a lack of facilities for individuals to be appropriately evaluated and treated for mental health illnesses as outpatients and inpatients. Until more financial resources are allocated for mental health patients, we will continue to hear about the toll of mental illness on society, the welfare of these individuals, and the aftermath of these mass shootings. There are laws that hold parents accountable for allowing disturbed children to have access to firearms and for not providing appropriate supervision of their children. Parents must seek help for their children from mental health professionals. They must be involved in their children's lives, especially if the child is aggressive and acting out in a disturbed manner. Parents have the responsibility to prepare their children for the real world and to teach them how to function effectively as adults.

After so many mass school shootings in America, and especially after the death of seventeen individuals at Parkland High School in Florida, the public and government officials are more focused on gun control, and the rules and restrictions relating to selling guns to young people under the age of twenty-one. Most important and hopefully, the states will increase funding to treat children and adolescents' mental health issues. How many more massacres do we have to witness? The rights of individuals with serious mental health issues need to be reviewed and restricted.

Gun Violence vs. Gun Control

Semi-automatic weapons may not have a place in a community, but especially, as part of an arsenal of a young person. Adolescents are not permitted to drink legally until the age of twenty-one. The "tobacco 21" law signed on December 20, 2019, raised the age nationwide to twenty-one to purchase any tobacco products or e-cigarettes. The majority of states allow 18-year-olds to purchase and own long guns (rifles and shotguns). Florida restricts it to age twenty-one. However, a sixteen-year-old minor can possess a shotgun or rifle for hunting. Many states do not impose a waiting period law between the time of purchase and the actual transfer of the firearm. Some states impose a waiting period of ten days, others three days. "A waiting period law requires a certain number of days to elapse between the purchase of a firearm and when the buyer can take possession of the gun. By delaying immediate access to firearms, waiting periods create 'an important cooling off period' that can help prevent impulsive acts of gun violence, including gun homicides and suicides."[134] A thirty-day waiting period for semi-automatic shotguns is a most responsible legislative action based upon the results of the mass shooting events that we have witnessed. There should be stringent background checks if any of these weapons are sold. Buyers must give up their rights and have their mental health history checked before securing these firearms. It is unrealistic to assume that individuals will be truthful about their mental health. Felons with violent pasts are not likely to follow the laws unless they have been reformed.

Collectively, we are all to be blamed for this breakdown within our society for mass shootings. "These tragedies are the result of a lack of investment in our children, our ability to raise respectful and responsible adults. Our children need adults to model something other than materialism and self-centeredness that they have witnessed on social media and in their homes."[135] We have focused our energies on trying to give our children everything they want without the responsibility and self-respect to earn these rewards themselves. When we do not meet their expectations, they become angry and hostile. After all this violence, some are asking if the politicians will do the right thing.

Unfortunately, not all the politicians are on board, no matter how horrific the situation has become about school shootings. Even after the violence, the battle of gun control and legislation continued in California, Ohio, and Texas in July and August 2019. In response to the shooting, Senate Majority Leader Mitch McConnell directed Senate Republicans to come up with options to address gun violence. Party members have expressed interest in a bill to revamp the background check system.[136] In Texas, the pendulum has swung the other way. "A series of new firearm laws went into effect in August 2019, further loosening gun restrictions in a state that had four of the deadliest mass shootings in modern U.S. history. A school district cannot prohibit licensed gun owners, including school employees, from storing firearms in a locked vehicle on a school parking lot, if they are not in plain view. Another bill allows handgun owners to carry their weapons in places of worship legally. There were also additional bills permitting handgun use."[137] It is a balancing act between the 2nd. Amendment and gun control.

Corporate Greed vs. Worker & Consumer Benefits

It appears that some people in our society focus solely on how much money they can make regardless of how it is earned. Most problems revolve around corporate greed. Companies will do anything to increase their profits instead of investing in benefits for the workers or consumers. Executives have worked out "golden parachute" deals with companies. It is an agreement between the CEO and the company, formulated for the CEO to receive substantial benefits and a large compensation as a severance package when the company is taken over by another company or for several other reasons, like being fired or quitting the job. In essence, it is a guaranteed financial insurance policy before they have even begun their new position, valued at millions of dollars and even with stock options.[138]

Abigail Disney, the heiress to the Walt Disney Company, recently said she was appalled that Disney's CEO received sixty-six million dollars in 2018. "It's time to call out Disney and anyone else rich off their workers' backs. Abigail recommended that Disney start remedying the problem by slicing their bonuses in half and distributing the money to the lowest-paid 10% of the workers."[139] A day trip to Disneyland for a family of four, two parents and two children over the age of ten years old, will cost $450, with an individual ticket price per person of $112.50.[140] This entrance fee does not include parking for a single vehicle which is $25.00, nor does it include a hotel stay for one night for four people, or the cost of meals for the day. Do Disney executives realize that many families must work a week or more to be able to afford close to one thousand dollars for a day's outing? It is outrageous. Since the parks are packed, I guess many families are making sacrifices. There is not much of an incentive to lower the price and capitalism flourishes.

Working conditions for employees in corporations do not always include payment and compensation for overtime, vacation and holiday time, job security, work intensity, teamwork, autonomy and freedom, flexibility and working hours, and health and safety. Before the pandemic, across America, the unemployment rate was low, but we are still hearing about plants closing, workers being laid off, stagnant wages, and poor, unsafe working conditions. Since CEOs are so well-compensated, why are the workers not receiving a wage increase or improved working conditions, especially if the company is very profitable? Apparently, this is a subject many business schools debate with various outcomes, depending on which side of the argument you are on. It has been reported that even when CEOs have not well-managed their companies, they are still receiving an outstanding financial package. Yet, some employees are fired immediately for poor performance.

"In the 2015-2016 election cycle, businesses outspent unions 16-to-1, $3.4 billion to $213 million, according to the non-partisan Center for Responsive Politics. Each year all of the nation's unions spend about $48 million on lobbying in Washington, while corporate America spends $2.5 billion, more than fifty times as much. This corporate spending has made many legislators in Congress far more attentive to corporations than to workers, thus the rush to cut corporate taxes, but the failure to increase the minimum wage."[141] Unfortunately, the assumption is that unions represent workers, which sadly is not always the case. They usually represent their own management, hence why many of them are in jail.

Elizabeth Warren, a senator, who was running for the Democratic bid for president in the 2020 election, has proposed legislation that will increase workers' participation in large American corporations. It also permits employees to become forty percent of the members of the corporate board of directors.[142] Co- determination provides the workers with the rights to participate in the management of their company.

In Germany and other countries in the European Union, workers sit alongside corporate board members. They have a right to seats on corporate boards. "In companies with 500 to 2,000 employees, one-third the number of seats, and half the number of seats in companies with more than 2,000 employees. This supervisory board can appoint and dismiss management. They can review management's performance. They give advice and assist in developing the company's strategic goals and objectives. The members receive financial and other crucial information related to the company's performance. They also receive a list of operations to approve before implementation within the corporation."[143] Unfortunately, even in Germany, there is great debate about how well this works, most evidenced by the fact that German industry has been stagnant for decades. There are few innovations or patents coming out of German companies, few are in the top 100-list in Europe. Co-determination is an interesting idea, but its success is questionable.

America is already seething with anger and civil unrest, which may well lead to a civil war. The stimulus package from the pandemic proved that the rich continue to fill their coffers with little concern or care for the struggling poor citizens who were desperate for aid during this unprecedented time in our history. My fear is that America will not be destroyed by external forces but from inside the nation, just like the Roman Empire was torn down from within the country and community, due to corruption, greed and unwillingness to take care of the workers. All the military power will not stop this erosion of community and societal values, like an apple rotting from its core. We will continue to experience severe cultural demise until major changes are initiated and instituted.

Financial Crisis of Student Debt

Another troubling financial dilemma within the United States is the extraordinary amount of student debt. In 2019, student debt has reached $1.5 trillion spread across 45 million borrowers with a loan delinquency rate of 11.4%, (90 days plus delinquent.)[144] The rising cost of college has reached an average of over $26,000 per year for a four-year public university, and $35,000 for a four-year private college. At the end of 2018, the average student loan debt was over $35,000.

While training as a medical doctor living in the United Kingdom, most of my education was paid for by the British government. Here in the United States, most medical students graduate from the university with a student loan debt of over $200,000. The United Kingdom had a great system in place to assist students financially if their families were unable to afford to pay for their college degree. However, as of 1998, attendance at public universities in the United Kingdom is no longer free, but the fees are much more reasonable than here in America.

"In 2017, in the United States, New York State became the first state to offer a tuition- free education at all CUNY and SUNY (City and State Universities of New York), two and four-year colleges. It is the Excelsior Scholarship Program."[145] Eleven states have adopted promise programs offering students two years of free college tuition for associate degree programs and vocational programs. Nine other states are working on legislation to assist students with tuition at state public colleges.[146]

In the United States, many scholarships and grants are available, but post-graduate colleges, like medical school and law school, must be funded by the students' families and college loans. According to the AAMC (Association of American Colleges), the average annual cost of public medical school, including tuition, fees, and health insurance is $34,000 for in-state tuition and $58,000 for out-of-state students in 2016-2017.[147] Instead of going straight into medical, dental or other post graduate schools, students have to get a four-year degree. This is not the system in the United Kingdom or Europe.

According to a report in CNN Money, a congressional committee was looking into the issue of wealthy universities with big endowments, charging their students way too much money for tuition."[148] And despite these endowments, many colleges and universities have raised tuition far above inflation,"[149] wrote the committee heading up the inquiry. "Harvard's endowment, the largest in the country, was at nearly $36 billion. According to the National Association of College and University Business Officers, about 90 other colleges have endowments valued at more than $1 billion."[150] Private colleges, which are the most likely to have big endowments, charge an average price of $43,370 a year for tuition, fees, room and board. That amount is 80% of the median family income of an American family. These figures are from 2016. They have certainly increased since then.

The larger question is why is it necessary for everyone to obtain a four-year degree? We spend a lot of resources offering people four-year degrees that they are not really qualified to seek and will never use. In this case, Germany and other European countries, and South Korea have instituted vocational training and an apprentice system. It would be much more beneficial to give students coming out of high school an opportunity to train in a skill or vocation to make a living. America is facing an unprecedented skilled labor shortage. According to the Department of Labor, the US economy had 7.6 million unfilled jobs, but only 6.5 million people were looking for work as of January 2019.[151] This issue ispartly due to our culture's emphasis on going to college. Many high schools look to their university placement as the best judge of a quality education. That statistic discriminates against students for whom college is just not a good fit, especially when schools do little to inform students of non-collegiate options. Employers are having trouble filling jobs for skilled trade workers (especially chefs/bakers/butchers, mechanics, and electricians). There is a shortage of drivers, especially for truckers transporting heavy goods, delivery and courier service, and construction truck operators. Another cause for the labor shortage is that automation has moved slower than predicted. Robots haven't successfully replaced the cashiers, tellers, and customer-service reps that interact with customers.

Bernie Sanders, a Democratic candidate who ran for the presidency of the United States, is a champion of debt-free college. In June 2019, Mr. Sanders, along with other House Democratic Progressives proposed a bill to eliminate all federal loan student debt and to forgive the debts of 45 million graduates. He has stated that within six months, all debts would be removed. To pay for this $2.2 trillion debt, there would be a Wall Street Speculation Tax on all financial investment transactions. Legislators agree that it is time for Wall Street to bail out college graduates after we bailed out Wall Street after the banking and real estate crisis in 2007–2009.[152] In fact, very few legislators agreed with him, hence the bill has not gone anywhere. There are many unanswered questions. Will there be student loan forgiveness for students who dropped out of college and never completed their degree requirements? Who will decide which students are released from their college loan debt obligations? Are the students who secured these educational loans learning financial responsibility through loan forgiveness? And what are the rewards for the students who have paid off their college loans? What about the disparity between irresponsible students who have defaulted on their loans, and those who have been financially responsible?

Misplaced Societal Values

Societal values in the United States are misplaced. Do football players who tackle and throw a ball down the field, basketball players who dunk a shot, and golfers who drive a golf ball down a fairway several hundred yards, deserve to be paid millions of dollars while teachers make next to nothing? What has happened in America with our system of justice and fairness, honesty, responsibility, service to others, and consideration to our families and communities?

Wherever we turn in our society today, there is an abuse of power, corruption, greed, and a substantial loss of respect for one another. The sole emphasis is on money, how much you can earn, and how quickly you can amass a fortune. Even teenagers today can make a substantial living playing video games and entering national competitions. This year the Fortnite World Cup Championship awarded prize money of $30 Million. The national event featured the game "Defense of the Ancients," a multiplayer online battle arena where each team is trying to destroy their opponents' heavily guarded structure at the opposing side of a map.[153]

In direct contrast, teachers in the United States receive astronomically less in annual salaries. Yet, the success of our economy rests on their shoulders. They are responsible for educating and preparing our children for future professions. Where is the social justice or awareness that our emphasis on athletic ability is not improving the welfare of our community? Americans can name their favorite sports team and football quarterback, but they cannot name a single individual who was awarded a distinguished Nobel Prize this year. These prestigious awards are for intellectual achievement in the six categories of physics, chemistry, medicine, literature, economic sciences, and peace. "The 2019 Nobel Prize for Physiology or Medicine was awarded to William G. Kaelin Jr., Sir Peter J. Ratcliffe, and Gregg L. Semenza. The trio identified molecular machinery that regulates the activity of genes in response to varying levels of oxygen. Their work has paved the way for promising new strategies to fight anemia, cancer, and many other diseases."[154] These Nobel Prize awardees have contributed significantly to our society by advancing the progress of medicine and assisting in saving lives through their breakthrough discoveries. They will receive this distinguished honor, a medal, and a share of a cash prize of about $1.1 Million. Saving humanity receives less than twenty percent of the average football quarterback's salary of $6 Million in 2019.[155] And we wonder why our children focus solely on self-gratification and consumerism to the extreme. Sadly, our values have become all about fame and earning millions of dollars, not what one can contribute to our society.

Climate Change and Our Responsibility to the Planet

Scientific analysis has pointed to our role in warming the climate through human activity since 1896, as documented by Svante Arrhenius.[156] In 1903, he was awarded the Nobel prize for chemistry. He was extremely interested in the fields of meteorology, climatology, and cosmology. In 1895, he wanted to quantify the influence of CO_2 on the greenhouse effect. He determined that "a reduction in the atmospheric CO_2 levels to half the existing ones would result in a drop of temperature of the planet between four and five degrees Celsius, which could lead to a massive cooling like the one that takes place during glaciations."[157] He also identified human industrial activity as the main source of CO_2 into the atmosphere.[158] An article in a New Zealand newspaper from August 14, 1912, stated: "The furnaces of the world are now burning two billion tons of coal per year. When this is burned, uniting with oxygen, it adds about seven billion tons of carbon dioxide into the atmosphere. The air becomes a more effective blanket covering the earth and raising its temperature."[159] Over a hundred years later, humans have continued to ignore these warnings and has turned a blind eye to the problems of climate change. The greenhouse gases produced by human activity have led to extreme disastrous effects. The environmental hazards have caused an increase in human health issues, natural disasters such as torrential flooding, uncontrollable wildfires, massive storms, cyclones, and severe erosion along the coastlines worldwide. Millions of east Africans were pushed to the brink of starvation when torrential rain created perfect conditions for desert locusts to reproduce at an alarming rate and devoured every crop in their path as they flew across the country. Swarms like these have not been seen for centuries. Same scenario in some parts of India. Due to a depletion of our ozone layer, there is an increased risk of skin cancer, stresses on our food production, unavailability of freshwater, and a spread of infectious diseases.[160]

Today, most young people are attached to their cell phones and other electronic devices. Climate change has not been a hot topic on their agenda. However, a young teenager from Sweden has recently changed that paradigm. She has ignited young people around the world to pay attention and demand a change by their governments. Greta Thunberg, a Swedish activist, arrived in New York after spending two weeks on a sailboat crossing the Atlantic Ocean. She refused to fly from her home in Stockholm to New York because the burning of jet fuel releases greenhouse gases such as carbon dioxide into the earth's atmosphere and oceans.[161] In September 2019, Greta presented a speech at the United Nations Climate Action Summit. She stated, "You have stolen my dreams and my childhood with your empty words. And yet I am one of the lucky ones. People are suffering. People are dying. Entire ecosystems are collapsing. We are at the beginning of mass extinction, and all you can talk about is money and fairy tales of eternal economic growth. How dare you! The popular idea of cutting out emissions in half in ten years only gives us a 50% chance of staying below 1.5 degrees Celsius, and the risk of setting off irreversible chain reactions beyond human control."[162] Greta has become an international leader for climate change and has led young people around the world to demonstrate. She was selected as one of the most one hundred influential people for 2019 and awarded Person of the Year 2019 by Time Magazine and was also nominated for the Nobel Peace Prize for 2019.[163]

Major climate change predictions for cities and countries around the world include a rise in temperature in cities in the Northern Hemisphere of 3.5 Celsius to 4.7 Celsius. Tropical cities will experience increased periods of extreme precipitation, and then drought. The change will bring about such severe droughts that cities will be forced to import drinking water. Regions that are already extremely hot will have food and water shortages.[164] The summer of 2019 was stifling around the world with extreme heatwaves. Europe suffered extremely from the intense heat. There were wildfires in the Arctic and Siberia, mass melting of Greenland's ice sheet, and the hottest month ever recorded in Anchorage, Alaska.

Deforestation has been occurring at an alarming rate. This mass destruction of clearing trees and wildfires has contributed to a reduction of 502,000 square miles of forest, according to the World Bank between 1990 and 2016.[165] Trees contribute greatly to our well-being. They absorb the carbon dioxide in the air and greenhouse gases. Over 20% of the Amazon rainforest has been destroyed over the past fifty years. The Amazon rainforest has been described as the 'lungs of the planet.'[166] The rainforests contain thousands of species of plants, animals, and insects. All these species can assist us in finding cures for life-threatening illnesses. Ranching in the Amazon region has increased dramatically with over 200 million cattle in Brazil. Methane produced by cows is much more destructive than CO_2 for global warming. Over one-quarter of the world's beef supply is exported from Brazil. Are people willing to decrease beef consumption to save the planet? Destruction of the Amazon surged to an 11-year high last year and continues to climb in 2020, which environmentalists blame on the policies of right-wing President Jair Bolsonaro who has emboldened illegal loggers, miners, and ranchers.[167]

Recently, Sir David Attenborough, an English broadcaster, writer, and naturalist, narrated an eight-part series, "Our Planet." It addresses issues of conservation featuring animals in natural habitats and humans' impact on the environment. He also produced a documentary on "Climate Change–The Facts," which states: "It is no longer a matter of opinion, the science is certain, and the evidence is unequivocal. Ice melt is worse than expected with the Arctic and Antarctic experiencing five and three times more ice loss, compared to twenty-five years ago. Rising sea levels are causing a football field of land to be lost in Louisiana every forty-five minutes. Atmospheric CO_2 concentrations have rocketed, and twenty of the warmest years on record have occurred in the last twenty-three years."[168] Attenborough forces us to come to terms with the facts–"irreversible damage to the natural world and collapse of our societies is imminent and that only through decisive and immediate action can it be averted."[169]

Looking Back Instead of Moving Forward

In light of Black Lives Matter Movement, the issue of reparations has come to the forefront. First, all lives should matter, not only black lives. Every individual should have the capacity and opportunity to study and receive an education or acquire a skill and work in the trade or profession of one's choice. President Lincoln issued a preliminary proclamation on September 22, 1862 and made it official on January 1,1863: "slaves within any State shall be forever free." However, slavery ended with the passage of the 13th Amendment after the Civil War ended in 1865. An estimated four million African Americans were set free.[170]

There is a significant divide among the black and white citizens of America regarding slavery reparations. Now the focus is on supporting special education, job training programs, and making investments in areas where Black residents face disparities. They want to increase minority home ownership, affordable housing, business ownership, career opportunities, and ways to grow equity and generational wealth. These accomplishments can only happen with responsible behaviors and not with handouts. Success in life is earned by surmounting obstacles, working diligently, and focusing on a goal. The current citizens, and millions of immigrants who are American taxpayers, had nothing to do with slavery that was abolished 150 years ago. They feel they should not be held responsible for any reparations. This issue has become a 2020 campaign issue. If we examine the history of our country, many disenfranchised groups could insist on equal payments. It is an unrealistic idea.

While many black people support the idea, it is enlightening to hear from a black college professor, Terry McCann, in North Carolina. "It is not going to cure anything. It is not going to help." He has two children and is a descendant of slaves. He believes that other disenfranchised groups in the country will demand reparations. McCann concluded: "I work hard, working each day to provide for my family, teaching my kids right from wrong. There is good and bad in all people, but I can't hold people today accountable for something that happened 200, 300 years ago."[171]

Some of the rioters and looters in Portland and Seattle rationalized their looting, stating that stealing things from the stores was a start to the reparations they were entitled to! Another person interviewed on the television stated that the things they stole were to feed the hungry and be able to pay rent during the chaotic times of the pandemic. I wander how many logical people would agree that those behaviors were in response to the past and present problems or merely justifying their irrational criminal activities.

Solutions: Mentoring Our Children

If we as adults do not get our priorities straight, how do we expect our children and the next generation to do the right things? It is the job of parents to mold their children into productive, well-functioning adults; otherwise, they will become society's problems. In turn, these young adults have the responsibility to make the world a better place. Adults must be willing to put aside their political differences and help the children who are hurting and broken. They need to demonstrate what it takes to invest in another human being. We need to pay attention, listen, and tell the truth to young people who are around us and those who live in surrounding communities. We need to teach children how to handle conflict with integrity, not unbridled anger. We must explain that failure is part of life that we all experience and demonstrate by modeling how to respond to the criticism of others with character and confidence.

Teenagers will not listen to our advice just because we ask them to. They learn by watching adults handle the problems of everyday life. It is so important to ask ourselves as adults, what are we modeling for the young people around us? How are we demonstrating patience and understanding with conflict, criticism, disappointment, financial stress, and even bullying? If we respond with anger, hate, harsh words, and aggressive behaviors, young people are likely to imitate the same response.

Most of us were horrified watching a mother and her daughter beating up another woman, pulling her out of her car over a road rage incident.[172] Young people need older, wiser, invested adults in their lives to show them how to live a life with

116

empathy for others, self-respect, and love for humanity in the face of adversity. Children require lessons in how to treat people when they feel misunderstood and are taken advantage of. Even for our enemies, we must model respect and tolerance.

Solutions: Anger Management

"While I understand the passions and the anger that arise over the death of Michael Brown, giving into that anger by looting or carrying guns, and even attacking the police, only serves to raise tensions and stir chaos."[173]

Barack Obama

The "Black Lives Matter" political demonstrations protested police brutality. Sadly, many of these individuals destroyed property, looted stores in their neighborhoods, and incited riots injuring other protest participants. Instead of peaceful demonstrations, the burning and looting created many images of rage, violence, and destruction. Many rioters chose to resolve issues with irrational behaviors like burning buildings and cars, breaking windows, spray painting obscenities that left the neighborhoods looking like war zones. Were these knee-jerk reactions or did a few incite all this chaos to vent their frustrations? How did the peaceful protestors allow the rioters to cause all this unjustified mayhem? Why didn't the police or government officials step in to stop the destruction in the cities across the country?

Protests with violence continued every night in Portland, Oregon since late May 2020 for over 100 days. This started after the death of George Floyd. The issue of how to contain and stop the violence became a source of conflict between the President who wanted to deploy federal agents and local leaders, the

Mayor of Portland, and Governor of Oregon. The latter did not take enough action to stop the looting, burning and destruction of property, including several fires started near the courthouse which could have spread and hurt the agents in the building. After the federal officers were called in to deal with the violence, some protesters threw rocks and water bottles, agents were burned by fireworks and a "caustic substance," others shone lasers at the federal agents and security cameras to block their view. The US attorney's office in Oregon said that 28 federal law enforcement officers had been injured during protests in Portland. "The most serious injury to an officer to date occurred when a protester wielding a two-pound sledgehammer struck an officer in the head and shoulder when the officer tried to prevent the protester from breaking down a door to the Hatfield Courthouse. Other injuries included broken bones, hearing damage, eye damage, a dislocated shoulder, sprains, strains, and contusions."[174]

Right or wrong, when citizens deem that their elected officials are not solving the problems, individuals feel like they must act. Some protestors who were interviewed on television stated that buildings could be rebuilt but once a life is lost, it cannot be brought back. Would that protestor feel the same way if his home, business, or livelihood were torn or burnt down in an act of defiance and protest?

Similar scenes were being played out in Seattle as well. Some protesters lit several construction trailers on fire at a youth detention center, smashed windows of businesses and, according to the police, injured Seattle police officers with explosive devices. The Seattle Police Department released partial body camera video that showed explosions erupting near officers and photographs of cuts and burns suffered by officers that they said were from explosives set off by the protesters. To contain the violence, officers doused protesters with pepper spray, rushed into crowds and knocked people to the ground. The same fires erupted in Kenosha, Wisconsin because people were angry over the police shooting of Jacob Blake, a black man. Sadly, two people were killed and one injured as shots were fired during the first night of protests. What was a 17-year-old doing with an AR-15 style assault rifle, thinking he had to stop people from rioting? He apparently wanted to be a police officer. Someone that age has no experience dealing with stressful situations and intimidation from one or many in a crowd. His reaction and firing his rifle were probably out of fear, as two protesters tried to take his gun away. He did not have support from others who were also present to protect businesses and buildings. Is this how changes will occur in a civilized society, with anger and violence, rather than peaceful protests and putting forth realistic suggestions to improve the situation for all concerned? It takes time for changes to come around. However, trying to solve any problems with violence only causes more dissension and friction between the parties involved, bringing more chaos and grief. Even the 1960s civil rights movement led by Martin Luther King, Jr. followed Gandhi's footsteps, emulating his concept of "Satyagraha," non-violent resistance. This approach produced positive results.

Responding to a message on Facebook for people to take up arms to defend properties and businesses in Portland, many people showed up causing even more instances of violence between demonstrators and counter demonstrators. These citizens were wrong in shooting protestors with paint balls and spraying them with different substances, instead of just guarding and stopping people from looting and destroying property. Officers had to intervene and made some arrests. Unfortunately, a man was shot and killed. The man who died was wearing a hat with the insignia of Patriot Prayer, a far-right group. Finally, the local and State officials acknowledged that a stronger response was needed to stop citizens killing each other. "The tragedy of last night cannot be repeated," Wheeler (Mayor of Portland) said.[175] "It doesn't matter who you are or what your politics are, we must stop the violence. It happened in Kenosha. And now, unfortunately, it is happening in Portland, Oregon." What really needed to stop was the bickering between the Democratic officials and the President, and what was needed to preserve the welfare and peace of all the citizens they were elected to serve!

Local news reported that 50 businesses and properties were destroyed in Pittsburg, another 50 in downtown Seattle and in the Chinatown district. Chicago had 45 properties damaged in the downtown and rioting spread to the suburbs as well. Madison, Wisconsin saw 75 businesses damaged and some were looted. The National Guard was finally deployed in 24 states as the innocent business and restaurant owners continued to suffer losses. Law enforcement personnel were also attacked. How many would want to return to these neighborhoods where local rebellious citizens and opportunistic groups of outside agitators exploited the situation? The protests were supposed to bring about constructive change, but the rioters turned it into destructive chaos.

The Insurance Information Institute offered the only ray of hope that riots, vandalism, looting, and fire were covered in the US under most insurance property policies. However, the heartache of someone's hard work being destroyed by no fault of his own and the necessity to start all over again cannot be compensated. This emotional turmoil on top of the losses caused by the shutdowns from the coronavirus pandemic dealt a double whammy.

There was no yelling, no screaming, no fighting when thousands of people stood in complete silence. They were protesting in squares and public places in Turkey. Instead of tension and aggression, they created a calm curiosity for the police.[176] Non-violence is the force that will change the world. When will our unhinged US citizens learn this important lesson from others in the world?

Currently, our culture feels like an erupting volcano spewing ash of devastation and death. So much chaos has erupted over the needless loss of one man's life and started endless protests and riots. People have donated an excess of $13.7 Million to the Floyd family.[177] George Floyd's sister also launched a GoFundMe campaign to help with travel and other expenses for his memorial. This fund raised $377,080 before she deactivated it. Americans are very generous and empathic, willing to help when there is a need. We should be concerned about the 95,000 health care workers who have been infected and 700 plus individuals who have lost their lives taking care of Covid-19 patients. Who is helping them out financially during this pandemic? The hospitals and insurance companies are trying to avoid paying their families workman's compensation, stating they cannot be sure where they contracted the illness. 431 police officers have been injured or killed in the riots since the death of George Floyd in Minneapolis. 101 police officers have died of Covid-19 in the US. About 82 have died this year by other means, meaning the disease has killed more officers than all other causes combined.

Where was the empathy and concern by the peaceful protestors when the police officers across the country were hit with bricks, rocks, Molotov cocktails, fireworks, and bullets by the rioters? Was this peaceful protesting to bring about constructive change? It was shameful to watch protestors willing the two Los Angeles County sheriff's deputies, who were shot in the head, to die.[178] They were ambushed while sitting in their police car. Are we going to start a fund and show concern for the police officers and frontline workers? Where is our sense of decency and humanity in this country, the US?

> *"Chaos does not unify. Chaos only serves the most extreme element of society that seek to destabilize any semblance of order to fulfill their selfish lust for power."*[179]
>
> Daniel Lubetzky

Amid all this devastation, protestors are asking officials to defund the police. Citizens must be worried about how these changes will affect them and how the cities will deal with crime. The police are present in our communities to protect and serve the people. How will law aiding citizens deal with these individuals' lawlessness? Police are often the first responders dealing with mental health, domestic violence, problems with neighbors, homelessness, various non-criminal activities, and actual violations of the law. We seem to have knee-jerk reactions to disband police departments and divert funds to public health and social programs. Will American citizens defund the politicians who are corrupt and bow to the lobbyists instead of taking affirmative action on issues that would benefit the people they were elected to serve?

Do local citizens have a vote on how their tax dollars should be spent? Polls suggest that 64% of Americans oppose the idea of defunding the police, and 34% agree with this move. 60% are against reallocating police budgets to other public health and social workers. 39% are in favor. Significant changes are now demanded because of a few corrupt police officers. Instead, people should expect police departments to uphold and maintain national standardized regulations. Reforms are possible and supported by most Americans. Unfortunately, some cities like Chicago are on track to witness their most violent summers. Lawless demonstrators are not going to deal peacefully with social workers! We should not encourage people to take matters into their own hands if they feel threatened without the support of adequate police protection. Street battles between the far right and some antifa on the far left seem to look forward to armed confrontations. We have armed militias patrolling the city streets; it is very scary. If all this chaos gets out of control, will we be igniting sparks for a civil war in the US? Civil unrest combined with the horrors of the pandemic, hurricanes, floods, and wildfires is not a good combination for anyone to look forward to in the near and distant future.

"Our lives begin to end the day we become silent about things that matter."[180]
Martin Luther King Jr.

While the exact quote is nowhere to be found in King's speeches or writings, it does seem to be a paraphrase of a more complex thought he uttered during a sermon in Selma, Alabama, on 8 March 1965, the day after "Bloody Sunday," on which civil rights protesters were attacked and beaten by police on the Edmund Pettus Bridge.

Many citizens are also tearing down national, historic monuments in cities and towns across America. They feel that they glorify white supremacy and memorialize an unrecognized government. Here again, who permitted these few individuals to destroy and erase the history of this nation? It is the past generation that fought the hard wars, gave birth to this nation to become the vibrant, democratic, technologically advanced, freedom fighting country. The younger generations of today have benefitted from the sacrifices of their ancestors, yet they think they can rewrite or erase history at their whim? They were neither elected nor permitted to take matters into their own hands to create hysteria and herd mentality, destroying the historical statues. Good or bad, this is our history. We must learn from history, not rewrite it. We cannot judge actions of people in the past by today's standards.

*"Go to Auschwitz and see the absolute torture
that went on there, then ask the Polish people
why the whole place hasn't been burnt to the
ground? They will tell you 'People must know
what happened here, so it never happens
again.' History whether good or bad should
be remembered."*[181]

Author Unknown

On an individual basis, during the 2018 US Open finals
tennis tournament, Serena Williams, a 23-time Grand Slam
champion, lost her temper and got into a heated dispute with the
umpire Carlos Ramos. She called the umpire "a thief" and
accused him of sexism after she received a series of code
violations during that final match. She received a point penalty
for smashing her racket, followed by a game penalty for verbal
abuse. She confronted the umpire and stated: "You stole a point
from me, and you are a thief."[182] At the news conference
following her loss, Williams said that she has seen male players
berate umpires. She claimed that she was fighting for women's
rights and women's equality.[183]

The issue here is to ask how Serena Williams advanced
the women's cause for equality by smashing her racket in anger
and her tirade? Professional sports figures are supposed to be
role models for young people. It is highly doubtful that she was
teaching a lesson in anger management. One can understand the
stress that she was under to make a comeback as the number one
female tennis player in the world. At the same time, losing
control on the international stage and not apologizing for her
behavior, is not teaching the younger generation how to resolve

problems with dignity and professionalism. Men tennis greats like McEnroe, Năstase, Connors, and Agassi berated umpires and were disciplined for poor behavior, suspended, fined, and several even received point penalties. At times, life is unfair. Everything cannot be about women's rights or even men's rights. We must take ownership of our behavior and accept what we did wrong. We cannot cry foul, become hysterical, and declare that it is sexist when you are disappointed or angry.

Solutions: Teaching Respect & Dignity

A mandatory two-year draft for all high school graduates has been suggested for our country's youth, and especially for all eighteen-year-olds who have dropped out of high school. Military service focuses on teaching respect, responsibility, and discipline. Soldiers learn how to make decisions under extreme conditions and stress. Enlisting in the Army, Air Force, Marines, Navy, or Coast Guard, offers technical and training programs that will enhance professional lives after service. Serving your country is the highest form of patriotism. US citizens have always bestowed the highest respect for the militaries' contributions to our society.[184] Senator Tammy Duckworth, from Illinois, suggests that we should all do national service, make giving back to society a standard practice across the country. "She joined other senators in introducing legislation to help young Americans strengthen their communities for service across the country, increase living stipends, establish a 21st Century American Outreach program, and much more on April 3, 2019."[185] It will offer an opportunity for young people to serve their country, and at the same time receive a living wage. After serving two terms, volunteers will receive the financial equivalent of the average cost of four years of tuition at a public college or university. Both the education benefit and the living stipend will be tax-free.[186] It is an opportunity for young Americans to learn about their communities and to come together to help those in need when disasters and emergencies strike. As Americans, we should be most thankful; we have so many privileges. Giving back by supporting our communities helps those in need and contributes to the common good. Volunteerism builds skills and understanding and fosters a stake within our communities. School systems across the country should promote and encourage student community action groups. Through participation, students will experience the value of assisting others in need and receive a lasting education in promoting community values.

The Pledge of Allegiance was written in August 1892 by the socialist minister Francis Bellamy (1855-1931). It was originally published in The Youth's Companion on September 8, 1892. In its original form it read: "I pledge allegiance to my Flag and the Republic for which it stands, one nation, indivisible, with liberty and justice for all." Today it reads: "I pledge allegiance to the flag of the United States of America, and to the republic for which it stands, one nation under God, indivisible, with liberty and justice for all." Our American flag is also a symbol of honor for every fallen soldier who has given their life for this great country, the United States of America. Standing when singing the National Anthem or saying the Pledge of Allegiance with our hand over our hearts, demonstrates our deepest respect for those who have fought to save our democracy.

All Americans, regardless of color, gender or religious affiliation would do well to remember the pledge, when honoring the flag and freedom it represents. The practice of taking a knee to support "Black Lives Matter" while playing the national anthem has caused alienation and shows disrespect to their country. This sign of disrespect is so painful for us to observe since we have lost thousands of our family members who volunteered to serve our country and truly believed in fighting for our freedom. Perhaps these individuals could find another way to find support for their cause without showing such disrespect for our fallen soldiers. After all, the US belongs to all citizens and should be respected by everyone.

Solutions: Understanding Religious Controversies

Religion tries to dictate how you choose to live your life, when and with whom you can have sex, whether you should use birth control or not, and if you should marry or live together. Most religions have a common theme about how to live your life while practicing good moral behavior. They believe that all people should be treated with respect and dignity. However, religions also dictate many restrictions and try to exert control over their congregations. Extremists interpret their holy books in whatever manner suits their way of thinking, deciding what is appropriate. We do have free will and can determine what is best for our needs. We all should understand the underlying philosophy of not causing harm to others.

In November 2018, a Pentecostal pastor of an Assemblies of God megachurch with a congregation of 10,500 in Springfield, Missouri delivered a paranormal-themed Sunday sermon before Halloween. He discussed the practice of yoga and stated that it was created with demonic intent because Hinduism is demonic. He expressed his disapproval of meditation when you practice clearing your mind. He feels that it is spiritually dangerous for people to empty their minds. And basically, he concluded that yoga is opposed to Christianity.[187]

This kind of ignorance is what is driving people away from formal religion. Congregants are being brain-washed by pastors like this individual. His statements are ludicrous. Individuals who have yoga studios in this geographic area suffered from a drop in attendance after this sermon. One wonders if people have lost their ability to think and do simple research for themselves. Everyone today has access to the Internet on their home computers or at the local library. According to the government of India's Ministry of External Affairs, yoga does not adhere to any particular religion or belief system.[188] It is a series of poses that promote flexibility and balance, increases muscle strength and tone, improves respiration and energy levels, helps with weight reduction, and improves cardio and circulatory health. It has also been known to decrease stress, to relieve anxiety and depression, and even assist patients to lower their blood pressure, reduce chronic pain, and ease migraine headaches. It is known to promote better and more restful sleep. So, one wonders what was the motive of this pastor to spread false ideas about a series of exercises that increase one's health and well-being? Had he run out of positive ideas to share with his congregants about Christianity? Why would he attack yoga, a meditative exercise practiced by over three hundred million people around the world? All religions are supposed to foster love, peace, and harmony. This type of preaching pushes educated men and women, and the younger generation away from formal religion.

Religion has also tried to dictate the sexual behavior of its ministers without success. The reputation of the Catholic Church has suffered irreparable damage due to the news of the sexual abuse cases reported about priests violating children around the world over the past fifty years, especially in the 1960s and 70s. Dr. Thomas Plante of Santa Clara University, a Catholic institution, reported that 4% of Catholic priests violated a minor during the last half of the 20th century, peaking in the 1970s and dropping off dramatically by the early 1980s.[189] The issues of sexual abuse, homosexuality, and celibacy in the church are extraordinarily complex. Both priests and nuns accept the vow of celibacy before receiving their final orders. Celibacy is a voluntary choice to remain unmarried or engage in any form of sexual activity, usually to fulfill a religious vow.[190] However, sex in the sanctuary is much more common than people think. In a recent article about the secret sex life of nuns, a nun stated: "We are all bound by the vows of celibacy, but we are also guided by human nature."[191] While taking their religious vows, especially celibacy, nuns promise themselves to be married to Christ. On that day, they are dressed in white and even receive a wedding ring as a bride of Christ. Celibacy is one of the most important sacrifices a priest or nun can make for the church. Both priests and nuns often struggle with their vows of celibacy under which even masturbation is a sin. The church believes that this act by men amounts to spilled seed for procreation and that women are vessels for childbirth. And women are prohibited from masturbating under Catechism rules because the church believes that self-pleasure "robs the potential of sex" from the partner and it often gives way to the potential for "adultery of the heart" if a woman is fantasizing while touching herself. And although celibacy has been the norm, "Pope Francis has just recently opened a meeting of bishops in Vatican City to discuss whether the Catholic Church should loosen its one-thousand-year-old requirement of celibacy for priests. The controversy centers on the possibility of ordaining married men to serve as priests in sparsely populated regions where Catholic parishes sometimes go for months without a visit from a priest. The church wants to ensure the availability of the sacraments that accompany and sustain Christian life."[192]

A study entitled "A Sexual Intimacy Survey of Former Nuns and Priests" by Margaret Halstead and Laura Halstead conducted in 1978 and recently updated in 2018, confirms that priests and nuns are aware of sexual activity within their convents, churches, and parish communities. Forty-four percent of those surveyed knew of sexual relations between sisters, and fifty-four percent were aware of sexual activity between nuns and priests. They were also aware of nuns having sexual relationships with lay parishioners and married men in the congregation.[193] The results of these surveys confirm that the church hierarchy has great difficulty controlling or dictating the sexual habits of their religious personnel, priests, and nuns, who are human beings struggling with celibacy.

Religious organizations must stop imposing feelings of guilt upon their congregants. Too often, this practice is used to force church members to conform and practice the beliefs of the church. Guilt and fear are not long-term motivators. Feeling guilty is not conducive to people making rational choices and decisions as adults. The idea of religion dictating birth control, stating what women should do or not do with their bodies, is a form of emotional abuse. The religious entities are not supporting families with multiple children. Families can suffer emotionally, physically, and financially if they are not able to provide the basic needs of food, clothing, and shelter for their family. Women also have medical problems if they conceive at an older age. They have a higher chance of giving birth to children with genetic conditions like Down's Syndrome.

Ironically, at a recent three-week meeting of bishops from the Amazon region and the Pope at the Vatican in Rome, November 2019, there were no women. For many years, women have been lobbying the Catholic church to allow women the opportunity to be represented and have decision-making power. The Catholic church is a male-dominated hierarchy. Little progress has been made about gender equality within the Catholic church, yet major religious decisions have been dictated about women's reproductive rights.

Solutions: Understanding Euthanasia

End of life decisions must be discussed. Euthanasia is frowned upon in our American society. However, there is nothing humane about seeing elderly patients lying in hospital beds screaming in pain because it is the only way that they can communicate their physical and emotional distress. These individuals are incontinent and unable to feed themselves, have no dignity left, and are receiving numerous medications just to keep them alive. They are chemically chained to life for the time being. Many religions and people who advocate against euthanasia state that only God can determine when their life ends.

Physicians are expected to tether these individuals to life with medications and oxygen, intravenous feedings, and ventilators, sometimes for years to keep them alive. Many family members suffer from extreme guilt for not taking care of their elderly relatives before a catastrophic illness struck. They try to convince the doctor to do everything possible to keep their family member alive, so they will have time to renew their relationship before the person dies. It is essential for every person to have a medical proxy, indicating what your final wishes are and how your end-of-life decisions should be carried out. Another family member may not have your best interests at heart. When questioned, the majority of people have no interest in being kept alive if they cannot recover from a medical catastrophe and lead an independent or an active and fulfilling life.

"Many people question the moral act of assisted suicide. Religious individuals feel that it is a sin to terminate a life. Advocates of the idea "right to die" believe that people should be allowed to end their suffering if faced with a terminal illness."[194] Physician-assisted suicide is legal in nine US states. It is an option given to individuals by law in the District of Columbia, Hawaii, Maine, New Jersey, Oregon, Vermont, and Washington. It is available to individuals in Montana and California via court decision. "The most common illness of patients turning to physician-assisted suicide is all cancers combined, often followed by amyotrophic lateral sclerosis (ALS). In general, these patients are motivated by symptoms, decreased quality of life and autonomy, a loss of sense of self, and fears about the future."[195] Why are we more humane to our pets than fellow human beings?

Solutions: Understanding a Woman's Right to Abortion

Abortion, the right to terminate a pregnancy is a choice. It is legal in the United States. In 1973, Roe vs. Wade was a landmark decision in which the Supreme Court ruled that the constitution of the United States protects a pregnant woman's liberty to choose to have an abortion without excessive government restriction. As of mid-June 2019, six states have only one abortion clinic left: Kentucky, Mississippi, Missouri, North Dakota, South Dakota, and West Virginia. Missouri could become the first state without any abortion clinics.[196] The Reproductive Health Services of Planned Parenthood in St. Louis, Missouri, has operated for forty-six years. They service their clients for cancer screenings, sexually transmitted infections like chlamydia, gonorrhea, trichomonas, herpes, human immunodeficiency virus, and syphilis, in addition to performing abortions."[197] Planned Parenthood states that across the country, there is a battle raging between licensed abortion clinics and state governments. There are on-going efforts to shut these clinics down due to failure supposedly to comply with state health regulations and inspections. "The Planned Parenthood Federation of America states that the moment has come; they have been warning about this day when abortion access is eliminated without ever overturning Roe vs. Wade."[198]

Ironically, there is a vast disparity in the number of women as compared to men in local, state, and national government entities in the United States. Yet these government officials are the ones who are determining the fate and access to women's rights to abortion. "As of February 2018, only about a quarter of elected positions in the United States were held by women. There were 1,977 women in power across governorships, congressional seats, and state legislative seats, which means 2,006 more legislative positions have to be won for women to reach equal representation."[199] Our local, state, and national governments are comprised mainly of individuals who cannot biologically become pregnant; still, many of these officials are pushing for the closure of abortion clinics. They are making it extremely difficult for women to receive an abortion in their state. Instead, they should be improving healthcare for women and children, and increase related state funding. In 2019, in the United States of America, women should not have to drive out of state to receive healthcare for an abortion procedure that they choose.

As a psychiatrist, I have treated numerous women who were riddled with guilt from having had an abortion, either early in life or during their later reproductive years. The decision was always extremely difficult. There were various reasons why they made this life-altering decision: financial instability, single status without a partner, unwanted pregnancy from an affair, rape by a family member or an assault, or simply, too many children already. Women are aware of this painful decision to terminate a pregnancy.

"TRAP laws are dangerously chipping away at abortion access under the guise of women's health. The American Medical Association and the American Congress of Obstetricians and Gynecologists oppose TRAP laws because they don't improve safety, but hurt women by blocking access to safe medical care."[200] "TRAP (Targeted Regulation of Abortion Providers) laws single out the medical practices of doctors who provide abortions and impose upon them requirements that are different and more burdensome than those imposed on other medical practices."[201] These laws force many women without access to an abortion clinic to drive out of state to get this procedure, but only if they can afford it. They will probably have to drive hundreds of miles away. They will still need funds for a stay in a hotel, at least for an overnight or a few days.

There are laws in several states that legally require women to receive counseling and undergo a twenty-four to a forty-eight-hour waiting period before an abortion, in addition to viewing the ultrasound image of the fetus before receiving the abortion. Women experience all these state requirements after they have already decided to obtain an abortion and drive to an out-of-state clinic. No one can say that this is an easy decision for any woman. And sadly, teenage girls have been known to try and abort an unwanted fetus by themselves, using a wire hanger and placing themselves in great medical danger. Although teen pregnancy rates have declined in recent decades, the U.S. rate is still one of the highest in the developed world. Between 1991 and 2018, the teen birth rate declined by an impressive 72% nationwide. The current rate is at 43.4 per 1,000 young women. The reasons include less sex, effective use of contraception, and availability of information about pregnancy prevention."[202]

Ironically, in our society, when a couple decides that they would like to have a child, a physician does not ask them if they have seriously thought through this decision, or can afford to raise a child, and most importantly, if they understand the responsibilities of being good parents. Giving birth to a child is a life-changing event. You are responsible for the well-being of this child forever. There are no required counseling sessions to be a parent. Usually couples make this life-changing decision and then choose to become pregnant, or in other cases, it just happens! Many women are not healthy enough to bear a child, but they go ahead anyway with this plan, risking their health and the future health of the unborn child. Millennials, young adults aged twenty-five-years old through thirty-seven-years old, are marrying at a much older age. In a "Current Population Survey of Annual Social and Economic Supplements," analyzed by the Pew Institute in 2018, only 46% of millennials are married.[203] It appears that this generation is giving themselves time to become responsible adults. There is a higher percentage of millennials who have chosen to be stay at-home parents.

One of the leading advocates for reproductive rights and universal healthcare is Dr. Linda Prine. She is the founder and medical director of the Reproductive Health Access Project (RHAP), and the leader of RHAP's Family Medicine Reproductive Health Network. "She is an outstanding educator who has trained more than 190 family medicine residents to provide full- spectrum contraceptive and first-trimester abortion care. These residents are now providing care all across the country."[204] She is a faculty member at the Beth Israel/Mount Sinai and the Harlem Family Hospital residencies, in addition to many other professional associations. Her work has been published in dozens of medical journals and featured throughout media outlets. Dr. Linda Prine is a nationally recognized leader and educator in reproductive health who has been most effective at tackling social issues of reproductive medical services.[205] She advocates that those men and women opposed to abortion, educate themselves about the facts related to the abortion procedure and women's reproductive rights.

A first-trimester abortion is considered minor surgery. The risk of complications increases with advancing gestational age. Early abortions that are not complicated by infection do not cause infertility or make it more challenging to carry a later pregnancy to term. Different methods of abortion are used depending on how far along the pregnancy has progressed. In the first trimester of the pregnancy from one to seven weeks, RU-486, a drug regimen is designed to end a pregnancy up to forty-nine days after the last menstrual period. A health care provider administers three pills in a medical office or clinic. These pills block the activity of progesterone, a hormone necessary to sustain the pregnancy. At thirteen weeks during the first trimester, a physician uses curettage, vacuum aspiration. This procedure is in a physician's office or clinic as an outpatient. From fourteen to twenty-three weeks, after the first day of the last menstrual period, dilation and evacuation (D&E), and labor induction are the two methods most typically used for abortion. In the third trimester of pregnancy, twenty-four to thirty-eight weeks, a doctor performs an abortion at this stage of the pregnancy, only if he reasonably believes that it is necessary to prevent death or to preserve the health of the patient.[206]

The political struggle for and against abortion rights has recently been fought in Ireland and Northern Ireland. After referendums in 2018 and 2019, abortions will be available to all women in these countries. These services were available to women in Ireland as of January 2019 and April 2020 to women in Northern Ireland. Abortion services can be provided up to twelve weeks to terminate a woman's pregnancy, and later where the pregnant woman's life is at risk, or in the cases of fatal fetal abnormality. "Orla O'Connor, director of the National Women's Council in Ireland, said: "It was a historic day in Ireland when women could finally access abortion at home, in care of their doctor. It is also very significant in lifting the stigma and shame that so many women experienced for decades unable to speak to family, friends, and seek the medical care they needed."[207]

For single women, couples who are together or those who have separated, the decision to have an abortion is gut-wrenching. There is no easy answer. Every woman and man must live with the emotional consequence of terminating a pregnancy. The least we can do in our society is to provide available and safe medical procedures and offer psychological counseling for all partners with this life-altering decision. There is no need for any of us to judge these individuals or their choices. They have already suffered deeply in the choices that they have had to make.

"Everyone makes mistakes in their life, but that does not mean they have to pay for them during the rest of their life. Sometimes good people make bad choices. It does not mean they are bad. It means they are human. It is how you handle your mistakes, that is most important."[208]

Anonymous

Solutions: Adoption

Advocates of adoption see this option as a very viable solution to abortion. However, anyone who has ever tried to adopt a baby, primarily a Caucasian, a white newborn baby, faces many obstacles and financial hardships. Many couples are unable to conceive or have genetic problems within their families. They are choosing to adopt a child. Adoption is a legal relationship established between an adult and a child, and the adult is not the child's original birth parent. The process of adoption is available through foster care, where the child's birth family is unable to provide for him or her. The local state government takes care of the child financially and then places him or her with an approved foster family. The family receives a monthly stipend to care for the child. The U.S. Department of Health and Human Services present the national data for Adoption and Foster Care Analysis annually. In 2018, there were over 437,000 children in the foster care system, with 43% of these children placed in a foster home of a non-relative. At the end of 2018, 25% of the children were adopted.[209]

In the United States, specific criteria exist for child adoption. You must be a U.S. citizen and at least eighteen years old. If you are single, you must be twenty-five years old. If you are married, you and your partner must jointly adopt the child. Additional requirements to determine if you are eligible to pursue a child adoption are a criminal background check, fingerprinting, and a home study. Foreign country adoptions, adopting children outside of the United States, will require you to meet strict criteria for adoption established by the child's native country.[210] The average total cost of adoption in the United States ranges from $35,000 to $40,000. International adoption can range from $30,000 to $50,000 plus, dependent on the country. Foster care adoption fees are up to $3,000.[211]

Before adopting, couples may decide to try fertility treatments such as in-vitro fertilization. Insurance coverage is not standard for this procedure, and it can cost about $11,000 to $12,000.[212] On a personal level, I assisted a co-worker who was struggling financially to complete several rounds of fertility treatments without success. Eventually, they turned to a private adoption in China, and adopted a little girl. It cost a large sum, but China was permitting Americans to select Chinese girls at the time. The couple was also able to adopt a little boy, through a private adoption, facilitated by the church they attended.

On a professional level as a child psychiatrist, I treated some very disturbed adopted children from America, and ones selected from other countries around the world. The American parents did not receive the family history of the adoptee, nor the child's prenatal history. The children's DNA or exceedingly early life experiences, like exposure to drugs and alcohol while in utero, could have profoundly affected the physical, mental, and emotional health of the child. In the end, many American parents have suffered greatly trying to raise these maladjusted and ill children. The heartache and daily disruptive behaviors of the adoptive child places a heavy toll on the well-being of every family member. The U.S. National Institutes of Health have completed studies on the developmental outcomes of internationally adopted children. It is essential to state here that not all internationally adopted children suffer from illnesses and other developmental delays in maturation. The decision to adopt requires very serious consideration and willingness to bear all the joys and heartaches of raising children. This is true for all children, whether they are your own or adopted.

Solutions: Birth Control

"In 2018, 16.4 million children were living with a single mother, 3.25 million children with a single father. A total population of 73.4 million children in the United States ages 0–17 years old was registered at that time. 21.9% of all children were living with a single parent.[213] In 2017, unmarried women gave birth to 1,533,901 children. 36% of unmarried women, mothers, were on Medicaid in 2017.[214] If unmarried women on Medicaid decide not to have any more children due to financial constraints and single parenthood, they will find that birth control services like tubal ligation, is not always available to them. Although many states cover sterilization procedures for women on Medicaid, "several states like Ohio and Oregon do not cover general or postpartum tubal ligation. Connecticut, Georgia, Mississippi, and Missouri do not cover tubal ligation performed postpartum in their family-planning programs, with Georgia noting that pregnant women are not enrolled in the state's family-planning waiver."[215]

Single, young mothers, who already have several children and are not receiving support from their children's fathers, can request to have their tubes tied if they do not want to have any more children, but will be denied through Medicaid in many states. Women in this situation have not been responsible for taking birth control pills regularly or using other forms of birth control. However, many government officials feel that a young mother is too immature to decide if she will want any more children. They think she may change her mind later on about this decision. What about the fact that she already has more children than she can afford to raise now, and she is on Medicaid? United States taxpayers are supporting these single-family households without the American people's consent to continue financial support based on the irresponsible behavior of these young men and women. The issue of providing birth control services and sterilization is of the utmost importance to lessen the financial burden of multi-generations applying for Medicaid services.

Problem & Solutions: Overpopulation

The earth is already overpopulated. Global human population has grown from one billion in 1804 to four billion in 1975, and was at 7.46 billion in 2018.[216] "The world's population is expected to increase by 2 billion persons in the next 30 years, from 7.7 billion currently to 9.7 billion in 2050," according to a new United Nations report launched on June 17, 2019.[217] The problem on earth is not a matter of land space for the growing population, but the sustainability of the planet's natural resources to supply food and water, in addition to meeting the consumption needs of the ever increasing population. In 2019, China and India were the most populous countries in the world. "Around 2027, India will overtake China as the world's most populous country, while China's population is projected to decrease by 31.4 million, or around 2.2%, between 2019 and 2050."[218]

China is an example of a country focused on trying to do something about overpopulation. In 1979, China introduced a one-child policy instituted by Deng Xiaoping, the Chinese leader. At the time, the population was 970 million. In 2019, it was at more than 1.38 billion.[219] In the late 1970s, the primary concern of the Chinese government was the availability of existing resources to support a ballooning population. It could outpace the available food supply. Young people were encouraged to delay marriage until their mid-twenties and were only permitted to have one child. Citizens risked huge fines and varying degrees of harassment from local authorities and at places of employment.[220] This one-child policy did meet with resistance, and eventually, the government relented and issued exemptions. The Chinese Communist Party's Central Committee considered the diverse and socioeconomic conditions across China. In 1984, couples in rural areas were permitted to have a second child if their first child was a girl.[221] China's one-child policy had been successful in preventing up to 400 million births. Then in the 1990s, the government focused on providing individual contraception rights. In 2001, the central government issued a uniform set of rules, rights, and obligations for family planning to be followed by Chinese citizens, in addition to addressing population issues on a national level.[222] In October 2015, a universal two-child policy was instituted to replace the one-child system.[223] However, there are negative aspects of these population control edicts. Within the younger generation, there is now a gender ratio of 117.6 boys to 100 girls born, which results in 30 million more young men to women in China. Millions of Chinese men may not be able to find wives.[224] Also, by 2030, a quarter of the population will be over sixty years old, and who will be taking care of this elderly population? Implementing a forced policy of only one child created a society where parents focused all their efforts on raising that one child, and perhaps even spoiling the child. The Chinese tradition of taking care of elderly parents is falling by the wayside. Young brides do not want the responsibility of taking care of their in-laws or their own parents for that matter. Solving the dilemma of overpopulation is a complex issue, as experienced by China. World organizations and countries must examine the use and consumption of the planet's natural resources. There is only a limited supply of resources that is accessible each year on earth.

Countries will be fighting over the availability of fresh water and water rights for their citizens. The energy production of coal, oil, and natural gas can have a negative impact. Deforestation will continue to create global warming. The loss of animal and plant species will create devastating effects on our ecosystem. Plants supply the oxygen we breathe and food that we eat. Overpopulation is one of our biggest challenges facing humanity. The environmental, social, and economic factors in all countries must be determined and examined. Comprehensive solutions must be tried and implemented to prevent global disasters.

Final thoughts on the Do-gooders

Do-gooders need to step aside, and let individuals and families make their own decisions that are beneficial to them. If the policy makers need to establish guidelines, do so taking into consideration what benefits the individuals without the policy makers' biases or prejudice. This respect for others is imperative, especially concerning birth control, abortion, end of life decisions, marriage, cohabitation, discipling and raising children. Access to mental health care should be available to all individuals, or we, as a society, will continue to suffer the consequences. Government officials need to allocate more money towards mental health care and insurance companies need to provide appropriate coverage when help is needed.

People in authority may think they are helping when certain policies are made. Unfortunately, their viewpoint may not be the best course of action for everyone. In this country, we believe in free speech. Individual and family rights should be honored and respected. In the end, all citizens should be responsible for their actions and welfare. Government representatives should put the needs of their citizens first and serve the communities who elected them.

"Moral authority comes from following universal and timeless principles like honesty, integrity, treating people with respect."[225]

Stephen Covey

Part 4

Moving Forward

Child Development and Parenting

Research regarding the brain has found subtle but significant biological differences between male and female brains. Among the findings are male brains are six to ten percent bigger, on average than female brains. Female brains have a bigger connecting area (the corpus callosum) between the two hemispheres of the brain and more synapses (connections). They tend to use both sides of the brain for a particular task more frequently than males do.

JoAnn Deak, PhD, an expert on brain research, reports that the differences in male and female brains start in the womb. Many female brains have more neurons in certain areas than male brains, as a result of having more estrogen bathe them during fetal development. A hormonal, chemical wash, estrogen for girls and testosterone for boys, enhance certain parts of the brain and changes them structurally before birth. Therefore, girls and boys are born with different hardwiring.[226]

Girls and boys appear to have different developmental timelines. Most girls are born with language processing neurons on both sides of the brain, but most males have them only on the right side. As a result, girls often become earlier readers than boys and begin the writing process sooner. Many girls have less spatial awareness than boys, but at the same time, develop fine motor skills earlier than boys. However, most boys tend to be more attracted to spatial tasks such as playing with Legos than girls.[227]

Girls are getting better grades in school than boys. These academic results are not just in the United States, but also across the globe. The results were based on a meta-analysis of 369 studies involving the academic grades of over one million boys and girls from thirty different nations. The study was done at the University of New Brunswick. Girls earn higher grades in every subject, including the science-related fields where boys are thought to surpass them.[228]

The latest data from the Pew Research Center showed that in 2012, 71% of female high school graduates went onto college, compared to 61% of their male counterparts.[229] Women are graduating from college at higher rates than men, and ever so slowly taking on major positions in corporations. It still may be harder for women to get into college due to competition and the male/female ratio, but women finish college at higher rates than men, who tend to drop out or take longer to complete a degree.[230]

"It is tempting to believe that boys are not "hardwired" to care about feelings or friendships. Niobe Way, a psychologist at New York University, has studied the development of adolescent boys. Research suggests that baby boys are as attuned to emotions and intimacy as baby girls."[231] However, most girls' and boys' brains are wired to process connections between language and emotion differently. JoAnn Deak, Ph.D., who has spent more than thirty years as an educator and psychologist, reports that many girls may have an easier time talking about their feelings than many boys.[232] This difference in processing between the two genders may contribute to men being oblivious to the impact of emotional infractions, and women responding at times like they were catastrophic violations of communication. Female brains tend to focus better on details, enabling girls to express their emotions at considerable length. (I am sure many men wish they did not have this ability.)

However, by the age of three years old, boys pick up on the idea that things like attentiveness, tenderness, and emotional perceptiveness are "girly." This recognized behavior may come about due to parenting styles, or what they are exposed to in pre-kindergarten, or what they are taught as far as expected behaviors. Boys learn to hide these emotions by first grade to fit in. By the sixth grade, boys start to objectify girls sexually. It is more important for a girl to be attractive to a boy than it is for a girl to be friends with a boy. As boys grow older, by the age of around sixteen years old, they have fewer close relationships even though they express the need to have someone to talk to.[233] They feel that they have to be "emotionless." It is important to recognize and acknowledge a boy's natural emotional and relationship skills and encourage those traits whenever possible.

Most parents believe that their children are not listening when they are trying to talk to them about important issues.[234] Research shows that peers influence the everyday behaviors of kids heavily, but parents are more influential when it comes to morals, values, and more significant beliefs.[235] Girls, particularly pre-pubescent ones, also have a higher sensitivity to noise and tone of voice. As a result, some girls may hear yelling when there is only firmness in an adult's voice, or take feedback on their work as negative criticism, even when it is constructive.[236] From personal experience, I am still very susceptible to the "harsh tone" of my partner, who is a "Southern man", even after living with him for thirty years. When he uses a specific tone of voice, he does not intend to be mean, but I am super-sensitive, and it causes friction between the two of us.

The message that young boys and men received growing up was to be more aggressive.[237] Now parents must show their sons how to be good, respectful human beings. They need instructions on how to be kind, patient, gentle, and treat everyone the way you would like to be treated.

Dr. Michael Reichert, author of "How to Raise a Boy: The Power of Connection to Build Good Men," offers seven phrases that all fathers need to say to their sons more often."[238]

"I've Failed a Million Times." - It is okay for boys to know that their fathers have failed and have made many mistakes. They are not perfect.

"You Have to Make Yourself Happy First Before You Can Make Others Happy." - If you cannot love and accept yourself, how can you care for others?

"Was That Really Your Best Effort?" – Boys must be pushed to do things again, putting forth the effort to encourage them to do better than they thought they could. A father, coach, or mentor relationship will want them to do better.

"Treat People as You Want to Be Treated." – This moral principle instills the idea of loyalty and commitment to the young man. It challenges individualism and teaches him that the whole is greater than the sum of its parts.

"Hurt People, Hurt People." – When a person hurts a boy, he wants to hurt someone else through words or actions to transfer the pain from being injured himself.

"Don't Always Blame Yourself." – Children tend to be self-centered, so if something bad happens, he needs to know that it is not always his fault.

"I Love and Understand You." – Fathers rarely express emotions of affection, but they need to do so, for their son to feel accepted and loved.

Bullying needs to stop. It is more the cultural perception of being weak if someone is depressed, has anxiety, is too skinny or fat, especially as a man. These attributes are normal for girls and women who are expected to be more emotional. Boys tend to be physically aggressive, while girls wage psychological warfare. It is so petty for girls to put other girls down because of the clothes they wear, their hairstyles, or whether they are part of a group that is popular or not. Where do they learn these selfish behaviors? When parents do not teach their children the right way to behave and hold them accountable for their actions, their children become society's problem, as witnessed too often today in our world.

Different men were interviewed and asked to define what aggression meant to boys. Their responses were part of a week-long series on "How to Raise a Boy," in the era of the Parkland High School Shooting in Florida, the presidency of President Trump, and the #MeToo Movement published in The Cut.[239] These are summaries of the following individuals who were interviewed, as described by Will Leitch.

One of the men, Eric Bates, described himself being on the receiving end of male violence at an early age. This experience seems to ring true with many of his male friends, especially youth growing up in impoverished inner-city environments. When he misbehaved, his father would spank him. When his parents were away or out of earshot, his older brother would chase him down and pummel him. At school, other boys would beat him up or bully him. Growing up, he was even punched when wrongly accused of making a move on someone's girlfriend. As a kid, he understood that these violent assaults were not an inherent or inevitable by-product of boyhood aggression.

To him, aggression was something else. It made him run faster, jump higher, think smarter, and become the best at everything he did. Aggression got him into jams and out of them. The violence around him was not about aggression but about rage. This hostility was about the ways boys and men around him had been hurt. It was their need to pass on the pain to others so that someone else would feel what they felt. With all the violence and cruelty, he knew what the boys who bullied him were going through. They were trying to become men, the same way he was, by figuring out what to do with what they had been given.

A Marine and a father of two sons, James Cook, felt that playing through competition is the best way to focus on young male aggression. Aggression becomes a maladapted trait when it is not channeled. The most important thing is to cultivate a sense of play.

A Navy Seal's take on raising sons noted that there is a lot of adult involvement in raising children these days. They are continually being supervised with grownups interfering. Boys are not allowed to work through conflicts or difficulties on their own. Everything in sports today revolves around training and practice. Boys are not permitted to be wild and free like in the old days while growing up in neighborhoods. As a result, they are having a hard time finding their place as men later in life. He feels masculinity has a voice, but fear keeps men from becoming their authentic selves. Society tells them that aggression is primitive, but it is not necessarily a bad thing for a man to be dominant and influential. Women are strong, and they want their men to be strong too. Fathers need to be firm with their children. They should not let them think that everything they do is okay. His take references parents who spend too much time trying to understand their children and relate to them on an emotional level. He does not think a father should behave in that manner toward his children. He wants his sons, especially to be a little afraid of him. He lived in fear of letting his father down, and it was not such a bad thing.

Craig Jenkins reported that inner-city teens do not have access to psychotherapy, and they could benefit most from it. They are shouldering the burdens of poverty and violence. When parents are struggling to meet basic needs like next month's food and shelter, they cannot focus on how their children are feeling. Youths growing up in the inner-city are fearful of even casual encounters with law enforcement. Their mothers train them to be attentive to what is going on in the streets. They must be taught how to behave when stopped by police officers. It is easy to be blamed for an altercation, even as a bystander in these communities.

Michael Kimmel, a professor of sociology at Stony Brook University in New York, asked the question: "What does it mean to be a good man?" to several thousand boys and young men around the world. He interviewed boys in Australia, police academies in Sweden, FIFA former soccer players, and even cadets at West Point.[240]

Their central answers included:

"Integrity, honor, being responsible, being a good provider, protector, doing the right thing, putting others first, sacrifice, caring, and standing up for the little guy." When they were asked where they learned these practices, they answered: "It was everywhere." These male behaviors are acquired through osmosis.

Next question: their response to "be a real man!" "Never cry, be strong, don't show your feelings, play through pain, suck it up, power, aggression, win at all costs, be aggressive, get rich, and get laid!" When asked where they learned these attributes to be a man, their response was in the following order: from their father, a coach, my guy friends, my older brother, sometimes, from a teacher and their mother.

Professor Kimmel hoped that from this exercise, men would understand how powerful the message is to prove that he is a real man. In every man's life, when he is asked to betray his values, ethics, or ideas of what it means to be a good man, he will give in and deceive himself. In doing so, men will do the wrong thing sometimes, fail to stand up for the little guy, and behave dishonorably to be part of the team. Kimmel feels that fathers need to tell their sons that at one time or another, they will face the pressure to prove their masculinity with "group think." They will feel pulled between their values and those established within the group. When they choose to join group-think, it is essential to understand that they will be damaging their heart and soul while trying to deny their humanity to be real men.[241]

Professor Kimmel sees a ray of hope. "These days, younger men are far more gender- equal than previous generations."[242] They will assist in childcare and perform more housework than the previous generations of men. They will have more friendships with women than any other generation before them. Presently, they are playing by new rules in the workplace. Nearly half of the men, 30 and under, said that it was unacceptable to comment on a woman's attractiveness in the workplace, while three-quarters of the older men said it was simply fine. In the past, most relationships started in the workplace or church. Now it is unacceptable to flirt or ask anyone out in the workplace for fear of accusations of sexual harassment. Now many professionals rely on the Internet to meet people which has many drawbacks and problems. Hopefully going forward, young people will appreciate the way people connected in the past. The "old way" needed fixing but as usual, the pendulum has swung way too far the other way.

Two teenage brothers were interviewed and commented on their thoughts about sex, social media, and what their parents did not understand. You may be offended by the crude language in this section. Feel free to skip this part.

The young men spoke about several recent suicides in their community. After it happened, people always say: "Bullying needs to stop." They want to tell the boys "to grow some balls." The boys feel it is a toxic mindset to have to carry themselves in a certain way, act in a certain way, and look a certain way. "[243]

The young men feel that this is part of what being an American is all about. "This nationalistic Uncle Sam wants you to go and fight for your country: shoot a gun, have sex, drink beer, look at boobs, and then go to church in the morning."[244] If they are scared or nervous to try something, or do not want to do something, their perception of what their parents think and say is simply: "shut up pussy, just go do it!" According to them, it is a very toxic, masculine thing.

They accept feminism but hate the super reaction that all men are bad. They understand serious issues around gender equality but feel women are right about toxic masculinity. "It changes the way you act; you are trying to act manly and impress people, and don't even realize it until you are called out for being a total asshole."[245] They view this behavior as disgusting. "Men thinking that they are the strongest, the biggest, and the best is why we see so much sexual abuse."[246]

The boys were also asked if they had seen or heard of instances of their friends or people, they knew of being raped or sexually harassed. "Yeah, all the time. Especially over the Internet. Send me nudes, bitch! If nude pictures are not sent, you are fucking ugly! I don't want your nudes anyway."[247] They reported that all of their female friends have gone through this experience. They try to fight all this abusive negativity as much as they can, but they cannot punch out a rapist, being scrawny, but they can all yell out at a rapist. They want every generation to become more informed of this abusiveness. They are glad that the Internet is monitored more closely now. They are aware that stuff like this has gone on forever, and rape has existed "ever since penises and vaginas have existed."

Their ideas on relationships focused on one primary key to success, to find someone different from everybody else and teach them about how other people think. One of the brothers was a virgin, and he was nervous about having sex before he had a girlfriend. Presently, he is in a healthy relationship, and they have talked about it. Talking and being able to communicate about sex has made them both more comfortable. He is no longer nervous, performing sexually. The other brother lost his virginity with an older girl when he was fourteen years old. Since that time, he has only gone on dates with older girls. He says their conversations are more like, "Let's do this," rather than "Would you wanna do this?" He was not ready to have sex at fourteen but feels comfortable now with what happened in the past. He was drunk, and it was awkward. He felt like he was doing it all wrong. He thought you must embrace that the first time is going to be uncomfortable. Both brothers agree "Sex can be scary, and parents should understand that. It is going to happen, and it is not going to go well if you try to make it not happen."[248]

The boys mentioned that some people struggle with things like how many "likes" they receive on social media connections. For girls, it is a huge thing. They feel that social media is making it harder to grow up in some ways, but more comfortable in other ways. They can watch everybody who is doing it and see how other people are coping. If they fuck up, they can feel better about themselves. Everybody fucks up.

Talking about parents, they just want them to understand that sometimes they are just having a bad day, and they do not want to talk to anyone. Also, it might not be the right time; they may be tired, or they did not get a lot of sleep the night before.

Dr. Shila Patel, M.D.

If their parents push them to talk, they may get angry. Growing up, they feel like they are adapting to new social norms that they are not used to. They want parents to have patience while they are going through this awkward stage. They want their parents to try out new tactics of communication for better relationships. They are not used to being an adult human. If their parents want them to be adults, they need to practice this new role with them. They cannot go from being children straight to adulthood. Sometimes, as young adults, they are going to be mean. They are not purposely trying to act this way. It just happens. They want help from their parents to transition into adulthood.

168

Raising Boys and Girls: Gender Biases

An article by Laurie Abraham in New York Magazine talked about how she was raised like a son, not a daughter. Her take was that we often hear about how we should raise boys more like girls these days. We should teach them to be more sensitive to others' feelings, not play at hurting other people, or not be so aggressive.[249] However, she was grateful that she was raised to some extent, like a boy. She got the chance to be very physical and learned to fight for fun. She wanted to win when playing sports. Her father would tell her before a game "to take no prisoners." Ms. Abraham thinks that there is so much out there in the world that pushes men to go beyond aggression, even shames them if they are not the toughest, the worst, the absolute winner. She feels that her father's rough play and martial rhetoric would have been oppressive for boys. Things worked out for her. Her family was well-balanced along traditional gender lines. Her mother's degree was in home economics; she and her sister were happy playing house and cooking regularly. These activities made her feel comfortable as a woman. Learning how to be more assertive and aggressive gave Ms. Abraham more confidence when dealing with people.[250]

Lisa Collier Cool, an American journalist, and author has written an article about how girls' and boys' brains work. The research claims "the most striking difference between the sexes was that women have a much higher level of activity in the prefrontal cortex, an area sometimes called 'the brain's CEO,' because it governs planning, organization, impulse control, and learning from mistakes. In another study, men's brains showed greater activity in regions associated with visual perception, tracking objects through space, and form recognition."[251] So when men and women achieve success after performing the same task, they are using different parts of their brains. Research does not claim that all girls' and boys' brains work the same way, or that a girls' behavior is predestined by brain chemistry. If twenty percent of girls do not fit a pattern, that is one in five girls.[252] Therefore, we should not make any assumptions about all girls exhibiting the same behavior. It is also important to note that no two brains are alike, and that biology does not determine destiny. Kids should not be stereotyped and locked into certain expectations. It is essential to let them explore and become involved in a wide range of activities.

Currently, raising children without gender presuppositions and barriers is a popular theme in parenting. Following are some recommendations for bringing up children with less prejudice and partiality. We should all be aware of our own unconscious gender biases. These beliefs are our inner thoughts that we demonstrate with our behavior. For example, when we see a woman in medical scrubs, we usually assume she is the nurse rather than the doctor. When a couple goes to buy a car, the salesperson will usually only direct his attention to the man when the couple is together. Rarely, does the salesperson think that the woman is the individual looking for, making the decision, and purchasing the car. Men assume that women do not understand monetary transactions and must be reminded that many women are business owners and CEOs, capable of a variety of business transactions. Most people believe that girls are more emotional than boys and cry more often. They believe boys are more aggressive. Interestingly, studies have been done depicting female gangs as much more aggressive in their behavior than male gangs. Biases about emotions are presented and passed along by parents, teachers, mentors, and peers. Society and the news media reinforce these biases repeatedly. Fathers will tell their sons to stop crying and not hug them. To them, it is considered "unmanly." This thought process was probably initiated by their fathers, who did not openly display emotion. We cannot expect boys and girls to grow and change unless we examine our own stereotypical thinking critically. Young children can model these negative biases displayed by the adults around them, but they become entrenched in adolescence and are proven to have negative impacts throughout adulthood. Parents must be aware of the unconscious messages they are modeling.

Parents must model behaviors that they want to foster in their children. They must show them what a healthy relationship looks like. At home, it is important to avoid sticking to traditional gender roles. The chores and activities should be divided in an unbiased way. Everyone, both boys and girls in the family should be responsible for doing the dishes, sweeping the floor, taking out the trash, helping with the cooking and the laundry. All the chores should be assigned on a rotation method. If the father never helps in the kitchen or cooks and the mother relies on the father to do the yard work or fixing things around the house, it sends a message to the children about the sexist roles of men and women. The different strengths of children need to be identified and encouraged. If a daughter prefers to do the yard work rather than the dishes, she should be encouraged to do so. Give responsibility to all the children to decide among themselves who is doing what chore and when it will be completed.

Friendships with the opposite sex are normal and healthy. When girls just play with girls and boys with boys, this reinforces gender stereotypes. At a young age, birthday celebrations for children should include both boys and girls. Co-ed activities should be explored. As children grow older and a boy and girl have a unique friendship, do not label them as boyfriend and girlfriend. Boys and girls need to understand that they can interact with one another in friendly ways that are strictly platonic. It is important to speak to them and teach them how to be respectful to one another within this friendship.

As teenagers, it is important to emphasize that sex is not about "the conquest." In a Harvard study, 76% of young people had never had a conversation with their parents about how to avoid sexually harassing others.[253] Their parents may have never talked about individuals displaying prejudice or contempt against women. And more than 60% of young people reported that their parents had never spoken to them about "being sure your partner wants to have sex and is comfortable doing so before having sex."[254] 50% of young people also stated that their parents had also never spoken to them about "the importance of never having sex with someone who is too intoxicated or impaired to decide about sex."[255] Some mothers raise their sons by telling them "women are the root of all evil." One wonders if this belief is to keep men from chasing women. Other mothers tell their sons "the penis is what causes all of the problems." The talk should be about safe sex and promoting healthy relationships, not disparaging remarks.

Parents need to be aware of the messages their children are receiving outside the home. In school, the teaching of American history often just focuses on our founding fathers: George Washington, Benjamin Franklin, John Adams, Thomas Jefferson, and others. Children need to become aware that there were many women in history who also paved the way for freedom and liberty in the United States. They too made outstanding contributions to our society. Susan B. Anthony paved the way for women's suffrage, the right to vote for women, which became the 19th Amendment to the Constitution in 1920. Clara Barton founded the American Red Cross and had served as a nurse in the Civil War. Amelia Earhart was the first female aviator to fly across the Atlantic Ocean. Grace Hopper essentially developed computer programming as we understand it today. Most of her team was female. Barbara Jordon was the first southern African American woman elected to the U.S. House of Representatives and the first African American woman to deliver a keynote address at the Democratic National Convention. As a parent, becoming involved in the activities of your children's school PTA (Parent-Teacher Association) will enable you to encourage celebrations of both outstanding women and men in our country.

Even when children are little, do not make assumptions about what your child would like based on gender. Let your children decide whether they like to play with Legos or dolls, or even both. Barbie doll's first-ever job was as a "Teenage Fashion Model" in 1959, but she soon broke boundaries in male-dominated fields, playing Major League Baseball, programming computers, and rising to the rank of sergeant in the Marine Corps. She has even made an incursion into space travel, reaching the moon in 1965, years before Neil Armstrong's famous first steps. It is not just about the differences between the sexes. We need to teach our children to acknowledge and appreciate the differences among human beings.

How to Raise Confident Children

Carl Pickhardt, a psychologist, and author of fifteen parenting books states "a child who lacks confidence, will be reluctant to try new or challenging things because they're afraid of failure or disappointing others. As a parent, it is your job to encourage and support your child as they attempt to tackle difficult tasks."[256]

A stable environment: If we want our children to be confident, this can only be achieved by children feeling confident within themselves. Chances are higher for children to become confident adults within a stable home environment. It does not mean that both parents must live in the same home. However, when both parents reside in the same physical space within a loving environment, the chances for emotional support increase exponentially. Unfortunately, many couples stay together even though they are unhappy with their situation "for the sake of the children." You are not doing any favors to your children by raising them in an unhappy home. Children are aware of their parents' contentious relationship. They feel the tension every day as their parents interact with one another. Children tend to be self-centered and feel that it is their fault that their parents are so unhappy. They have little understanding of what constitutes a healthy adult relationship. They are also unaware of the many conflicts between parents, such as finances, work responsibilities, caretaking of other children and parents, lack of intimacy, or extra-marital affairs. A stable home with two loving parents can assist children in becoming confident adults. Many children are raised in families these days with two mothers or two fathers. If it is a loving environment, children can grow up feeling good about themselves. Children growing up in an unhappy home may plan early in life to run away or turn to drugs to escape emotional pain.

A proper introduction: confidence is exhibited immediately with introductions. How likely will your child extend his or her hand to meet someone, address them properly, and be able to look at the person, making and maintaining eye contact? A handshake is a firm hold, not a weak grip. Body language reveals whether you are anxious or nervous, or ready to address whoever or whatever comes your way. Modeling and showing your children how to introduce themselves properly is the first way to assist them in building confidence.

Ability to ask questions and receive appropriate age-related answers: children are resilient. They should have the opportunity to ask questions and get suitable answers to questions, instead of being told that they are too young to understand what is going on. They should not be left in the dark. They can handle stressors better knowing what is happening than leaving it to their imagination and reaching false conclusions. Parents should not be afraid to talk to their children about financial limitations within the household. Today, children are exposed to an unlimited number of electronics, clothing, shoes, and other gadgets. Advertising is continually encouraging young people to update their electronic devices, which is very costly. As parents, it can be extremely difficult financially to keep up with these expenses. It is essential to sit down with your children and explain the limit to your financial resources.

Role modeling: children will learn to handle situations depending on what they see and hear from adults within the home when dealing with difficult or stressful situations. It is okay for fathers to show emotions like sadness and crying and hug their children and spouses. It is okay for mothers to show strength and be assertive in difficult situations. Also, mothers and fathers can work together on projects that may have been designated typically male or female projects in the past. Their children will understand that both sexes can achieve success when they set their minds to do so, no matter what the task. Parents are not the only role models in their children's lives. Teachers, coaches, relatives, and neighbors can also play a vital part in your children's lives as mentors. It is a mutual relationship where both members of the relationship have respect for one another. They spend time together, and especially for young people, they realize that they are not alone, another individual cares about their well-being and success. As with any adult individual in your child's life, careful consideration of your child's safety with this individual is paramount. Considering all the racial tension in the country, it is very important to teach children to treat everyone equally without looking at their color or nationality. Children will model parents or other adults in their lives as to the way they behave dealing with anger, racism, or other significant issues.

Healthy behavior within the home: role modeling extends to the healthy habits exhibited by parents. Smoking, alcohol, and drug use send a permissive message to your children. As parents, you are showing them that these habits are allowed. As parents, you must teach your children what is legal and illegal, what are the associated social behaviors, and what are the effects of these behaviors. If you, as parents, do not take the responsibility to teach your children about substance abuse, they will be influenced by their peers. Most children will start smoking if they see their parents smoking, and the same behavior will be imitated with drugs and alcohol. Presently, with all the literature promoting the dangers of cigarette smoking, states have continued to pass laws permitting marijuana use.

Fostering responsibility and independence: parents make the mistake of doing everything for their children, saying that they need to focus on their schoolwork, sports activities, socialization, and other things that interest them. They give the excuse that when their children mature, become young adults and live on their own, they will know what to do. No, they won't! Parents must begin from an early age to teach their children how to become responsible and take care of themselves. Today, many millennials are staying at home longer. College students are returning home after graduation to save money. The sad fact is the longer the amount of time these young people are under their parents' roof, they are delaying independence and adult responsibilities. It is too easy for parents to slip back into the role of taking care of their adult children. It is a habit, a difficult one to break. Also, many of these young adults are turning to their parents and grandparents for financial assistance. They are contributing minimally to the household expenses, or even assisting with daily chores. Life skills must be taught early, especially when children are teenagers, so they will be able to be independent after high school and or college. They should have mastered practical skills like cooking, doing laundry, cleaning a house, and grocery shopping. Children should have been taught budgeting skills by explaining what the monthly bills are and how they are paid throughout the month. Budgeting is a great skill to learn when they will be working at their first job and throughout their life.

Bullying and establishing healthy behaviors: parents are reluctant to talk to their children about bullying and how to stand up for oneself, and how to feel safe and report any bullying to school officials. Parents must address this issue head-on to protect their children from such harassment and destructive behavior. Communication is the key. Ask your children about their school day. Find out what they liked or did not like about the day. Do not be afraid to be curious about your middle school and high school children. Their problems can escalate very quickly on social media. Sadly today, many young people only communicate through social media on their cell phones and find it difficult to express themselves with adults in a face- to-face conversation. They are visibly uncomfortable. If these communication skills are not practiced in their teenage years, they will find it exceedingly difficult attending college and giving class presentations or a speech. And later, they will be very inept at interviewing for employment when they graduate from college. Lifelong skills must be practiced at an early age to promote confidence and strength of character.

Misbehavior and consequences: Children and teenagers must be taught boundaries. Teaching responsibility for one's actions must start at a young age, so teenagers do not make tragic mistakes. Too many high school graduates go out celebrating and end up in a fatal car crash the evening of their high school graduation. It is too late for parents to explain the consequences of making a bad decision after a fatal accident. Parents must enforce consequences for bad behavior. If there are no consequences to their bad behavior, they grow up thinking that they can get away with anything. They also believe that they will be able to act however they please in life. It is a dangerous behavior pattern with very destructive results. If parents are not able to address these issues or confront the unacceptable behavior of their children, enlist the aid of other adults like school counselors, coaches, other relatives, and therapists to help you with your child's behavior. Just because your children will listen to other adults, does not diminish their respect for you as parents. Sometimes, a third party must step in and assist your child.

Self-respect and respect for others: encourage your children from a young age to be respectful to others, even when they are angry or disagree with authority figures. It is appalling how some young people speak to their parents and other adults, even their teachers. Parents must teach their children how to interact respectfully with their peers and adults. Politeness to others must also be taught. Showing appreciation and thoughtfulness are outstanding personality traits. Children need to be made aware of the effect of their words. They need to focus on paying attention to become better listeners. Focusing on their cell phones while trying to listen to other individuals speaking will only create miscommunications. Parents and adults must lead the way and begin to put their cell phones away, especially out at restaurants. It is prevalent today to see an entire family sitting in a restaurant with everyone on their cell phones. No one is communicating with another family member. There is nothing wrong with establishing a rule that during mealtime, all phones are turned off. Family socialization is crucial to develop well-balanced family members who enjoy being with one another and are supportive of each other.

Last Thoughts to Ponder

It is truly disgraceful that people judge others by the color of their skin or gender and intimidate them. Education and tolerance about other cultures must begin at a young age, so children do not grow up with prejudice. Americans are a melting pot of many different cultures from all over the world. Everyone can learn and appreciate the goodness of different people and their ideas.

We need to change our culture. Communication is paramount to solve problems. Anger can start a revolution; it cannot negotiate the more delicate steps necessary for real social change. Private conversations, which cannot be legislated or enforced, are essential. This is the kind of challenge predicted by the futurist John Naisbitt, for the human mind.

> *"The most exciting breakthroughs of the 21st century will not occur because of technology, but because of an expanding concept of what it means to be human."*[257]
>
> *John Naisbitt*

I hope that I have made you aware of specific issues and increased your ability to analyze these subject matters from another viewpoint. Mine is a small voice crying out to the powers that be, whether political, economic, or religious leaders to take immediate steps to find solutions to these catastrophic cultural events and improve the well-being of all citizens. And to young adults, may I recommend that you do everything you can to save our planet from annihilation. Significant changes need to be made soon, or our earth will perish under the perils of climate change. My recommendation to parents is to instill ethical values in your children. Please do not give them everything that they want. Make them into kind, responsible human beings. Teach them how to be productive and appreciate what they have. Be their guiding parents, not just their friends. They will have plenty of friends, but only one set of parents. My advice to the baby boomers is to keep moving, exercising the brain and body. And along the way, try to impart wisdom from the past to whoever will listen. The politicians in the United States need to remember that they work for everybody in the country, not just their party affiliates. They need to stop wasting millions of dollars on elections, and instead, put the money to better causes that are too many to list here.

We all have an expiration date. What will your thoughts be when your end of time arrives? After my father's passing, I went to see his financial manager. We were discussing some of my father's business affairs that he had wrapped up before his passing. I will never forget the words he used when he spoke about my father: "He finished well." These words have stuck in my mind as I too, want "to finish well," when my time comes. I wonder how many of us will be able to say that we did all we could to make the lives of other people we cared about, a little easier after we are gone.

"To give of one's self; to leave the world a bit better, whether by a healthy child, a garden patch, or a redeemed social condition; to have played and laughed with enthusiasm and sung with exaltation; to know that even one life has breathed easier because you have lived-this is to have succeeded."[258]

Ralph Waldo Emerson (1803-1882)

The Coronavirus - COVID-19
Pandemic of 2020

Historians and writers are busy all over the world either dictating, typing, or putting pen to paper in the old-fashioned way to document this momentous event, COVID-19 that has affected the whole world in the year 2020. How could a virus begin in Wuhan, China as an epidemic, and then spread so quickly across countries affecting thousands and thousands of people around the globe turning it into a pandemic.

Since the previous chapters represent an historical perspective of American culture and we are now trying to manage this global pandemic and its effects here in the United States, it is essential to discuss the repercussions on all Americans and the international coronavirus news at the present time. It is an event beyond comprehension. Our world is shutting down and we are all sheltering in place, afraid to go anywhere. We are told that the virus is in the air, small vapor droplets expelled when an infected person is talking.

As I write this chapter, data from Johns Hopkins University is reporting that there are more than 190,000 deaths from coronavirus and more than 6 million confirmed cases have been diagnosed in the United States.[259] Globally, a million people have died, and more than 30 million have been infected. That figure calculates to about 3.4% fatality rate amongst those affected. These numbers are not accurate as the true number of people infected in the US and worldwide cannot be tallied as everyone who may be infected is not counted. The US has 4% of the world population but 21% of deaths associated with this pandemic. A crying shame for a country that spent 16.9% of gross domestic product (GDP) on health care, nearly twice as much as the average OECD (Organization for Economic Co-operation and Development) country. The second-highest ranking country, Switzerland, spent 12.2%. At the other end of the spectrum, New Zealand and Australia devote only 9.3%, approximately half as much as the US does.[260]

We cannot discuss the current situation without comparing it to the last few pandemics. The deadliest and most severe pandemic worldwide was during 1918-1919, but there were three others in 1957, 1968, and 2009.[261] The previous three epidemics were less severe and caused less mortality, even though both the 1957 H2N2 and 1968 H3N2 outbreaks resulted in roughly a million deaths globally. The 2009 H1N1 caused 300,000 deaths in its first year.

The last time the world inhabitants experienced anything like this current situation was over a hundred years ago in 1918, due to the H1N1 virus, sometimes referred to as the "Spanish flu."[262] Wartime censors had suppressed news of the flu to avoid affecting moral. Spain remained neutral during World War I. The Spanish media was free to report news of the flu, so nations with a media blackout could only read in-depth accounts from the Spanish news sources. There were almost 8 million deaths reported in Spain after the initial outbreak in May 1918. People assumed that Spain was the pandemic's ground zero.

There is still debate over where this Spanish flu originated, but the first known case in the United States was reported at Fort Riley, a military base in Kansas on March 4, 1918. By noon, over one hundred other soldiers had reported similar symptoms. It spread from the United States and Europe to the remote parts of Greenland and the Pacific Islands. President Woodrow Wilson died in early 1919 from this infection while negotiating the Treaty of Versailles.

Researchers have yet to discover why this strain was so lethal. Since testing was not available universally, accurate numbers were not documented. The world population in 1918 was around 1.8 billion. However, it was estimated that about 500 million people or one-third of the world's population was infected. 20 to 50 million, 3 to 5% of people worldwide died during this pandemic, with about 675,000 in the United States. In those days, there were no vaccines or antibiotics to treat secondary infections associated with influenza infections. Medical technology and countermeasures were limited or non-existent at the time.

Additional factors contributed to the virulence; the world was still engaged in World War I, during which roughly 17 million people were killed. As recommended, even today, interventions were to isolate, quarantine, use good personal hygiene, use disinfectants, and limit public gatherings. The global pandemic lasted two years.[263] The vast majority of deaths came about in the fall of 1918. Historians now believe that it was the "second wave" caused by a mutated virus, spread by wartime troop movements that caused the human loss. From September through November 1918, the death rate skyrocketed. During the second wave, unlike a typical seasonal flu, which mostly claims the young and old, the Spanish flu exhibited a "W curve." There was also a massive spike within the age group of 25 to 35-year-olds, who were otherwise healthy but succumbed to this virus.

Since then, many experts have predicted that a severe pandemic could occur again. The avian flu A (H7N9) caused concern internationally. Since 2013, it has so far infected 1,568 people in China with a case fatality of about 39%. However, it did not spread quickly or efficiently between people. Otherwise, it would have caused a pandemic similar to the 1918 flu.

Five years ago, during a TED talk in 2015, Bill Gates had warned us that many countries had worked for years to reduce the risk of nuclear war but needed to give similar attention to a killer virus. He stated: "If anything kills over 10 million people in the next few decades, it is most likely to be a highly infectious virus rather than a war. Not missiles, but microbes."[264]

In January 2020, the unemployment rate of 3.6% was at a fifty-year low.[265] Companies were hiring new workers in hospitality, healthcare, construction, and leisure. According to the US Private Sector Job Quality Index, the US jobs market has shifted dramatically over the last thirty years towards creating low-wage jobs. "In 1990, 53% of positions could be described as low-wage/low-hour jobs, and 47% were high-wage/high-hour jobs. Since 1990, 63% of the jobs created have been low-wage, and just 37% were high-wage."[266] Despite this fact, most people were able to pay their bills, and the consumer index was high. The country was rejoicing, having a strong economy, backed by an all-time high stock market. All that financial progress came to a screeching halt once the pandemic hit. The Bureau of Labor Statistics counted more than 158 million Americans as employed in February before the worst of the coronavirus-fueled economic upheaval hit the United States.[267] In just three weeks, more than 10.5% of that total had filed for unemployment.[268] The

Pew Research Center in the first week of April estimated one in three Americans had to take a pay cut or had been laid off because of the outbreak. In March, the unemployment rate increased to 4.4%, the highest monthly surge since 1975. The number of unemployed persons rose to 7.1 million in March, and 12 million Americans filed for unemployment benefits in the week that ended on April 4, 2020.[269] The unemployment rate was 14.7% in April, 13% in May, 11.1% in June and 10.2% in July, 2020.[270] Just before the pandemic, unemployment was at 3.5%. During the Great Depression, the highest unemployment rate was recorded at 10%.

Most of us want good times to continue and take life for granted, even though it is so fragile. Unfortunately, the expression "life can turn on a dime" has come true for so many of us in such a short period. It is difficult to phantom that the whole world would be brought to a stand-still, and our whole way of life was halted by something that none of our senses could detect. You could not smell, taste, or feel it until it made you sick. For some people, there were no symptoms even when infected with the coronavirus. That is why the term "invisible war" was coined. Regretfully, our government officials did not attack this scourge as if it was a war. At the beginning of the pandemic, Americans were not told to stay at home and isolate. Individual state officials passed rules, but Washington was ineffective, and the President's message may have been counterproductive. If this had been a nuclear war, we would either all have been eradicated or be speaking Chinese now! Our response was and continues to be pitiful. Restaurants were closed, and we were forced to cook at home. There were no more sporting events or activities. And we are inundated with the news of the pandemic 24/7.

A bigger question, is the world correcting itself? Is the reason behind this disaster for humanity to realize that we have messed up our priorities? Did the carbon emissions and climate change finally create something to alter the course of the universe? After all, we have had an increase in temperature with global warming, wildfires burning down millions of acres, melting icebergs and raising the sea levels. In addition, there has been an increase in tornados, hurricanes, earthquakes, and landslides causing massive damage, floods, and tsunamis. Some communities have been devastated, so many lives upended, and others worldwide are facing a severe drought bringing famine to the population. Who do we blame for this chaos, or is all of humanity guilty?

Should China be accused of starting the pandemic and refusing to immediately alert the world health organizations about the severity of the virus infection? In January 2020, Chinese officials were aware that a lethal disease had been unleashed. Instead of sounding the alarm, they chose to stockpile their inventories of masks, personal protective equipment, and ventilators. They reduced their export of these items and even bought out additional health supplies from other unsuspecting countries. Why have there been less deaths in China where the virus originated? After all it has the highest population of any country in the world.

Many health experts believe that the pathogen, COVID-19, (SARS-CoV-2 virus), most likely originated in bats, but more likely in pangolins, a relative of the armadillo and anteaters. Two researchers found a 99% match between DNA of the new coronavirus in humans with the DNA in pangolins, using genomic sequencing.[271] Dr. Sonia Shah, in her book 'Pandemic' warned over 300 infectious diseases have newly emerged or re-emerged over the past 50 years, and epidemiologists have been predicting that that one of them will cause a disruptive, deadly pandemic for years. Simply put, one of her concerns was that humans have been encroaching on animal territory for years and the loss of certain animals, insects and wildlife has upset the balance and created an opportunity for new pathogens to emerge.

Pangolins are an endangered species, and China's laws protect these animals. Selling pangolins can land the seller in prison for ten years. Despite this illegal activity, researchers describe it as "the most poached and trafficked mammal in the world." The Chinese use the animal's scales to treat conditions like arthritis, menstrual pain, and skin conditions. The meat is also considered to be a delicacy. Researchers suggested that the viral infection originated at a seafood and wild animal market in Wuhan, China. The pangolins may have been sold at this market illegally.

Vincent Racaniello, a microbiology professor at Columbia University has disputed the data and connection between the market and the virus's origin.[272] Two Chinese researchers have suggested that the virus may have "leaked" from one of two labs near the Wuhan market. This theory has not been supported by direct proof. The Wuhan Institute of Virology strongly rejected any suggestion of the virus originating from their lab. China is also fighting back any of these allegations.[273] According to a report by the Associated Press in April 2020, based on leaked documents from a confidential teleconference with China's National Health Commission, Chinese leaders allegedly failed to notify the public about the looming crisis. Their internal evidence had painted a dire situation. There was a six-day delay, during which 3,000 people got infected in China. This obstruction laid the groundwork for an outbreak that spread around the world. The Chinese authorities had counted the infected cases and the number of deaths differently three times in January and February 2020. By mid-April 2020, they revised their figures again with a 50% increase in deaths from the coronavirus in Wuhan.[274] Chinese authorities reported that the data was changed to show "accountability to history" as well as to ensure "open and transparent disclosure of information and data accuracy."

In March 2020, China established a new policy whereby all academic papers about COVID-19 will be subjected to extra scrutiny. The central government officials must approve them before they are submitted for publication.[275] The surveillance was an attempt by the Chinese government to control theories on the origin of this pandemic. An anonymous Chinese researcher said that this move was a worrying development; it would obstruct crucial scientific research. His opinion was that China does not want to take responsibility for the origin of this pandemic. There have been reports of censorship from whistleblowers. There is a clampdown on research into the origins of the virus. The first transmission to humans was reported in Wuhan, a city in the Hubei province of China. Cases appeared there in December 2019. During the first few weeks of

January, officials in Wuhan were insisting that only those individuals, who came into contact with infected animals, could catch the virus. No guidance was issued to protect doctors. An article in the South China Morning Post places the first case on November 17, 2019. Since then, the virus has spread most likely through person-to-person contact.

According to news reports on January 18, 2020, the Health and Human Services Director had been briefed on the dangers of the coronavirus in the United States. On January 24, President Trump tweeted that China was working hard to contain the coronavirus outbreak. On the same day, there were two confirmed cases of the disease in the United States. The day before, the World Health Organization (WHO) had put out a statement that all countries should prepare to contain the virus. China had started locking down the province of Hubei. On January 27, the CDC issued a level 3 warning about non-essential travel to China. On January 29, the President reported receiving a briefing on the coronavirus from health agencies working closely with China. Peter Navarro, Director of Trade and Manufacturing in the Trump administration wrote a memo to the National Security Council (NSC) that as many as half a million Americans could lose their lives in this pandemic. China had acknowledged by this time that the virus was highly contagious, more so than the regular flu. By January 30, the WHO announced a global world pandemic.

The United States was continuing to work with China at that time. China continued to engage in a cover-up. The WHO did not do enough to investigate the facts coming out of China. There were reports that the World Health Organization was reluctant to impose restrictions of travel back and forth from China beginning February 2020. The WHO cautioned against the overuse of travel restrictions but stopped short of saying that Trump's decision in the US, or anyone else's in other countries was inappropriate. WHO Director-General Tedros Adhanom Ghebreyesus told his executive board: "We reiterate our call to all countries not to impose restrictions inconsistent with the International Health Regulations. Such restrictions can have the effect of increasing fear and stigma, with little public health benefit. So far, twenty-two countries have reported such restrictions to WHO. Where such measures have been implemented, we urge that they are short, proportionate to the public health risks, and are reconsidered regularly as the situation evolves."[276]

Numerous flights landed in the United States from China and Europe before the travel ban. The virus had already spread, causing deaths in China, Europe, and the United States. It is now known that the first death from the coronavirus COVID-19 was a 57-year-old woman from Santa Clara County in California. She died February 6, 2020, of a massive heart attack. According to the autopsy report, there was evidence of the coronavirus infection in her heart, trachea, lungs, and intestines.[277]

The World Health Organization (WHO), on March 11, 2020, declared COVID-19 a pandemic, reporting over 118,000 cases of the coronavirus illness in over 110 countries and territories around the world and the sustained risk of further global spread. "This is not just a public health crisis, it is a crisis that will touch every sector, so every sector and every individual must be involved in the fights,"[278] stated Dr. Tedros Adhanom Ghebreyesus, WHO Director-General, at a media briefing.

The top government scientists battling the coronavirus estimated on March 31, 2020, that the deadly pathogen could kill between 100,000 and 240,000 Americans, despite social distancing measures. Schools were closed; large gatherings were banned; travel became highly restrictive, and people were asked to stay in their homes.[279] However, these numbers were based on government officials figuring on only 50% of Americans responding to the recommendations. People were instructed to limit the number of individuals who came within six feet of their proximity, especially when out in public. It was proposed that no more than ten people congregate for any social activities. I never thought the comment *"I wouldn't touch him/her with a 6-foot pole" would become a national policy, but here we are!*

It was essential to stay away from individuals infected with the virus and regularly wash one's hands. The new American mantra was to wash your hands frequently throughout the day for at least twenty seconds by singing "Happy Birthday." In 2020, we were teaching people how to wash their hands thoroughly. People were advised to use alcohol-based hand sanitizers and disinfectants and to avoid touching their face. When going outside, it was strongly recommended, but instead should have been mandated, to always wear a mask that covered your mouth and nose, especially when shopping. Adults over the age of sixty and those with underlying conditions like high blood pressure, diabetes, asthma, cancer, and being immunosuppressed were encouraged to stay at home and remain isolated. The virus was more lethal to older adults, African,

Asian, Hispanic, and other minority race Americans, and those individuals with underlying conditions. Due to the high number of people who responded to the recommendations initially, the number of deaths was less than those projected at the end of March 2020.

People in Wuhan minimized fears about the virus, despite knowing the dangers, and even punished doctors who spoke up.[280] Dr. Li Wenliang, who diagnosed the virus, was hailed a hero for raising the coronavirus alarm in the early days of the outbreak. Sadly, he died of the infection on February 6, 2020. He was 34 years old. Dr. Li tried to send a message to fellow medics about the outbreak at the end of December. Three days later, police visited him and told him to stop spreading rumors. He returned to work and caught the virus from a patient. Dr. Li was working at the center of the outbreak in December 2019 when he noticed seven cases of this infection. He thought the illnesses looked like SARS, the virus that led to a global epidemic in 2003. Dr. Li did not know then that this disease was an entirely new coronavirus. Four days later, he was summoned to the Public Security Bureau, where he was told to sign a letter. In the letter, he was accused of "making false comments" and had "severely disturbed the social order." He was one of eight people who were being investigated for spreading rumors by the police. Officials from Beijing, China refused help from the CDC and gave WHO limited excess to Wuhan. There has been unreliable data from China about the number of people who were infected and the number of deaths. The Chinese officials have always manipulated the numbers to serve their purpose and broader interests. China is now retaliating by saying that the US military started the infection in Wuhan.

None of this information changes the fact that the President was made aware of the looming dangers by the end of January 2020. He was concerned about "spooking" the stock market and minimized the risks of the virus. These misjudgments have caused severe health and economic consequences in America. Instead of the back and forth and where the blame lies, broad worldwide alliances should be built to take coordinated action, not withholding funds to the WHO, restricting trade, and playing the blame game with China. China may well have to pay the consequences and examine how they conducted business. Even during the "Cold War," the USA and Russia were mortal enemies, but they worked together to vaccinate and eradicate smallpox.

COVID-19 was not an infection spread by rats like the plague in Europe. No one knows what happened to the "Spanish flu" virus after two years of utter devastation and significant loss of life. Did it just disappear or mutate and became less potent? COVID-19 is an invisible enemy. Initially, it was thought that this disease was like the regular flu and was only deadly to the older population. Now we know differently. There have been many reported cases of young, healthy individuals also succumbing to this infection. Many people did not heed the recommendations of the medical experts and take this disease seriously. *Can everyone please follow the government instructions so we can knock out this coronavirus and be done with it? I feel like a kindergartner who keeps losing more recess because one or two kids can't follow the directions.*

Finally, the government authorities had to step in and enforce the closure of schools, restaurants, beaches, and sports activities. *This virus has done what no woman has been able to do: cancel all sports, shut down all bars, and keep men at home!*

The coronavirus forced individuals to adopt many unfamiliar and uncomfortable changes. Even though many people felt that the state and federal guidelines were correct, others thought they were too strict or not strict enough. Unfortunately, there was much at stake for our way of life: the freedoms we enjoy, maintaining employment or collecting unemployment, the survival of small and large businesses, and the health of American citizens. Everyone was encouraged to be vigilant and do their part to battle this invisible enemy. The majority of people were fearful. There was the terror of catching the virus and dying. Unfortunately, this pandemic started at the same time when seasonal allergies were gearing up, displaying similar symptoms such as coughing, sneezing, a runny nose, except for an increase in temperature with the coronavirus infection.

Coronaviruses are a group of viruses that can cause disease in both animals and humans. The novel coronavirus seems to primarily spread via respiratory droplets produced by an infected individual during coughing, sneezing, talking, or breathing. The next person becomes infected by inhaling these droplets into his or her lungs or by getting them in the nose or mouth. If people got sick right away after they were infected, they might stay at home in bed, giving them few opportunities to transmit the virus. Instead, individuals with COVID-19 are contagious before they have symptoms, says Lauren Ancel

Meyers, executive director of the University of Texas at Austin COVID-19 Modeling Consortium. The CDC estimates that about 40% of transmissions occurs before the infected person has any symptoms and that the symptoms take an average of six days to begin. However, it can take up to fourteen days for the disease to elicit physical ailments. Around 80% of people with COVID-19 experienced mild, flu-like symptoms and recovered without specialist treatment. However, one in six people experienced severe symptoms, especially trouble breathing. COVID-19 coronavirus affected people in different ways. The most common symptoms were fever, tiredness, and a dry cough. People could also have aches and pains, persistent pain or pressure in the chest, nasal congestion, runny nose, sore throat and diarrhea, the onset of confusion, agitation due to encephalopathy, or inability to be woken, bluish lips or face. Others were reporting a loss of sense of smell and taste in otherwise asymptomatic patients. Another strange symptom is the presence of purple or blue lesions on a patient's feet and toes. They are typically painful to touch and can have a hot burning sensation. This condition has been dubbed "COVID toes." These patients were usually children and young adults. They were also free of other COVID-19 symptoms. Increased clotting of blood vessels, kidney failure, acute liver damage, ongoing GI issues, skin manifestations, neurologic damage, and endocrine problems causing blood sugar control issues have also been reported, especially among very sick, hospitalized patients. Additionally, people admitted to intensive care were at increased risk for mental health issues like post-traumatic stress disorder (PTSD), anxiety, and depression. COVID-19 had also been causing sudden strokes in adults in their 30s and 40s who were not otherwise terribly ill. The virus can cause the blood to clot in unusual ways, and stroke could be an expected consequence. These patients were unwilling to call 911 or go to the hospital.

Many hospitals were overwhelmed with coronavirus cases. Physicians reported that this virus can attack almost every organ system and may or may not present with respiratory symptoms. It is unlike any other viral infection they have ever dealt with, propagating theories that it may have been a laboratory manufactured virus. Even though most experts have ruled out this hypothesis, it is difficult to comprehend why the virus is so devastating to some families while it leaves others who are infected, without any symptoms. Question to be pondered here is whether this was a DNA, genetically engineered virus that is virulent to certain DNAs. There has never been a clear understanding why China suffered so few casualties despite their huge population and the infection originating on their soil.

People with mild symptoms were asked to isolate, but ones with fever, cough, and difficulty breathing were requested to seek medical help. The patients who developed acute respiratory distress syndrome (ARDS) were the unfortunate ones who died due to intense, systematic inflammation. It was frightening that some people were infected but had no symptoms. They spread the infection unknowingly, especially if they were not tested and unaware that they were infected. This period gave an infected individual a long window to encounter other people and to perhaps get into a situation ripe for superspreading the virus. In fact, research on actual cases, as well as models of the pandemic, indicate that between 10 and 20% of infected people are responsible for 80 percent of the coronavirus's spread. Therefore, the health experts from the very beginning of the pandemic stressed that we needed to test people, get the results ASAP, so we could isolate and contact trace to prevent the spread of the virus. The US was not prepared nor had the ability to take this route.

Patients with COVID-19 who developed acute respiratory distress syndrome (ARDS) were at a higher risk of long-term health issues. Now we know that even a 'mild' case could leave someone with disabilities and long-term chronic issues. Many patients who have 'recovered' continue to have lingering health problems. The list of symptoms is longer and more varied than most doctors could have imagined.[281] Ongoing problems include psychological problems, muscle weakness, unable to stand for long periods of time, shortness of breath, and long-term fatigue. Many people also said they could not sleep. They had relentless fevers, violent diarrhea, and throbbing headaches. The tips of their fingers and toes often burned intensely, like they were shocked from an electrical socket. Some women described having extremely heavy periods or no periods at all. Some complained of their hair falling out in clumps. Many had a racing heartbeat, achy joints, and a persistent loss of sense of smell and taste. Most of them were trying to figure out what was going on with their bodies while navigating what they call a "brain fog," a mix between short-term memory loss and an inability to focus. Impaired lung function from the infection could negatively affect other organs like the heart, lungs, kidneys, and brain.

These patients have been dubbed as "long haulers".[282] BuzzFeed News staff spoke with more than 100 of these long haulers who described a set of similar symptoms. David Putrino, the Director of Rehabilitation Innovation at New York City's Mount Sinai hospital, has been studying and caring for long-haulers at one of the nation's only post-COVID clinic since May. He has been in contact with about 90,000 people in almost 100 countries who are all reporting nearly the same serious, post-viral symptoms. Their average age is about 38, and they are mainly women. These chronic symptoms should be enough to make everyone pause and think, that even if they are young and healthy, could they afford to be out of action for six months? Before COVID, many of them were vibrant and active. Now, they can't work and often need help with basic tasks, like feeding themselves and taking a shower. A small handful of scientists have started collecting data on the longer-term effects of COVID-19. A study out of Germany found that 78 out of 100 patients, most of whom recovered at home, had heart complications two months later. An Italian study found that 87% of hospitalized patients still had a variety of symptoms after two months. In America, 35% report problems two weeks after the acute infection.

As of April 2020, 3.5 million cases were confirmed worldwide, and over 245,000 people lost their lives.[283] The current world population is 7.8 billion, according to the most recent United Nations estimates recorded by Worldometer. One million people had died worldwide from the COVID-19 in less than 9 months after the first death was confirmed in Wuhan,

China. Only 4 countries, the US, Brazil, India, and Mexico accounted for 50% of these deaths.

Not only Americans but all citizens' lifestyles worldwide were stifled within a few weeks as this pandemic spread. In this day and age of travel by air, boat, and cruise ships, the virus had multiple avenues to spread at will. Americans are used to the lethal illness of the flu every year. During the flu season, handwashing and receiving the vaccination are certainly advocated, but not all the other safeguards are required or mandated as with this coronavirus. The CDC estimates that up to 42.9 million people got sick during the 2018-2019 flu season; 647,000 people were hospitalized, and 61,200 died.[284] Only 18.8% of 18 to 49-year-olds, 40.7% of 50 to 64-year-olds, and 66.4% of people over 65 got the "flu shot" in the United States. The 2018-2019 flu season was the longest one in a decade, lasting 21 weeks. It began in November, peaked in mid-February, and trailed off in April. The death rate from the flu was at 0.018% in the United States, with a population of 330 million people. The current death rate from COVID-19 is at 0.057%, with a loss of 190,000 lives so far, and counting. CDC reported overall death rate to be less than 1% for everyone except people over 70. Compared to the regular flu season in the United States, the number of deaths from the coronavirus had already surpassed the number of deaths from the flu within two months, by the end of April. Countries, including the United States, tried to institute lockdowns.

Some countries were more successful than others. The countries that had fewer deaths had citizens who were willing to listen to the health experts and follow guidelines. Some governments were willing to take harsh action against their citizens who did not follow protocol to save the lives of their fellow countrymen. However, this was not the case in the US. There were rules for social distancing. Since late April, health experts and medical professionals stressed the importance of wearing face masks, as more research found that the virus spreads through face-to-face close contact like talking, sneezing, and coughing. As infected cases and deaths continued to rise in the US, scientists were finding that men were more likely to die from COVID-19 and did not know why.[285] Was wearing a mask to avoid death part of the feminization of America? Was it too emasculating to wear a mask to protect the others around them? The survey found that 34% of men compared to 54% of women responded they "always" wore a mask when outside their home and that 20% of men said they "never" wore a mask outside their home (compared to just 8% of women). Some see masks as a weakness, and men, regardless of politics or race or sexuality, do not like being seen as weak. President Trump resisted wearing a mask and did not set a good example as a leader for this lifesaving measure. Many governors were announcing that face masks were required in public places when social distancing was impossible. Other politicians like Georgia's Governor Brian Kemp were explicitly banning mayors in Georgia's cities and counties from ordering people to wear masks in public places.

A mask is better than a ventilator. Home is better than ICU. Prevention is better than treatment. It is not curfew, it's CARE FOR U.

Until this pandemic, most people did not realize how lethal the flu season could be. Many people opt not to get the regular flu vaccination. One wonders how many people would have responded to requests of social distancing, quarantine of elderly citizens, wearing masks and gloves, if told to do so when the pandemic first started. Would the American people have stopped hugging, shaking hands, socializing, going out to eat at restaurants, exercising in the gyms, going to concerts, watching their favorite sports, and going to movies in theaters? Truthfully, they would not have stopped any of these regular activities voluntarily. Once they started hearing about the number of people getting infected and dying around the world, Americans took notice. Some listened to the medical experts and began self-isolating in their homes. Despite more than 200,000 deaths and almost 7.5 million cases of infected people in the US, many remain stubborn, quoting loss of freedom in having to follow the safety measures. Do people understand the meaning of freedom? Do they understand that with freedom, comes responsibility, not only for themselves but also for their fellow citizens? One American was dying every 80 seconds. 40 out of the 50 states in the US had increasing numbers of infected cases in August, 5 months after we realized the seriousness of the pandemic.

As scientists have learned more about COVID-19, it has become clear that so-called super spreader incidents, in which one person infects a disproportionate number of other individuals have played an oversized role in the transmission of the virus that causes the disease.[286] Scientists have identified factors that catalyze such events, including large crowd sizes, close contact between people and confined spaces with poor ventilation. Current evidence suggests that it is mostly circumstances such as these, rather than the biology of specific individuals, that sets the stage for extreme spreading of the novel coronavirus. In late February 2020, about 175 executives from around the world attended the biotechnology company Biogen's leadership conference in Boston. Over a course of two days, people shook hands, mingled, and ate meals together. Several attendees and others at the event unknowingly got infected with COVID-19, then took it home. At least 99 people ended up sick in Massachusetts alone. Now this event has been linked to about 20,000 cases of infections. The spread of COVID-19 began with about 90 cases among the attendees and their direct contacts. Around the same time, the coronavirus was spreading among more than 100 people who went to a funeral in Albany, Georgia. This sparked an outbreak that soon led to the surrounding rural county posting one of the nation's highest cumulative incidences of COVID-19. The next month a single individual with the disease infected 52 people during a two-and-a-half-hour choir practice in Washington State. Two people died. In Arkansas, an infected pastor and his wife passed the virus on to more than 30 attendees at church events over the course of a few days, leading to at least three deaths. And these new cases spread to 26 more people, at least one of whom died. Large gatherings were banned from the beginning of the pandemic, but some people were not taking the warnings seriously. The Boston conference and the funeral in Georgia were among several super spreader events that played "a notable role in the early US spread of COVID-19," according to a report by Anne Schuchat, principal deputy director of the Centers for Disease Control and Prevention.

Time also plays a factor in the rate of transmission. The longer a group stays in contact, the greater the likelihood that the virus will spread among them. Exactly how much time someone needs to pick it up remains an unanswered question, says Syra Madad, a special pathogens expert at NYC Health and Hospitals. She adds that the benchmark used for risk assessment in her contact-tracing work is 10 minutes of contact with an infectious person, though the CDC uses 15 minutes as a guideline. Essential workers such as grocery store checkers and nursing home employees interact with large groups by necessity and work in situations primed for superspreading. The same is true now for teachers who are interacting face-to-face with a large number of students in the school setting or at college level. If we want to contain COVID-19, we will have to find ways to protect them and make their workplaces less favorable to such events.

At the beginning of the pandemic, young people continued to gather in masses on beaches during "spring break." They lined up at bars in Boston, New York, and other cities, and celebrated Mardi Gras in New Orleans. They must have felt invincible. There were "coronavirus" parties where young people deliberately got together to get infected, and then thought that they would recover.

After an initial shut down, some states lifted restrictions, to try and bring some normality to an incredible abnormal situation. People relinquished their responsibilities to stay safe and experts blamed the massive upsurge in infected cases on lockdown fatigue and summer travel. Instead of cases rising in the urban areas, now the infection was ravaging people in the rural counties, especially in Ohio, Missouri, Wisconsin, and

Illinois. During Memorial Day weekend, large crowds gathered at Lake of the Ozarks in Missouri. In early July, 43 cases were linked to a Michigan house party, mainly consisting of 15 to 25-year-olds. Thousands gathered at a rodeo in protest of government restrictions in Minnesota, after someone invited people to attend on Facebook. 700 guests showed up at a party at a rented Airbnb in New Jersey (which is only second to New York for the greatest number of infections and deaths), and it took police 5 hours to break up the party.[287] These individuals were obviously not concerned about the men and women in uniform and their families being needlessly put at risk to the infection. Another party led to 20 teens who tested positive after attending a party which led to a cluster of cases. They were 15 to 19-year-olds. There was a 'Safe and Sound' Benefit concert in Southampton, where 600 vehicles were found. Governor Cuomo was appalled, calling this an "egregious social distancing violation" and wanted to pursue charges against those involved. Nonessential gatherings of more than 50 people could be fined $1,000.

The Sturgis Motorcycle Rally is an American motorcycle rally held annually in Sturgis, South Dakota, usually during the first full week of August. An estimated quarter of a million motorcyclists were expected to descend on the city. What was appalling and unpatriotic, undaunted by the virus, tens of thousands of motorcyclists roared into Sturgis to celebrate the 80th year for the rally. When asked about catching the COVID-19, the response was "If we get it, we chose to be here!" It was reported that a tattoo artist who was working 16 hours a day had tested positive with the COVID-19, and also a bartender next door to him. Since masks and social distancing were not mandated during this rally, it is very difficult to imagine how many people could have been infected from just these two sources. About three weeks after the rally kicked off, the repercussions became clear. More than 100 cases of COVID-19 connected to the rally were reported in at least eight states, according to the Associated Press reports.[288] I guess the people that attended this rally had no care or concern for their families, neighbors, or co-workers. Officials from Sturgis were asked why they did not cancel the event. Their response was that people were going to come whether they had the rally or not and a lot of businesses would suffer by not holding the rally. After many residents objected to holding the rally during a pandemic, city leaders decided to pay for mass testing with money they had received as part of federal coronavirus relief funding. Two weeks after the rally, the average number of daily new cases increased by 32, an increase of about 43%. Since the pandemic started, South Dakota has had 10,884 confirmed cases, with a death toll of 159 by end of August.

With the fall semester approaching and coronavirus infections still rampant, numerous colleges and universities nationwide started reversing course and abandoning plans to bring students back to campus.[289] The plan was to bring a portion of their students back to campus and teach both in-person and online. Many students wanted to return to campus after months of isolation, and many were skeptical about the online learning experience. Experts were not optimistic that if colleges did bring students back, about how long they would be able to stay open in-person this fall. These dangerous situations are similar to where people live in close proximity and the chance of spreading the infection is high. The goal should have been no transmission of infections before schools and colleges opened. Everyone was trying to get back to normalcy during abnormal times. They should have waited a few more months before colleges reopened. Once colleges opened, they became the new hot spots. Students were either infected even before getting to college or caught the virus soon after arriving at college. Experts were worried "young people were going to behave like they always do." Hundreds of students started congregating, which led to drinking, dancing, not social distancing or wearing masks, packing the streets and front yards of off-campus houses, near the University of North Georgia.

This behavior continues across college campuses, despite rising cases of COVID-19 in students returning to colleges and Georgia having the fifth highest number of infections. The University of Alabama reported more than 500 COVID-19 cases less than a week after classes started. At Ohio State, more than 220 students were suspended for violating pandemic precautions before the school year even began. The University of Notre Dame reported a record spike, confirming at least 147 COVID-19 cases on its campus, after just 58 cases were reported the day earlier. The university traced nearly 60 of those cases to an off-campus party.

The numbers of infected students started rising and colleges like UNC-Chapel Hill moved all undergraduate classes online after 130 more students tested positive for the coronavirus. This happened within one week of opening. The decision to move classes online "has come entirely too late," said the union, which sued the UNC System on August 10 on behalf of housekeepers, professors, and other staff. Four COVID-19 clusters were reported over three days in dorms, apartments, and a fraternity house. UNC has reported 324 confirmed cases, 279 students and 45 staff members the decision to send students back home was a nightmare for parents as well. They may have brought their child to the college campus from out of state and then had to return to bring the student back home with all their belongings. Health experts suggested having the infected college students remain at college to avoid them going home and infecting other family members. The irresponsible behaviors of super spreader students partying at get-togethers off campus and bringing the virus back on campus, caused major hardships for students who were following the rules and looking forward to getting away to college. It was a lot of extra work on the faculty to arrange for online teaching. Colleges were concerned about loss of income, amounting to millions of dollars, from the room and board revenue from students. Some offered students small tuition discounts. Due to the irresponsible behaviors of a few, all students had to suffer as many colleges switched to exclusively online. At this juncture, it is unclear whether these students were more interested in having short term pleasure or needed more evidence of pain suffered by families of the 200,000 dead, before reality hits them. Many of the young people who were acting recklessly may not have experienced a loss of a family member or friend to COVID-19. Otherwise, they would be more cognizant of their responsibility to others living in America. U.S. is not only unhinged but may be fracturing due to abnormal responses to the same crisis that is affecting the entire world.

Some college professors were reporting that online learning was not taken seriously by some college students. They were not dressed appropriately, some in their pajamas, eating breakfast, etc., when they were attending Zoom online classes. This was in full view of the professors and other students taking the class. Instead of trying their best and making the most of difficult learning situations, these young people were showing their total lack of responsibility and self-discipline during tough times.

Amid a global pandemic, tens of thousands of couples postponed their weddings. Even wedding planners were reporting that with all the social activities involved in a wedding, it would be difficult to practice social distancing. One of the most blatant disregard for rules and the safety of their loved ones was demonstrated, with the help of the church, at Saints Peter and Paul Church, in Washington Square Park, in San Francisco.[290] The couple wanted a storybook wedding at the same church where the bride's parents and grandparents had previously married. Instead of waiting for a safer time to hold the wedding, the couple decided on a large covert wedding amid strict pandemic health orders. The San Francisco City Attorney's Office arrived at the last minute to closed church doors as they were allowing attendees to enter the church through the back doors. At the city attorney's request, the wedding was moved outdoors to a connecting basketball court. But according to the San Francisco Chronicle, the bride and groom and as many as eight other participants may have contracted COVID-19. The virus did not spare them. Other attendees had to take flights to other states, hence continuing the risk of spreading the virus. Another e-mail also revealed the city attorney had already warned the San Francisco Archdiocese in June about hosting other illegal weddings. A statement was released, which said in part it hoped this incident would shock the archdiocese into taking responsibility for what was happening at its churches. Another indoor wedding in Maine that violated attendance limits was responsible for three deaths and nearly 150 infected people, according to the state's Center for Disease Control and Prevention. Despite the rush to get married, the divorce rate rose by 34% between March to June 2020 compared to same time frame in 2019.[291] 31% of divorcees were blamed on the pandemic stress. 20% were newlyweds, married for less than five months. During this pandemic, the churches have shown a lack of leadership in providing appropriate information and have not taken measures to ensure the safety of their congregants. Some churches continued to have services, choir singing, funerals, weddings, etc., hence infecting several members of their congregation with COVID-19.

To add insult to injury, the U.S. Roman Catholic Church used a special and unprecedented exemption from federal rules to collect at least $1.4 Billion in taxpayer-backed coronavirus aid. This in light of the fact that churches do not pay taxes. Millions of dollars went to dioceses that have paid huge settlements or sought bankruptcy protection because of clergy sexual abuse cover-ups. The amount of money garnered by the churches may have surpassed $3.5 Billion, making a global religious institution among the biggest winner in the U.S.

government's pandemic relief efforts, reported by an Associated Press analysis of federal data.[292] As small businesses were shutting down permanently, workers were out of jobs, the rate of poverty was increasing across the U.S., people could not pay rent or have money for food, the Congress let faith groups and other nonprofits tap into the Paycheck Protection Program. The $659 Billion fund had been created to keep Main Street open and Americans employed. Instead, the Archdiocese of New York, for example, received 15 loans worth at least $28 Million just for its top executive offices. If churches are allowed to tap into taxes, they need to be treated as a business and made to pay taxes on all their sources of income. Where is the outrage? Are Americans aware of such egregious deals made behind closed doors?

The evidence about superspreading activities has led researchers to believe they were responsible for much of the new coronavirus's transmission. "Preventing super spreader events would go a long way toward stopping COVID-19" said Samuel Scarpino, a network scientist who studies infectious disease at Northeastern University.[293] "All of the data I'm seeing so far suggest that if you tamp down the super spreader events, the growth rate of the infections stops very, very quickly," Scarpino said. The virus can fade out if it is denied circumstances for spreading. Due to the irresponsibility of people who did not want to abide by the restrictions, there was a massive surge in the number of new cases. The people continuing to congregate in mass numbers were ignoring what the officials and experts were saying, and what other countries in Europe were doing, reopening SLOWLY and cautiously. Distancing and using face masks were paramount. In some states, police officers were given the authority to fine people from $100 to $500 for not following the pandemic rules. The requirements included wearing masks while out in public, not hosting get-togethers of more than ten people, and maintaining six feet from other individuals.

Most people can pray at home and do not have to attend church services which have infected many in the congregation. The Internet provides many venues to watch shows and movies. It is not necessary to go to movie theaters especially if someone is infected or at a higher risk to get infected. Enjoy outdoor activities but do so with a small number of people you know who are not infected. The large gatherings that continue to defy all advice from health experts are to say the least, reckless, and uncaring, not only for themselves but also for their families and friends. We are in this mess together. Everyone must do the right thing to survive.

According to Forbes, CareerBuilder found that 78% of US workers were living paycheck to paycheck in January 2019. This current financial crisis was not caused by greed, mismanagement, or corruption. The government's response was not a "bailout" to reward bad behavior, as was the case in the 2008 financial crisis. It was an effort to protect public health and compensate those whose livelihoods had been taken away through no fault of their own. On the federal level, Congress passed three broad economic relief bills to assist families, businesses, and communities as the pandemic threatened the economy. In March 2020, Washington enacted the largest economic stimulus package in US history with $2 Trillion in coronavirus aid. There was funding allocated for research and development for the coronavirus treatments, medical supplies, testing, and the creation of a national sick leave program to provide temporary relief to employers and employees, who were laid off due to the coronavirus. Loan programs were put in place to assist businesses of all sizes to continue to pay both employees and operational costs while closed temporarily due to the virus. It authorized economic relief payments to workers and families, and increased unemployment benefits to assist those workers, who may not qualify under other programs. It also included a provision to protect the jobs and salaries of defense and space contract employees to keep the workforce and these important programs intact.

Extensive oversight was not implemented, despite negotiations between the Democrats and Republicans over the $2.2 Trillion coronavirus relief package.[294] The White House wanted to let the Treasury Department distribute $500 Billion to industry and states without anyone overseeing the process. Finally, a law was passed and an inspector general at the Treasury Department would oversee the fund, but two weeks later, after hundreds of billions of dollars had already been distributed through the Paycheck Protection Program, this post had not yet been confirmed! The President also was not going to allow the inspector general overseeing the executive branch's committee to submit reports to Congress without his supervision, arguing it was unconstitutional. Liz Hempowicz, Director of Public Policy at the Project on Government Oversight wrote in an e-mail to TIME, "It's imperative that these oversight mechanisms are fully functional so we can have confidence that this money won't be lost to waste, fraud, or abuse."[295] Glenn Fine, who was acting Inspector General at the Pentagon, was quickly appointed to lead the committee, but he was removed by President Trump just a week later.

Officials at the banks approved large amounts of loans to big corporations and did not cater to many of the smaller businesses, who were left out without any financial help or funds. Huge loans were given to big businesses that caused the money to run out quickly. The American people were hoping that this rescue plan was not a repeat of the financial crisis of 2007 when banks would not release funds for mortgages, even though the government had given them large sums to do so. I guess it was wrong to assume that large corporations should have a healthy nest egg to see them through any difficult financial times. However, they may have spent it on enormous salaries for their CEOs and other administrators.

The program paid out $521 Billion to almost 4.9 million companies to provide relief for small businesses and their workers. Publicly traded companies have received more than $1 Billion in funds meant for small businesses.[296] Nearly 300 public companies have reported receiving money from the fund. The first pool of $349 Billion ran dry, leaving more than 80% of applicants without funding. Due to the outcry, publicly traded companies returned almost $600 million that would eventually be directed to smaller businesses. Treasury Secretary Steven Mnuchin defended the program as a success, saying three-quarters of the loans were for totals of under $150,000. Officials urged publicly traded firms with access to other capital to return the money by May 7. Mnuchin said that all loans of more than $2 million would be audited with potential penalties for those who don't comply. The Los Angeles Lakers, a basketball franchise, repaid a $4.6 Million coronavirus relief loan that they received as part of the federal government's Paycheck Protection Program. Potbelly and Ruth's Chris Steak House, two publicly traded chain restaurants with locations across the country, decided to return $30 Million in loans that were meant for helping small businesses survive during the pandemic. An analysis by the Associated Press shows that as much as $273 Million was loaned to more than 100 companies that are owned or operated by donors to President Trump.[297] Just one example of this abuse was a case of Manhattan law firm whose attorney has defended President Trump for almost two decades. Kasowitz Benson Torres LLP, whose managing partner, Marc Kasowitz, was at one point the president's top lawyer in the special counsel's Russia investigation, was set to receive between $5 Million and $10 Million from Citibank. (The largest loan a company could seek was $10 million.) They were entitled to apply for these loans but was it morally the right thing to do?

This information has to give pause to all Americans about the abuse of power and corruption at the highest levels of our governing system, together with the greed of the banks. If the government wanted the stimulus money to help the struggling families and stimulate the economy, they missed their mark. As a non-economist, I certainly understand the logic of putting money in the hands of people who need the money to pay bills, rent and feed their families. And in turn, they are the ones who put the money back into the economy. Giving money to rich companies, churches, and CEOs who are only going to pocket the money will not grow the economy. The US Congress passed a new COVID-19 relief package totaling $484 Billion, the fourth aid bill in response to the pandemic. This amount was added to the small business aid fund, while also funding hospitals and testing. The total federal spending on COVID-19 relief rose to $3 Trillion, swelling the US budget deficit towards record levels.

Families were confined to their houses. All the people who could work from home did so. Unfortunately, children were also at home; their schools were closed. Many parents had multiple jobs now, completing their work online, homeschooling their children, and preparing three meals a day for the family. Since the elderly population had been asked to stay confined to their homes, their children or neighbors stepped up to make sure their needs were met for groceries and medications. Everyone had to wear masks and gloves to venture out to grocery stores to keep the households supplied.

Americans are not used to seeing bare shelves in grocery stores. Fear of necessary supplies running out caused people to start hoarding items like sanitizers, disinfectant wipes, face masks, disposable gloves, chicken, ground beef, canned goods, paper products, and especially toilet paper. No one understands the reasoning behind hoarding toilet paper. After a month of stockpiling food and other essentials by panicked shoppers, the supply networks had been strained and tested as never before. Unfortunately, the US relies on China and India for many of their medications and vitamins. These products were in dire supply. Farmers were producing their crops, but millions of pounds of tomatoes, potatoes, squash, strawberries, and other fresh fruits and vegetables were going to waste. They did not have people to pick the produce, nor transport it. They also did not have enough buyers since the restaurants were either shut down or severely limited in seating customers. People were scared to eat out. Dairy farmers had to dump their milk; schools, restaurants, and manufacturers using milk products were shut down.

The trend of what people bought was interesting. Initially, people wanted to protect themselves. Masks, cleaning products, and hand sanitizers were sold out, and then came the onslaught for toilet paper.[298] Other paper towel products and aerosol disinfectant sales spiked. As more people stayed home, spiral hams, and baking yeast became a favorite as people started baking. Shelves were emptied of flour and sugar. Next, there was a rush to purchase hair clippers and hair dye since barbershops and hair salons were closed. After stocking up on food and consumable products, shoppers turned to buy puzzles, games, and other forms of entertainment, as well as educational products. Appliance dealers saw a massive increase in demand for freezers as people rushed to buy more groceries than usual amid the pandemic.

Americans received a stimulus check that accompanied the CARES Act in March, maximum of $1,200 each, depending on the individual's adjusted gross income. Families with children received extra money. Most Americans used their stimulus checks to cover basic needs such as groceries, mortgage or rent. However, people also spent the money on non-essentials including electronics, clothes, and toys, according to major retailers. Again, a lack of long-term needs superseded instant gratification. We were far from the pandemic being over, but Americans did not want to save whatever money was left to buy necessities, like food for the future if the workers lost their jobs or were laid off temporarily again.

Many selfless and conscientious people were serving our communities to get us through this pandemic. Grocery store workers had to restock the shelves with necessary products. They put themselves at risk while working with the public and were exposed to infected people who were unaware of having the virus. Many infected people were asymptomatic. The health care workers were constantly exposed to the virus, due to the enormous number of patients going into the hospitals with symptoms of COVID-19. These staff members included doctors, nurses, aides, and cleaning staff. The first responders and home health personnel had to go into homes, nursing home facilities, and accident sites. They did not have enough protective gear to keep themselves safe. These frontline people were increasingly losing their lives trying to deal with the massive influx of patients. Young medical students and nurses were able to graduate early to start helping with the increased patient load. The virus did not discriminate. It took some of the most brilliant doctors, healthcare workers, nurses, and first responders to their early deaths. No one was immune from this highly infectious disease.

On April 14, 2020, the American Medical Association called on the Federal Emergency Management Agency to act as a central distribution point for masks, gloves, and other protective equipment for frontline American health workers. They stated that state and local governments were still needlessly competing with the federal government for equipment.[299] The federal government's Strategic National

Stockpile had nearly been emptied, and states were left to find their own personal protective equipment supplies. The surge in demand had left importers, suppliers, and purchasers scrambling. And price gouging had exacerbated the problem. Amazon, the major e-commerce giant, stated that it had a "zero tolerance" for coronavirus-based price gouging and scams. It deleted more than a half a million offers for violations during the COVID-19 pandemic. Amazon also suspended the accounts of nearly four thousand vendors in order "to protect customers from bad actors," who were trying to exploit customers during the coronavirus pandemic.[300]

The toll from the disease of COVID-19 on frontline healthcare workers was significant, with more than 9,000 infected by the virus as of April 10, according to figures released April 14, 2020, by the U.S. Centers for Disease Control and Prevention.[301] The agency added that its findings likely underestimated the number of cases among healthcare workers because "data completeness varied" among states. In states with full reporting, more than 10% of all confirmed cases involved health personnel. By mid-August 2020, more than 900 US healthcare workers had died of COVID-19 and the toll was rising.[302] Some of these deaths were preventable. Poor preparation, government missteps, and an overburdened healthcare system increased that risk. Inadequate access to testing, a nationwide shortage of protective gear, and resistance to social distancing and mask wearing forced more patients into overburdened hospitals and drove up the death toll. Half of the healthcare workers were also suffering mental health problems from the stress and trauma of treating patients with the COVID-

19. About a third of the National Health Service staff was reported to be infected in the United Kingdom.

United Food and Commercial Workers International (UFCW) reported at least 82 grocery store workers had died from COVID-19 and 11,507 had been infected or exposed to the virus in the first 100 days of the outbreak. The nation's largest private sector union, UFCW represents 1.3 million employees in grocery, meatpacking, food processing, retail, healthcare, and other industries in the United States and Canada. By the end of June 2020, the Washington, D.C.-based union reported that among its membership, 238 workers had died from coronavirus in the 100 days since the pandemic started, while almost 29,000 had been infected or exposed.[303]

New York Governor Andrew Cuomo made an impassioned plea on April 18, 2020, to remain united as the nation fought the pandemic. "The emotion in this country is as high as I can recall. People are frustrated; we're anxious; we're scared; we're angry,"[304] Cuomo said during his daily briefing, emphasizing that the crisis was mentally and economically devastating. "Look, if you have partisan divisions splitting this nation now, it's going to make it worse. This is no time and no place for division. We have our hands full as it is. Let us just stay together and let us work it through."[305]

On the same day, protests took place in Texas, Maryland, Indiana, Nevada, and Wisconsin against ongoing stay-at-home restrictions enacted to fight the spread of the coronavirus. Several such demonstrations had already taken place across the country in mid- April, in California, Michigan, Ohio, and New Jersey. Dozens of people drove in circles in their vehicles and honked during a lunchtime protest. One woman waved a sign out her window that said, "I want to save my business! I need to work!" Another man scrawled on his pickup truck, "The face mask you were duped into wearing symbolizes that you are losing your freedom of speech." It was dangerous to other citizens that people seemed to be getting restless and reckless when there were 40,461 deaths among more than 755,533 coronavirus cases in the United States, according to data from Johns Hopkins University COVID-19 tracker on April 20, 2020. Protesters showed up in the capitals of Colorado, Washington, Indiana, Maryland, New Hampshire, and Texas that weekend to decry their states' stay-at-home orders.

Didn't people understand the seriousness of this pandemic? What other motives would the health experts have other than saving lives? Even though many people across the country continued to implement social distancing measures during the coronavirus crisis, some parts of the country were not keeping those efforts in mind. Florida Governor Ron DeSantis gave the green light for some beaches in the state to reopen amidst this pandemic on April 17.[306] Twenty-eight beaches in Florida were initially closed as of March 20. When they opened with some specific rules in place, it was reported that thousands of people were seen on the beach within twenty-six minutes of the beach opening, and people continued to pour in the next day despite overcast weather. A local mayor had asked them to please respect and follow the outlined limitations. People were to stay within the guidelines for their safety and their neighbors' well- being. This event occurred only three days after Florida's deadliest day yet, when it was reported that seventy-two people had died from the coronavirus in twenty-four hours. The number of confirmed cases in the state was still increasing on Saturday, the day after the beach was opened. The Governor thought people were going to be responsible. "They are going to be safe, but they want to get back into a routine."[307] However by mid-August, Florida became the fifth highest state with more than half a million infections and inching closer to ten thousand deaths. Four million people had been tested by that time in Florida.

If people cannot police themselves and be responsible, life will never get back to a routine until vaccinations are available for the population. Harvard researchers warned that if the country wanted the economy to open back up and stay that way, testing had to go up to at least 500,000 people per day. Testing nationwide in April was at 150,000 per day. Regrettably, the results from the tests performed were so delayed that they were almost useless for contact tracing. What would happen if the virus mutated, and immunity was not available?

Going outdoors was not canceled; listening to music was not canceled; quality time with family was not canceled; reading a book was not canceled; sharing with friends on the phone and other social outlets was not canceled; singing out loud was not canceled; laughing was not canceled; and sharing HOPE with others was not canceled. People were asked to EMBRACE what we had.

The first chance people had an opportunity to show some self-discipline, they were irresponsible. The fear factor did not seem to be universal. Even though so much information was available about the severity of the coronavirus and the need to follow guidelines, some people still refused to accept reality. Individuals were in denial which was manifested by refusing to wear masks and attending large gatherings. Short term denial helps a person to adjust to a new stressor. However, when the denial becomes long term, it can be dangerous to self and others. Americans and some people around the world suffered from a loss of control coupled with cabin fever, and the inability to come and go as they pleased. During this time of self-incarceration, people experienced more depression and anxiety. The pandemic added extra stress on young students because of the social isolation, family financial instability, or death of loved ones. This presented distinct challenges to parents and educators in preventing and responding to student suicides, which are the second leading cause of death among 10 to 19-year-olds in the United States. One in four Americans between 18 and 24 years old said they had considered suicide in July because of the pandemic, according to a survey from the Centers of Disease Control and Prevention.[308] Surveys were conducted among adults aged over 18 years across the United States during June 24-30, 2020. Overall, 40.9% of respondents reported at least one adverse mental or behavioral health condition, including symptoms of anxiety or depression (30.9%), symptoms of a trauma or stressor related to the pandemic (26.3%), and having started or increased substance use to cope with stress or emotions related to COVID-19 (13.3%). The percentage of respondents who reported having seriously considered suicide in the 30 days before completing the survey (10.7%) was significantly higher among respondents aged 18-24 years, (25.5%).

People get angry and frustrated with a lack of control. Who do they blame for this pandemic? Why aren't resources available now? People had to prepare meals because restaurants were closed, and there was limited delivery and pickup. People were scared to order food from restaurants. Many of the smaller businesses in their neighborhoods were closed. Was the government moving fast enough? The stimulus money was not reaching the people quickly, which added to the unrest. One cannot even imagine the logistics faced by the government officials who had to find financial solutions to the economic devastation of so many families and businesses during this time. I wonder how many officials wished they had never run for office or won the election. How were so many people going to cope without money, the ability to take care of their families, and the prospect of losing their businesses or their homes? And so many families had lost family members from the coronavirus. They were not able to be with them at the end of their life. It had to be heart-wrenching, not to be able to say a final goodbye to a family member. Mothers and fathers, who were infected, could not hold their newborn children until after the quarantine period.

Despite access to multiple social media outlets, people felt isolated. The Internet not only kept people connected but endless streaming shows also kept them entertained. There was just so much news one could follow without it affecting the psyche. Human beings need to touch, hug, see smiles, and give high-fives. People were robbed of these simple pleasures during this pandemic. Family members had to remain confined together for longer periods than usual. This closeness can give rise to frustrations, where people want to create some distance. Couples who were suffering from "too much" time together could try these strategies.[309]

1. Instead of criticizing, try and show appreciation for what each one is doing. Ask for what you need.

2. High levels of stress can increase coping skills for some, while the anxiety may immobilize others. Make anxiety the common problem. Set aside time to share your feelings openly without judgment, no criticism, no problem-solving (trying to fix it), no critique, just you and your partner sharing and listening to each other.

3. Individuals should ask for some alone time, away from their spouse and children. It is normal for relationships to be stressed during these abnormal times. Regroup and take time to take care of yourself.

4. Try not to argue over insignificant matters. Take a time-out and listen to the other person's point of view. Accept each other's emotional coping styles.

5. No one is a mind reader. Ask politely for everyone to help out. List all the chores that need to be done and assign them.

6. Laugh at yourself and rarely at others. Laughter is a great stress reliever.

7. Build a shared sense of purpose like taking care of an elderly family member or neighbor who needs help during this stressful time.

8. Develop routines of shopping for groceries, mealtimes, exercising, and relaxing together. Consistency helps to avoid anxiety during unsure times. Work together to establish expectations that help you cope with togetherness.

Relationships are a good judge as to how well we are coping. Will there be an increase or a decrease in the number of new babies being born in the next nine months? While navigating through this pandemic, we may learn some new ways to enhance our relationships.[310] Over time, the negative social repercussions from the coronavirus, like an upsurge in divorce rates and domestic and child abuse cases, will need to be analyzed. Consider individual or relationship therapy if additional guidance is needed. Teachers and school counselors, who suspect child abuse are supposed to report it to authorities, but schools were closed. These cases may go unreported. Younger children are worried about whether they will ever see their friends again or if they will return to school. Once schools opened, they turned into hot spots as well. More than 70,000 new Covid-19 cases in children were reported across the US since early August, marking a 21% increase in just two weeks. Children have many questions, and presently, the adults in their lives have no answers. They wonder about the signs of coronavirus, if they will be tested, if there are medicines to make them well, and how long the pandemic will last. Most children are feeling anxious and wonder when life will be normal again. Many older students have already graduated through online ceremonies due to COVID-19.

Every day, people did different things to put smiles on people's faces. They organized a neighborhood zoo. Neighbors placed stuffed animals in different local areas so people could see them while taking their socially distanced walks. On Easter Sunday, a band member in our complex organized his band to play on a neighboring balcony. The rest of us danced on terraces outside our condos. Playing in the group was the only source of income for many members; we gave tips to help them financially. It was one of the most joyful occasions during the pandemic. We recalled watching people on television in Italy, singing, and playing music from their windows and balconies.

Dr. Sanjay Gupta on CNN Health has been posting weekly reports on the coronavirus pandemic. It was refreshing to hear that he was also losing track of the days of the week. It is happening to all of us because we are homebound. He emphasized that we must focus on the things that we can be thankful for, and fill our days with lightness, whenever possible, to get through these gloomy days. He mentioned dancing to release endorphins. He encourages families to hold a dance-a-thon, to dance like no one is watching, because no-one is! My 86-year-old mother has been walking on the treadmill daily and doing other exercises to keep active, since she is homebound. I can get away from the fast-paced coronavirus news by going for a swim, walking, doing cardio exercises and Pilates, lifting some weights, fixing meals, and writing. Due to all the streaming shows and movies, evenings are occupied. Eating healthy is not always possible since we all need comfort foods. It's important to limit them. Keeping up with friends and family with so many social media outlets can be time-consuming. However, sending out and receiving positive energy is very rewarding. Laughing at the jokes and videos about the coronavirus on social media can also be entertaining. We all suffer from the fatigue of not being able to come and go and spending extended periods of time at home; it wears you down. Summers are for people to take vacations and travel, not to be stuck at home.

We must balance our sadness at the loss of life, livelihood, and struggles with the good feelings we can raise from within ourselves. People can show up for one another, even when not physically present. Social isolation can be worse than physical illness. However, clarity comes from being quiet and listening to our feelings. That connection is more vital to our health and happiness than we may care to admit. It can mobilize us to get to a better place with ourselves and others. Boredom can increase alcohol, drug, or food intake. Unless people are attending virtual AA/NA meetings, they are at an increased risk of a relapse in all addictive conditions without the usual support.

When this is over, what will I choose, a Weight Watchers or AA meeting? Out of quarantine, will I be 20 pounds lighter with balanced chakras, living in a decluttered house full of completed projects, or 20 pounds heavier with a drinking problem?

These psychological problems can lead to an increase in pre-morbid medical problems in people already suffering from high blood pressure, diabetes, and other illnesses. Older people faced the most risk, so they were specifically asked to stay home and ask others to get their groceries, medications, etc. This isolation and lack of stimulation may lead to dementia like symptoms due to depression. Other people who are already suffering from an obsessive-compulsive disorder, especially if they are germophobic, suffer even more intensely. The coronavirus has to be an absolute nightmare for them!

People working from home reported being more tired. Nerina Ramlakhan, Ph.D. states that sleep is controlled by our circadian rhythm, which is regulated by how much daylight we get, what time we eat our meals, when we exercise, and perform other routines.[311] This rhythm was disrupted since we were forced to stay indoors for longer periods of time. We had to adapt to new rhythms. We were spending too much time online or messaging on phones, video calling, and using social media to connect with the world, as well as constantly checking for the latest updates on the coronavirus.

I have addressed the emotions of anxiety, frustration, anger, depression, and stress. We do not know when things will return to normal. It is emotionally draining. A book was recommended by Fareed Zakaria, CNN host, 'Life Is in the Transitions: Mastering Change at Any Age' by Bruce Feiler. He addresses how life in not linear and by embracing the non-linear life, we can give meaning to our lives in times of change. He presents a new model for life transitions and how to navigate obstacles, especially after life-quakes. This may be a good source of information for people who are struggling with many major unwanted changes that this pandemic has brought. The COVID-19 has created uncharted territory for many individuals regarding health and finances.

Some simple daily solutions include maintaining a set sleep schedule, eating for energy, but understanding that reaching for comfort food during stressful times is normal. It is essential to stay hydrated with water, but coffee is dehydrating. Alcohol intake needs to be monitored since it can also make you tired and affects the quality of sleep. Try not to stay on the computer for long periods of time, take breaks, and stretch. Moving around helps to raise your energy level and makes you more productive. Exercise, take socially distanced walks, do at-home online workouts that several gyms like Planet Fitness have produced. Get outside and work in the yard. Daylight and nature are integral to your well-being at this stressful time. Connect with friends and family to decrease your loneliness. Do not spend all your free time staring at the screen, binge watching endless streaming programs. Limit listening to news reports and stick to fact- based information. Try an energizing meditation technique. Learn to take deep breaths. Take up a new hobby, experiment with new recipes, bake, learn a new skill, pick up an instrument you have not played in a while. Everyone needs to problem-solve as to what they can do to reduce the stress of being stuck at home. This life crisis shall eventually pass. We just don't know when.

During the pandemic, people were reporting that they were having unusual vivid dreams.[312] Some dream experts believe this may be due to withdrawal from our normal environments and daily stimuli as most people were staying at home. The subconscious mind has to draw from themes from the past. Data collected from at least five research teams across multiple countries were finding that the pandemic dreams were colored by stress, isolation, and negative emotions which made them different from typical dreams. Emotions flood the consciousness, especially during REM sleep. Most of the time, people do not remember dreams. However due to isolation, stress, anxiety, lack of activity, decreased sleep quality, and frequent awakenings, these conditions can lead to increased dream recall. There was a 35% increase in recall among participants in an ongoing study in France.

In South Korea, health officials were investigating why 163 people who recovered from coronavirus had retested positive.[313] According to the Korean CDC, 2.1% of the individuals retested positive. The same situation occurred in China. However, official figures are not available for China due to a news blackout. This report raises the question as to whether someone can get reinfected. In South Korea, this reoccurrence was profoundly concerning. Health authorities thought that they had brought the disease under control. In the last week of August, the US saw a first case of reinfection in a 25-year-old man from Reno who had been cured of the coronavirus infection. The second time it was a different strain of the same COVID-19 virus and was more serious than his first illness. Immunologists had expected that if the immune response generated after an initial infection could not prevent a second case, then it should at least be a less severe illness.[314] They always presumed people would become vulnerable to COVID-19 again, sometime after recovering from an initial case, based on how our immune systems respond to other respiratory viruses, including other coronaviruses. It's possible that these early cases of reinfection are outliers and have features that won't apply to the tens of millions of other people who have already recovered from the infection. Everyone should assume they can get sick for a second time and must continue to take proper precautions.

In March, while the US was still battling the first wave of the infection, South Korea, China and Singapore were among the Asian countries facing a second coronavirus wave, fueled by people importing it from outside.[315] Japan reported being in the middle of a second wave in August and that a third and fourth wave could be expected in the future. By end of August New Zealand marked 100 days without any community transmission, but then there were 137 active cases of COVID-19 a couple of weeks later.

The stats for the US were grim. In August, Director of the US Centers for Disease Control and Prevention, Dr. Robert Redfield told the Journal of the American Medical Association, as many as 60 million Americans could have been infected with coronavirus.[316] The CDC released a report in June, published in JAMA, showing an infection rate in the United States of about 10%. Redfield said he believed testing had missed 90% or more of cases. "Maybe for the 2 million cases we diagnosed, we had an estimated 20 million people infected." Many states were reporting errors made in getting an accurate count of people infected. Some were following U.S. Centers for Disease Control and Prevention instructions, considering people with a positive antigen test to be a "probable" case of COVID-19. Others were asked to report only confirmed cases to the public. The health experts were concerned that without better data, the states were unable to communicate to the public a clear picture of the pandemic's scope.

It is worth noting how many wonderful things people were doing, and how they were helping during this pandemic. Companies and wealthy individuals were stepping up to slow the virus's spread and help find a cure. Just as automakers shifted to make tanks and planes during World War II, today's corporations were retooling their production lines to make everything from hand sanitizers (LVMH) to respirators (Ford, GE). Companies donated money, meals, masks, ventilators, other personal protective equipment (PPE) to hospitals and other front-line personnel and businesses. Billionaires were putting their money behind pharmaceutical companies to develop a vaccine. Everyday people were helping their neighbors and communities. Many were listed in the article published by 'The Hill.'[317]

Elton John hosted a televised coronavirus relief concert featuring several popular stars and raised $8 million for relief efforts. Kanye West, Angelina Jolie, and other actors and musicians from all genres were donating money to help feed families and support health care workers.

Tyler Perry picked up the tab for senior-hour shoppers at 73 grocery stores in Atlanta and New Orleans. Blake Lively and Ryan Reynolds donated $400K to NYC hospitals. Singer Lizzo donated food to multiple hospitals in Washington State and Minnesota. Singer James Taylor and his wife donated $1 Million to help Massachusetts General Hospital. Neil Diamond released a remix of "Sweet Carolina" with changed lyrics to help boost people's spirits. John Legend, Chris Martin, and several other musicians were going virtual, performing concerts from their homes and live streaming. Taylor Swift sent $3,000 each to two fans after seeing their social media posts. Matthew McConaughey played virtual bingo with a Texas senior living facility.

Dan Gilbert, owner of a real estate company and the Cleveland Cavaliers, was offering free rent to small restaurants and retailers. Bedrock, which is downtown Detroit's biggest landlord, was waiving rent, building expenses, and parking fees for restaurants and retail tenants that qualify as small businesses for April, May, and June. A New York City landlord told tenants in 18 of his buildings not to worry about April rent payments. A new Facebook group entitled RVs 4 MDs has launched to provide temporary mobile homes for health care workers to isolate themselves during the outbreak. The Four Seasons Hotel in Manhattan provided free rooms for medical personnel responding to the coronavirus pandemic.

A school principal at a Michigan high school visited a drive through where a student was working to tell her that she was named valedictorian. A sheriff visited over 300 students' homes to personally congratulate them on graduating since these ceremonies were all cancelled. Several health care workers were caught in a photograph smiling and making "heart" hand gestures as they prepared to fly from Atlanta to New York. A man in New Jersey tearfully held up a sign thanking medical professionals for helping to treat his wife. A Minnesota trooper pulled over a doctor for speeding, and instead of a ticket, gave him his supply of protective masks. A FedEx employee shared a photo of a care package left for delivery drivers with a message thanking them for their work. People were converting book-sharing libraries into mini-food banks, replacing shelves of books with pasta, peanut butter, and packets of ramen in Little Free Libraries across the country.

The American Humane Society launched a fund to help cats and dogs displaced by the pandemic. Animal shelters around New York were running out of pets eligible for adoption or foster care. People wanted them as quarantine companions. Animal hospitals and veterinary schools were sending critically needed ventilators to hospitals.

In the third week of April 2020, Publix grocery store chain, based out of Florida, announced that they would buy fresh produce and milk to help farmers who have been financially hurt during this pandemic. They planned on donating these products to Feeding America member food banks operating in the communities they serve.[318] The Food Lion grocery chain was donating $600,000 to people affected by the pandemic, providing about 6 million meals. Grocery stores, wholesale stores like Sam's Club and Costco, pharmacies like Walgreens had special hour openings for seniors, immunocompromised citizens, and first line workers.

Feeding America works through food banks across the country, including feeding children that rely on school meals. Since the food banks were struggling to meet the demands, and many farmers were facing decreased demand and struggling themselves, the Farm Bureau and Feeding America asked the Department of Agriculture to step in. The farmers could deliver food directly to the food banks, ease the supply chain, and recoup some of the cost of planting and harvesting. John Botti of Westchester, New York decided to do something after watching the news about farmers pouring milk down the drain and watching vegetables rotting in fields. He called a few friends, sent semi-trailers to the nation's farms, and took free food directly to the food banks. This amazing group of individuals was creative and resourceful. They made an immediate difference in the fight against hunger.

Companies were either producing masks or donating their stockpiles.[319]

~ General Electric had to lay off 10% of its U.S. workers at its aviation unit as the coronavirus hurt the aircraft demand, but instead raised production of ventilators and other crucial medical equipment.

~ Detroit automakers created a new 'arsenal of health' to cope with growing coronavirus pandemic.

~ Automakers, Ford and General Motors were assisting where they could to produce life-saving respirators, ventilators, and masks to assist those infected by the disease as well as health-care workers on the frontlines. Their efforts come nearly 80 years after the Detroit automakers responded to President Franklin Roosevelt's call to arms during World War II.

~ At Braskem petrochemical plant in Marcus Hook, PA, 43 co-workers became roommates. For 28 days, they did not leave the plant, sleeping and working all in one place. Each one worked 12-hour shifts, night and day to produce millions of pounds of raw material, (polypropylene) that will end up in face masks and surgical gowns, worn by frontline personnel during the pandemic. They wanted to ensure that no one caught the virus, so they "lived in" at the factory.[320]

~ Many restaurants stayed open to provide pickup or delivery service so that people could still get meals at reduced rates. This service was a lifesaver for many individuals who were inundated with other responsibilities during the pandemic. It was very sad that people had to stay indoors, especially the elderly, and people were scared to go outside to purchase food. This epidemic created major hardships for the restaurant industry. Even after the ban for in-person dining was lifted, a report from the U.S. Centers for Disease Control and Prevention showed that people diagnosed with COVID-19 were nearly "twice as likely" to have eaten out at restaurants within the two weeks before they showed symptoms. 40% of individuals who contracted the virus had eaten out at a restaurant. The report suggested that because of the difficulty in social distancing and people unable to use masks, dining inside of a restaurant presented a greater risk of contracting the virus.

~ Spotify was donating up to $10 Million for the music community. They will match donations on a fundraising page on its website.

~ Starbucks was giving free coffee to any front-line responders, donated 700,000 meals to food banks, and announced a $500,000 donation to support first responders and health care workers. They also donated more than $3 Million to global relief efforts.

~ Tyson Foods announced it would be paying roughly $60 Million in bonuses to frontline workers and truckers.

~ Google donated $800 Million to small and medium sized businesses, health organizations, and health care workers as well as governments around the world. The company was working with Apple on a contact tracing app to track and potentially prevent the spread of the virus.

Individual people stepped up to help where they could.

~ Apple CEO, Tim Cook donated 10 million medical masks to health care workers around the country.

~ Oprah Winfrey donated $10 Million for coronavirus relief efforts.

~ Drew Brees, quarterback for New Orleans Saints donated $5 Million to help feed the hungry in Louisiana.

~ The biggest individual contributors so far had been Bill and Malinda Gates who donated $250 Million towards the relief fund. Bill Gates earned $12 Billion in 2019 and is worth $104 Billion.[321] He has given away 27% of his wealth to charity as of 2019. He alone could have taken care of feeding the hungry in this country together with Amazon CEO Jeff Bezos who was estimated to be worth $118 Billion. Bezos, the world's richest man, has previously been criticized for not contributing more of his wealth to philanthropy, but has donated billions of dollars in recent years to causes including climate change and food banks.[322] MacKenzie Scott, formerly MacKenzie Bezos, has already donated nearly $1.7 billion of her fortune to a variety of organizations and causes after pledging last year to give most of it away during her lifetime. Her net worth is currently estimated to be around $60 billion, according to the Bloomberg Billionaire's Index. What about all the athletes and entertainers that make millions a year due to patronage from everyday families going to see them and supporting these activities?

~ Athletes raised $25 Million for the coronavirus relief fund.

According to "Global Wealth in 2019" there are 18.6 million millionaires in the United States. However, only 3.5 million are considered wealthy. 95% of millionaires in America have a net worth of between $1 and $10 Million. As of 2015, there are 536 billionaires. Hopefully many of them saw fit to be generous during this time of need for their fellow citizens. How many of the big company CEOs were willing to give up their salaries? The Texas Roadhouse CEO gave up his bonus and base salary this year to pay his chain's workers.

While the government has been struggling to administer tests and get enough supplies for healthcare workers, small and big organizations, and companies were helping. It would only be fitting to also list them.[323] The organization "Doctors without Borders" was sending aid to the countries that had been hit the hardest. The World Health Organization was coordinating efforts around the world. Oxfam America was organizing efforts to increase the delivery of clean water and sanitary supplies to refugees. The Red Cross was seeking blood donations. World Central Kitchen was delivering chef-prepared meals to those in need. Team Rubicon, a veteran-based company provides services during disasters and emergencies. Half-Table Man Disaster Relief had been working to feed those in need.

In contrast, it was tragic how Americans of Asian descent were treated by some of their fellow Americans as coronavirus spread across the United States. There were reports of being spit on, yelled at, and even threatened in the streets. Asian-Americans reported verbal and physical attacks from school yards to trips to the grocery stores. The origin of the coronavirus in China caused this backlash. Calling it a Chinese infection did not help matters. Hundreds of attacks on Asian people were reported.[324] Asian businesses were also targeted. Rather than feel helpless, many Asian-Americans recorded their interactions on their phones, or Go-Pro, and decided to carry guns.[325] Many Asian Americans said they wanted to safely confront racist bullying and harassment, and grassroots groups were sharing virtually, ways to defuse the confrontations and abuse. Asian Americans were wrestling with a second epidemic, hate. How were Asian-Americans responsible for the virus? Why were some people turning on different races during times of significant stress from the pandemic?

Numerous assault cases were reported on people who tried to enforce or encourage people to wear masks. A security guard was killed in Michigan at a Family Dollar store. A 54-year- old woman's leg was broken after she was thrown to the ground by another customer at a Staples store in New Jersey. A nasty fight erupted on an American Airlines flight after a passenger reportedly refused to wear a face mask on a flight from Las Vegas to Charlotte, N.C. Several tussles with security guards at businesses were reported. These are just a few examples of irrational behaviors of our citizens. The insanity of a few kept pulling many back into this nightmare where people were treading lightly or staying put. We just needed to get to safety without any more loss of life. We should all have been working together to help everyone get through these tough times.

A troubling fact was that gun and ammunition sales spiked during the pandemic.[326] Many gun buyers said that they wanted to be ready with protection, if there was panic. California had an early rise in the number of COVID-19 cases, and there were long lines at gun and ammunition stores in March. The sentiments were that if people started panicking, rioting, and looting in the few weeks to months after the pandemic started, the government and the police may not have the ability to protect them. There was a 227% increase in 2020 of background checks received by the Colorado Bureau of Investigation, from the same timeframe in 2019.[327] In times of crisis, whether it is financial, political, health related, or spurred by gun violence itself,

Americans buy guns. In August alone, 1.6 million guns were sold.

As of July 31, there have been 339 shootings resulting in 297 deaths and 1,437 injuries, for a total of 1,734 victims, according to Wikipedia.[328] These are mass shootings that have occurred in the United States in 2020. These incidents are referred to as mass shootings since they involve multiple victims of firearm related violence. The only shooting that made it to the news headlines was the one in Nova Scotia.[329] A 51-year-old assaulted his girlfriend, and then went on the deadliest 12 hour shooting rampage in Canadian history. Twenty-two people died that day, including the gunman after a confrontation with the police. Speculation was that the assault on his long-term girlfriend was the catalyst to the burning of properties and killing innocent people. Frustrations run high during times of stress and domestic violence can get out of control as in this scenario.

Two major issues, school and other mass shootings, and the #MeToo Movement and sexual harassment cases dominated the headlines for the past two years. The only case of sexual assault that has surfaced recently involved Tara Reade, a staff assistant who had worked in Mr. Biden's Senate office.[330] She accused Joseph R. Biden Jr. of inappropriately touching her. She made an allegation of sexual assault against the former vice president, the Democratic Party's presidential nominee for 2020 election. The assault allegedly took place in 1993. Mr. Biden has said that the allegation was false, and she should show some reports to back up her allegation.

In this time of turmoil, there were two very opposing headlines on March 11, 2020. The one that gripped fear in everyone's heart was that the pandemic was very real on our doorsteps in America. The other headline that people may have missed but was on many people's minds in the not-so-distant past, was that Harvey Weinstein was found guilty of two of five felonies on February 24, 2020. He was sentenced to 23 years in prison on March 11, 2020 and was initially held at Rikers Island prison before being transferred to Wende Correctional Facility.

Time will tell which topics retain interest with the public: life and death, surviving the pandemic, or who was accused of sexual harassment. In the meantime, all we can do is wait for the world to be cleansed, not just from the pandemic, but from our misunderstandings of one another. Where is our compassion, our love and respect for each other? Perhaps in the "quiet" around the world, we will all reawaken with a renewed vision of kindness and thoughtfulness to all.

Repercussions from the Coronavirus - COVID-19 Pandemic of 2020

In the United States, a somber milestone has been reached. More Americans have died from COVID-19 than from any other disease in the last 100 years, according to a tally from Johns Hopkins University, surpassing the number killed in the Vietnam War of 58,220, according to the Nation's Archives. America is always proclaiming to be "the best in the world." Now we have to add that we had the greatest number of deaths and infected people in the United States from COVID-19 pandemic. What is even more alarming is that the true numbers of the coronavirus infections are not available. Many people have not been tested. All the deaths that have occurred during the timeframe of the pandemic cannot be accurately diagnosed if these individuals were not tested before death.

It has been a challenging time but devastating for so many people around the globe. I am trying to wrap my brain around this invisible virus, how it has infected millions of people worldwide and killed thousands of individuals in this day and age of advanced technology and resources. An analogy was made between the pandemic and a tornado, which tears apart some homes while leaving others standing without any damage. The virus swept through different parts of the country and the world. It devastated many families whose members perished, or others who lost their livelihoods, while others were lucky enough to remain unscathed.

A wise friend told me that life is so painful at times; we wonder how we find the strength to carry on through great turmoil and sadness. Yet, we push on, one foot in front of the other, one thought to calm us and the other to carry on, one prayer to give us strength for the day, and another for the next day. And so, there is a new day, a new beginning, perhaps a new challenge.

> *The art of living is to make the most of each moment and give your very best.*[331]
> *Author Unknown*

In the words of Dr. Sanjay Gupta, "This pandemic is going to challenge us all in new ways, but it will also teach us a lot about ourselves."[332] Going forward we will have many questions as we venture into unknown territory. What will change within our culture? What will our society look like? What societal woes will have been resolved due to the new norm? What new problems will arise from the chaos and aftermath? Will we forget what we have been through and create the same problems or make them worse?

First and foremost, nobody should feel invincible, and nobody should let their guard down. Dr. Fauci, the nation's top infectious disease doctor, continues to reiterate that a second round of coronavirus is inevitable. If the second wave of the coronavirus coincides with the seasonal flu in the fall, there could be many more lives lost. Once the pandemic arrived on US soil, people were asked to do things outside. The outdoors provided an opportunity where people could eat, drink, relax, exercise, and socialize at a distance. The risk of spreading the virus was greater in enclosed spaces. Now with winter approaching, these outdoor activities will be limited and chances for more indoor gatherings will increase the risk for more people to get infected without a vaccine.

How bad the death toll will depend on what treatments we have available. Currently, there are several drugs, like remdesivir that are being tried on patients with some promising results. It has been able to shorten the hospital stay by four days and shows that there can be drugs that affect this virus. Dexamethasone is the other medication that has helped some patients receiving invasive mechanical ventilation or oxygen but not those who did not require respiratory support. A report out of the U.K. suggests that autopsies indicated the use of anti-platelet medications, in addition to blood thinners, may be helpful to stem the effects of COVID-19 due to the presence of blood clots seen in multiple organs like the brain, heart, liver, and lungs.

Will we be any closer to getting a vaccine? Health experts believe a vaccine coupled with recommended public health measures will be the path back to societal normalcy. The worldwide effort to create a vaccine for the novel coronavirus started in January, soon after scientists in China posted online the genome of a virus causing a mysterious pneumonia. Many countries are trying to get a viable vaccine in place as soon as possible. There have been reports of 200 experimental vaccines aimed at ending the pandemic. However, only a handful are getting the attention of the world and are recognized as a scientific quest moving forward at record-breaking speed. There are 35 vaccines in human trials around the world, nine months into the pandemic.

According to health experts, it is possible that a vaccine may be available by the end of 2020. On the other hand, most experts agree that it will take 12 to 18 months since the start of the pandemic, before a safe and effective shot is developed, tested, manufactured, and made widely available. President Trump has been advocating that a vaccine will be available by the end of 2020. He has allocated a large amount of money behind this venture. Food and Drug Administration Commissioner Stephen Hahn told the Financial Times he would be willing to fast-track the coronavirus vaccine process with an emergency use authorization before phase 3 trials are over but insisted, he would not do so for political reasons. The novel coronavirus is RNA-based, like H.I.V., which makes it all the more difficult to design and test an entirely new vaccine. We must be so thankful to the thousands of people around the globe volunteering to be tested with a vaccine. Making mistakes or taking short cuts in developing a vaccine could give false hope, and maybe, have disastrous consequences. In 1955, 200,000 children were given the first polio vaccine; 40,000 of them contracted polio and around 10 children died. It would take only one bad side effect to detract the vaccine program that the world desperately needs.

The nation was caught off guard. There was a lag time to get tested. In fact, even now, the different states are left to their own resources to test people in their states rather than a universal effort by the central government. Ill-informed politicians and business leaders did not take the warnings seriously that were issued by health experts. President Trump tried to reassure Americans that this virus was similar to our flu epidemics and would infect a few people, and just disappear. Experts feared that this virus was a new strain of influenza, like the pandemic of 1918. We now have the technology to create, and mass produce a new flu vaccine in only a few months' time. Now we know that this is a highly infectious disease, the likes of which have never been seen before.

A severe lack of personal protective gear, masks, gloves, equipment to keep patients alive, like ventilators, compounded the problem. The US was already behind as the Trump Administration had exacerbated the problem by disbanding the National Security Council's pandemic team. However, problems due to millions of masks stored in the federal government's Strategic National Stockpile had been used up during the 2009 flu pandemic. Congress had failed to reappropriate the necessary funds to replenish them. A shortage existed not only in the United States, but all over the world, except in China. Despite being portrayed as a selfless provider of medical aid to other affected countries, Beijing was reaping hundreds of millions in profits by selling equipment to panic-stricken governments abroad. Much of it was useless, and Spain, the Czech Republic, and Malaysia returned the equipment.[333]

Many countries around the world did not take appropriate action in response to the coronavirus. The countries exhibited denial, mixed public messaging, and eventually, lockdowns. Government officials relied on models of the potential spread. Slight delays in taking action had huge consequences. The first lesson that all officials need to learn when dealing with a future crisis, is preparedness with personal protection equipment. Second, health officials must increase the speed of an early diagnosis of disease, then quarantine individuals, and provide treatment.

Third, there needs to be a central command coordinating efforts rather than every state acting independently. Lastly, there should be rigorous contact tracing. New Zealand's Ministry of Health devised a voluntary app on cellphones to track the movements of people with the virus. All individuals need to participate and be responsible in this war against the coronavirus.

After the initial shutdown in the US, many people in the country were begging for the businesses to open. There was a major economic fallout from the shutdown. However, Dr. Anthony Fauci said a shutdown would not be necessary if we did just five things: wear a mask, maintain physical distance, avoid, or close bars, stay away from large gatherings, and finally wash hands.

Getting a coronavirus test in many countries was nearly impossible unless you were already very ill. In Iceland, anyone who wanted a test received one. Iceland's response to the coronavirus was not particularly innovative. It was meticulous and fast. Their plan was to be aggressive in detecting and diagnosing individuals, putting them into isolation, and being very thorough in their contact tracing. They used the police force and the healthcare system to analyze, and institute contact tracing of every newly, diagnosed case of the coronavirus. Many lessons need to be adopted from countries that did well during the pandemic.

Countries like South Korea implemented quarantine for people driving from Wuhan more than two weeks before their first infection. They kept their mortality rates way down compared to other countries. South Korea had tested 338,000 in April. They reported 10,800 cases with 250 deaths from the coronavirus. On April 30, 2020, they announced that they had no more new cases of infection. In June 2020, South Korea reported that the country was experiencing a second wave of the coronavirus. They warned that stronger physical distancing measures would be reimposed if the daily increase in infections did not decrease.

Vietnam does not have the resources to conduct mass testing. They had tested only 15,637 people and Vietnam had 194 confirmed coronavirus cases and no fatalities as of March 2020.[334] Swift action by the authorities helped contain the infection. On February 1st, Vietnam suspended all flights to and from China. It also decided to keep schools closed after the lunar New Year break. Two weeks later, a 21-day quarantine was imposed in Vinh Phuc province, north of Hanoi. That decision was sparked by concerns over the health status of migrant workers returning from Wuhan, China where the virus originated. Vietnam is now experiencing a spike in cases in August,2020. According to the Worldometer, 929 cases have now been reported with 21 deaths. Vietnam has very low numbers compared to the US and Europe.

Taiwan was hit hard during the SARS (severe acute respiratory syndrome) outbreak of 2003. More than 150,000 people were quarantined, and 181 people died. This experience helped many parts of the country react faster to the current coronavirus outbreak. On January 25th, as the world was still waking up to the potential danger of the novel coronavirus spreading rapidly out of central China, Taiwan took the danger more seriously, both at the governmental and societal levels. They implemented border control and wearing face masks as early as January 2020.[335]

Taiwan was one of the most at-risk areas outside of mainland China, owing to its close proximity, ties, and transport links. They banned travel from many parts of China, stopped cruise ships from docking at their ports, and introduced strict punishments for anyone breaching home quarantine orders. They ramped up the production of face masks, performed nationwide testing for the virus, retested people with previously unexplained pneumonia, and announced new punishments for spreading disinformation about the virus. Taiwan's government had established a public health response team for instituting rapid procedures for the next crisis after the SARS epidemic. Medical officials held daily briefings. Taiwan merged the national health insurance data with customs and immigration databases to create real-time alerts to help identify vulnerable populations. An excellent health data system helps with monitoring the spread of the disease and allows for its early detection. They had initially banned the export of face masks to ensure the domestic supply, but then donated 10 million masks to the United States, Italy, Spain, and other countries. At the end of June 2020, Taiwan reported 446 confirmed cases and just seven deaths for nearly 24 million citizens. In the same time frame, the United States had more than 2.5 million cases and 125,000 deaths.

The Ministry of Health in New Zealand reported 1,251 confirmed cases of people infected with 22 deaths from the

Covid-19 by mid-August 2020. Jacinda Ardern, the prime minister imposed a national lockdown much earlier in its outbreak than other countries and banned travelers from China in early February before New Zealand had registered a single case of the virus. It closed its borders to all non-residents in mid-March when it had only a handful of cases.

Only 10% of countries in the world are led by women, presiding over 4% of the world's population.[336] It would be difficult to report any robust data regarding gender differences in leadership performance. However, most of the countries that have female heads of state are doing well containing the spread of the virus. Another interesting fact is the young age of some of these female prime ministers. Normally with age comes wisdom, but during this historic pandemic that has affected the whole world after 102-years, the young women are showing the rest of the world how to be successful in taking care of their country's population. In Germany, Angela Merkel, the oldest female prime minister at 65-years-old, has tested more people per capita than any other country in the world. Denmark's Mette Frederiksen at 42-years-old, Finland's Sanna Marin at 34- years-old, Norway's Erna Solberg at 59-years-old, and Iceland's Katrin Jakobsdottir at 44-years-old, in addition to several other Nordic countries are all led by women. Their countries have lower death rates from the coronavirus compared to the rest of Europe. In contrast, Sweden, the only Nordic country not led by a woman, Prime Minister Stefan Löfven refused to impose a lockdown and has kept schools and businesses open. The death rate has soared in Sweden at a much higher rate than in most other European countries.

In Barbados, Prime Minister Mia Mottley, 54-years-old stood out for her ability to handle the crisis. Prime Minister Silveria Jacobs of Saint Maarten, 51-years-old, governs a tiny Caribbean Island of just 41,000 people, but her no-nonsense video telling citizens to "simply stop moving" for two weeks had gone viral around the world. "If you do not have the type of bread you like in your house, eat crackers. If you do not have bread, eat cereal. Eat oats!" She said emphatically.[337]

Cultures with women in charge may be more likely to act with empathy, cooperation, and in an unselfish, risk-adverse way. All these qualities may reduce the harm done by a contagious virus. A more masculine approach to facing illness (a stoic, macho attitude conveying a sense of invincibility) is not helpful during a pandemic. Women are better equipped for handling a health crisis. Health-related behaviors favor women. They take better care of their health problems, get regular physical examinations, and outlive men. Acting reckless, risk-taking, and overconfidence are generally male qualities. The general population may be more willing to listen to the health directions from their female leaders.

Due to the delayed action on the part of Americans to take the coronavirus pandemic seriously, the available options going forward were limited. The physical distancing strategy worked, but at a very high economic cost. This behavior could not be sustained indefinitely. The number of infected cases went up significantly once the restrictions were lifted, and more people were tested. There was much uncertainty, but life, as most people knew it, could not return to pre-pandemic lifestyle. The question is how do we continue living from day-to-day with the coronavirus?

We must address the lack of tests and medical supplies. Testing companies rely on the same chemical agents. These supplies were already running low. They could not just be purchased but had to be manufactured. Testing is crucial. In reality, it might take several months before companies could meet the global demand. We need to get more creative at finding ways to control the spread of the virus with less economical, devastating measures. Government officials must ensure that when companies finally develop a vaccine or drugs for treatment, they do not become a "rainmaker" for the shareholders of the company. They should be affordable and available globally to all. There should be no price gouging. The lawyers should also be kept at bay from suing companies that are offering the drugs and vaccines that are released earlier than normal, due to the urgency of preventing the coronavirus and treating the symptoms. There may be unforeseen side effects.

Politicians must work to stop the public from believing that this virus is a hoax. The COVID-19 pandemic fueled more than 2,000 rumors and conspiracy theories. Users with fake accounts posted official-looking articles with highly inaccurate information. Most Americans (71%) had heard of a conspiracy theory circulating widely online that powerful people intentionally planned the coronavirus outbreak. One version of this theory went something like this: The COVID-19 pandemic is part of a strategy conceived by global elites, such as Bill Gates to roll out vaccinations with tracking chips that would later be activated by 5G, the technology used by cellular networks.[338]

And a quarter of U.S. adults saw at least some truth in it, including 5% who said it was definitely true and 20% who said it was probably true, according to a June Pew Research Center survey.[339] It was illogical and disgraceful for people to start and spread rumors that were linked to thousands of hospitalizations and hundreds of deaths. A myth that consumption of highly concentrated alcohol could kill the coronavirus was linked with more than 5,900 hospitalizations, 800 deaths, and 60 cases of blindness due to methanol poisoning. Some of the misinformation included the idea that drinking bleach could kill the coronavirus or a theory that the virus was created in a lab as a bioweapon.[340]

At the beginning of September, a follower of the conspiracy theory group QAnon tweeted that only 6% of the 183,000 deaths attributed to Covid-19 were "actually" from the virus.[341] According to the Centers for Disease Control and Prevention, 6% of reported COVID-19 deaths listed the virus as the sole cause of death, and the other 94% had additional health issues at their time of death (called comorbidities). Listing these other health problems on the death certificate does not take away from the fact that people died from the COVID-19. Members of QAnon misinterpreted this statistic to mean that only 6% of those deaths were "actually" from the virus.

This created a lot of misinformation and confusion especially after President Trump retweeted it. Twitter later removed the tweet and told the Washington Post it violated the site's policies about coronavirus misinformation, but the claims still made their way around the Internet. This misunderstanding of the statistics gave credence to previous coronavirus conspiracy theories, like the incorrect claim that hospitals purposely inflated their reports of coronavirus patients or that public health departments were inflating COVID-19 deaths. Just looking at the number of deaths during the same period in 2019 and comparing them to 2020, would help people understand why this pandemic was so lethal. The number of deaths in the United States through July 2020 was 8% to 12% higher than it would have been if the coronavirus pandemic had never happened. That figure translates to at least 164,937 deaths above the number expected for the first seven months of the year, 16,183 more than the 188,000 attributed to COVID-19 thus far for that period, and it could be as high as 204,691.[342]

Misinformation fueled by rumors, stigma, and conspiracy theories can have potentially serious consequences on the individual and community if believed over evidence-based guidelines. Health agencies must track misinformation in real time and engage local communities and government officials to debunk misinformation.

President Trump has not helped and in fact, hindered the public in understanding the seriousness of this pandemic. The American citizens were misled by the Commander-in chief, instead of allowing the experts to give accurate and knowledgeable information. President Trump admitted he knew weeks before the first confirmed US coronavirus death that the virus was dangerous, airborne, highly contagious and "more deadly than even your strenuous flus," and that he repeatedly played it down publicly because he did not want to create a panic, according to legendary journalist Bob Woodward in his new book *Rage*.[343] When the daily briefings stopped, it felt like the virus had eased up. People were under the false assumption that we were somehow past the worst of it all. And we stopped hearing important updates and information about many pertinent issues. Then the President took over giving daily reports, instead of allowing medical professionals to do so. To make matters worse, in September, President Trump appointed communications officials at the US Department of Health and Human Services, who demanded to see reports out of the CDC before they were released.[344] They wanted to change the language of weekly science reports released by the US Centers for Disease Control and Prevention so as not to undermine President Trump's political message. How is anyone to believe what is really happening even though CDC officials fought back against the most sweeping changes.

Even six months after the first case of death from the COVID-19, the US has failed miserably to contain the rate of infection. Researchers from the University of Washington's Institute for Health Metrics and Evaluation (IHME) have issued a forecast of 300,000 deaths from coronavirus by December 1, 2020. However, if 95 percent of people were to wear a face mask in public, some 66,000 lives could be saved, they added. "We're seeing a rollercoaster in the United States," institute director Christopher Murray said in a statement.[345] "It appears that people are wearing masks and socially distancing more frequently as infections increase, then after a while as infections drop, people let their guard down and stop taking these measures to protect themselves and others which, of course, leads to more infections. And the potentially deadly cycle starts over again."

It is extremely difficult to understand how the world's richest country, with all the brilliant minds and technology, failed to meet this tragic and catastrophic calamity head on. America's tragic response to the COVID-19 pandemic made the US look more like a failed state. Instead of checking facts and reaching correct conclusions, the national response was fragmented with the politicians inflaming the situation with all their rhetoric and disagreements. It appeared like we had lost our capacity for an effective crisis response. All the doom and gloom news, political posturing and behavior of our citizens made it appear like we had failed. This was a time for the country to come together, not fight culture wars and highlight for the world, how unhinged the country is.

At the beginning of the pandemic in February 2020, President Trump tried to reassure the citizens that once the warmer weather arrived, it would weaken the virus.[346] That did not happen. In March he stated that all US citizens arriving from Europe would be subject to medical screening. Americans returning to the country were neither tested, nor was anyone forced to quarantine. Next, he wanted us to believe that the virus was just going to disappear. Here it is, still raging six months later. He was genuinely concerned that if the economic shutdown continued, deaths by suicide "definitely would be in far greater numbers than the numbers that we're talking about" for COVID-19 deaths. Yes, the heartache about people losing jobs, homes, and businesses was terrible but the oversight for distribution of the stimulus money was also fraught with mismanagement. However, so far, there have not been 180,000 suicides! Despite the coronavirus infection numbers going up daily, he kept advocating that the pandemic is "fading away." In July, President Trump claimed the pandemic was under control when the country's daily cases doubled to about 50,000. It is unclear where his assumption originated that 99% of COVID-19 cases are "totally harmless." The report from the WHO was that about 15% of COVID-19 cases can be severe, with 5% being critical. CDC reported that 40% of cases were asymptomatic. The President claimed that anybody that needs a test, gets a test. That is not true even six months out. His biggest conclusion about cases going up in the US is because we are testing far more than any other country, which is totally false. In some states, such as Arizona and Florida, the number of new cases being reported was outpacing any increase in the states' testing ability. All signs were pointing to a worsening crisis. His wishful thinking started in May that a vaccine will be available relatively soon, despite the experts informing the public that it could take 18 months to get a viable vaccine. A lot of money was given to the pharmaceutical companies to get a vaccine before the winter flu season or the election in November. President Trump stated this kind of pandemic "was something nobody thought could happen." Experts both inside and outside the federal government had alerted the public many times in the past decade about the potential for a devastating global pandemic. The President continued to push the efficacy of the anti-malaria drug hydroxychloroquine to treat COVID-19 and even took it himself, despite the experts denouncing this use. He also questioned the use of injecting disinfectants to treat COVID-19. This suggestion was alarming. People who listened to the

President, thought about ingesting disinfectants, which would cause devastating health consequences.

We must focus on finding and helping people who are infected. More accurate tests, such as the saliva-based kits being developed at Rutgers University, which can be used at home, must be standardized, manufactured, and widely distributed in the communities, schools, colleges, and workplaces. Abbott Labs have approval for a test that costs $5, and results are available in 15 minutes. It does not require specialized equipment and can be produced in bulk. Even tourism companies, airlines, and cruise ships could become operational again with these tests. They are cheaper and turnaround time for the results can be hours, rather than days. The results have to be obtained in a timely manner so that contact tracing can be implemented. One of the major problems in containing the spread of the virus in the US has been due to the delay in getting back results from the millions of tests diagnosed in the labs. They could not keep up with the number of tests they were receiving. A huge amount of money was wasted in doing the tests, as the only benefit from performing all the tests was to try and get a rough idea of how many people were infected. Getting the result in several days was useless since it allowed the infected person to move about in the community and infect a lot more people, especially if they were non-symptomatic. Labs doing the testing received payment whether they delivered the results in one day or two weeks. There also was confusion in how the labs were reporting results. All these issues need to be worked out. There should not be any excuse in an advanced country like the US to have this lack of accountability.

Recovered coronavirus individuals with antibodies may have a false sense of security and spread the virus during future surges. We need to continue doing the things we know to help decrease the spread of the virus, like wearing masks, social distancing, and washing our hands. Practicing habits like eating healthy, reducing stress, exercising, and getting adequate sleep will increase our chances of remaining well. If you must go out, it is a safety procedure to wear a mask. This behavior has to become a habit. Medical masks are still in short supply, and they must be reserved for healthcare workers. There are numerous sites on the Internet teaching how to make homemade masks. Ready-made masks are also available in stores and online. They help to slow the spread of the virus. Masks are worn widely in the Asian countries. They signify civic- mindedness and conscientiousness. In America, masks are usually associated with crime. This concept must change, and we have to understand that it is a means of protecting ourselves and others from a potential infection. As western countries increase their use, it will show that society is collectively acting against a serious threat.

Childcare will finally be recognized as essential work. Until the pandemic, children were taken care of at day care centers, by nannies, or teachers at school. During the summer, there were various summer camps. Suddenly, parents had to become full-time caretakers of their children, in addition to working at home. At times, it was amusing to see newscasters and weather reporters on television trying to report from their homes and seeing their children drifting in and out of the screen. Some children even interfered with the broadcast. Employers may be more sympathetic to employees and more flexible when parenting duties are necessary. Some cities have set up childcare centers, with officials now understanding that people like bus drivers, nurses, and other essential workers cannot go to work when their children are at home. Even the Federal Government has set aside $3.5 Billion for childcare during the coronavirus pandemic.[347]

Parents, school children, and college students were all looking forward to returning to normalcy once schools restarted. Here again, on August 5, President Trump tried to reassure the citizens and urged schools to reopen, falsely claiming that children are "almost immune from this disease." Both Twitter and Facebook removed the post shared by President Trump for breaking their rules against spreading coronavirus misinformation.[348] Research has shown that while children tend to get infected with the coronavirus less often and have milder symptoms than adults, kids can still contract and spread it. Some have become seriously ill and even died. By the beginning of September, according to the American Academy of Pediatrics, more than 550,000 children in the US had tested positive for the coronavirus since the pandemic started. The children represented 9.8% of all COVID-19 cases in the US.

Schools had from March until August to plan their reopening. However, as with most measures to deal with this pandemic effectively, no clear guidelines or rules were put in place. Now teachers are facing the same problems of getting infected as first-line workers, and the children are exposed to the virus. Despite recommendations from CDC health officials, some school districts in Georgia called mask-wearing a "personal choice" and said that social distancing "will not be possible to enforce in most cases,"[349] especially at high schools with more than 2,000 students. Masks are not a 'personal choice' during a pandemic. A narrow sign-up window for virtual classes meant many parents missed their opportunity to enroll their children online. However virtual learning was not an option for many low-income students without access to devices, or for students in rural areas with poor Internet access. One student pointed out, "I've only known three people to get it, other than the football players. If I get it, I get it. I believe that's what most people in my area's ideology is, if we get it, we get it."[350] It was a very difficult decision for all involved. Parents had to go to work. Parents had to process the information available and make the best decision for their own families. The decisions parents made were different for each household and each community. And some families arrived at different conclusions after looking at the same data. Children were desperate to get back together with their friends as they had been cooped up for months. They missed their friends and craved the social interaction that kids need. The teachers were fearful of catching the virus. Students who "chose not to go to school" could face suspension or expulsion. Teachers said they too felt they had no choice but to show up to work. Anthony Fauci, the country's top infectious disease official had asked school superintendents to not allow indoor dining, and mandate masks. If there was limited passing space in the halls, all teachers should have been wearing masks, and students' lunches should be delivered to their classrooms, so they don't eat together in the cafeteria. It's unclear whether these recommendations were followed.

Denmark had opened schools on April 15, 2020. Their schools had all gone online after there was an increase in surge of cases among the staff and children. Once they opened, they kept the students in smaller groups in class and at break times. The groups were not allowed to mingle. They kept the same group together so that if one person was infected, they would have to quarantine just a few people in the group. There was cooperation between the teachers, parents, and government policy makers. The Health Minister stressed "you cannot create union during stressful times, like this pandemic. Union has to be in place and present so that everyone is cooperative."[351] The US has no chance of success against the coronavirus with all the fractions among our citizens and policy makers.

Crucial medical drugs were running out. According to a University of Minnesota analysis, about 40% of around 156 critical care drugs were in short supply. Many of them depended on the supply chains from China, Italy, or India, who had halted several exports.[352] Global demand was very high, and supply was lagging. Doctors, nurses, and home health workers were overwhelmed and falling sick themselves. Now they had to catch up on elective surgeries, treating other medical conditions, and cancer treatments that were postponed because of the pandemic. All these services are necessary for the financial viability of hospitals. Tracking infected patients will require a lot of people. Due to chronic underfunding, local US health departments lost more than 55,000 workers from 2008 to 2017. Now, new personnel will have to be trained. It will be an opportunity for recently unemployed people.

If restrictions were lifted slowly, there may not be a need for a lockdown again. However, people were careless in choosing leisure activities over their own safety, like going to the gym or movie theaters, which increased infection rates. Like the underground bars during the Prohibition era, illegal gyms were opening everywhere, from LA to New Jersey. The German government has established a system that allows communities to reopen, close again if necessary and then reopen again. The reopening is done in a measured, cautious, data driven way, and to close down if the spread of the virus accelerates. Most Germans are accepting this system and the restrictions will remain in place until a vaccine or another treatment is available. The US needs to develop a similar standard of functioning during these difficult times.

Most experts and political leaders are cautioning about lifting all restrictions until a vaccine is available. This vaccine has presented a challenge for people who have been so opposed to mandatory vaccines. This deadly virus has made some anti-vaxxers change their minds.[353] After all, if it kills the young and old indiscriminately, who wants to take a chance if there is something that will prevent a severe illness and death? According to CNN Health report in May 2020, childhood vaccinations have plunged since the coronavirus pandemic started according to the Center of Disease Control and Prevention. There was a 30% decrease in March and 42% in April. Children will be even more vulnerable to diseases like measles. In April 2019, CDC reported 695 cases of measles from 22 states. This is the greatest number of cases reported in the

United States since measles was eliminated from this country in 2000.

The concept of herd immunity comes from vaccination policy to calculate the number of people who need to be vaccinated to have immunity to the virus, so that transmission can no longer take place. Many people across the country would have to get sick with the coronavirus to build up a natural immunity. As the virus spreads and infects people, many could die in the process.[354] Dr. Leana Wen, emergency physician and CNN medical analyst warned about 2 million Americans could die in the effort to achieve herd immunity to the coronavirus naturally. "If we are waiting until 60% to 80% of people contract the virus, we are talking about 200 million-plus Americans getting this infection and at a fatality rate of 1%, that's 2 million Americans who will die in this effort to try to get herd immunity," Wen said.[355] If herd immunity does not include testing, tracing, and isolating, then it is going to be extremely hard to protect populations most at risk. In June 2020, Anthony Fauci, the head of the National Institute of Allergy and Infectious Diseases, said that, because of a "general anti-science, anti-authority, anti-vaccine feeling, the US is 'unlikely' to achieve herd immunity, even after a vaccine is available."[356] In September the CDC directed public health officials in all 50 states to be ready to distribute a COVID-19 vaccine to high-risk groups, like health-care workers, as early as late October or early November. The FDA would have to use its emergency authority to meet that timeline. The top adviser to Operation Warp Speed stated that an October vaccine was 'extremely unlikely' but major trials were under way to reach that goal.

A detached society will become a "cold society." Many of us are ready to touch, hug, talk face to face, sing, and smile without having to hide behind masks and gloves, but everyone must remain cautious. I do not think that shaking hands, giving high-fives, and other forms of greeting will disappear or be replaced by a Namaste gesture as done in the Asian cultures. We need to connect with one another again. If children cannot play with each other, there will be no social learning. American society is already fragmented by technology and the overuse of social media like Facebook, Twitter, and other social media accounts. We do not need additional technology or reasons to replace human face-to-face connection. Sadly, after several months of isolation, people can become fearful of intimacy. The world may be seen as a dangerous place. The invisible enemy could be anywhere. Some people may refuse to leave their homes. They may even develop agoraphobia.

Eating out in restaurants or going to bars is a popular social activity for Americans. Some establishments have tried to create more space between tables until the danger subsides. The concern is for the employees who do not return to work. They were receiving more money from the government unemployed than what they were earning at their jobs. This economic solution created a whole new problem for most businesses trying to reopen. Workers want to feel safe, but everyone needs to be cautious. Hopefully, people are tired of being at home and feeling unproductive. They will want to get back out and be re-involved in their jobs and occupations.

Certain regions around the world have experienced hunger due to factors like extreme weather, economic downturns, wars, or political instability, creating refugee situations.[357] This current hunger crisis is different. It is global due to the sudden loss of income for millions of people who were already struggling to survive. Several factors have contributed to this current economic situation: the collapse in oil prices, shortages of hard currency from tourism that evaporated, overseas workers not having any earnings to send money to support their families back home, and the ongoing climate change, violence, population dislocations, and humanitarian disasters.

The coronavirus was sometimes referred to as an equalizer because it did not discriminate. It has sickened both the rich and poor. However, when it comes to food, the commonality ended. Large segments of the poor population are now going hungry and facing the prospect of starving. There is no shortage of food globally according to the International Food Policy Research Institute in Washington. The logistical problems in planting, harvesting, and transporting food have already been a major issue, even in America. The countries that rely on imports of food will suffer. It has been sad to see long lines of cars waiting to get free supplies of food, and hearing from people who did not get any, as supplies ran out. On the other hand, it has been very encouraging to see thousands of people and restaurants across the country contributing, cooking, and helping to feed the hungry, and school children receiving school meals.

The way Americans shop for groceries may change after the pandemic.[358] Despite huge increases reported in Internet shopping, grocery sales accounted for a very small fraction in

2019. In response to stay at home mandates, more Americans than ever, are ordering their groceries online, either for delivery or pickup. Instacart, the biggest independent grocery- delivery service had a 150% rise in its orders. They were looking to hire 300,000 new "personal shoppers," who pick up and deliver groceries to customers. Many of these individuals were recently laid off workers. Amazon cannot keep up with the demand. There is a concern that there will be an expansion of superstores which will buy out most supplies, squeezing out smaller grocery stores. This action would impact supermarket workers, low-income shoppers, and individuals who want to select their own fresh fruits and vegetables. During the pandemic, decisions were made to mandate small shops to close while larger stores like Walmart, big chain grocery stores, warehouse stores like Sam's Club and Costco, were allowed to stay open. It was most unfortunate as these smaller stores catered to a smaller number of patrons while the big stores had numerous people walking through them. This decision caused a demise of the small-owned businesses. And, to add insult to injury, many businesses suffered the riots and looting stemming from the Black Lives Matter Movement protests.

The Centers for Medicare and Medicaid Services (CMS) have previously limited the ability of providers to be paid for telemedicine services. During the pandemic, they increased their coverage to include these services, as did many private insurance companies.[359] Both state and federal governments relaxed the requirement that physicians must have a separate license to practice in each state. These changes boosted telemedicine companies' revenues and encouraged traditional providers, both hospital and office based, to give telemedicine a try instead of in- person visits. Until now, this practice was limited. Formerly, there were restrictions on reimbursements and the concern that telemedicine would jeopardize the quality of care rendered to the patient. CMS has committed to reimbursements noted for only the duration of the COVID-19 Public Health Emergency.

The role of a health care provider is expanding. Even before the crisis, there was increasing levels of burnout. The pandemic created a surge in demand for health care and at the same time, reduced how many health care workers were available to help, due to contracting the virus themselves. Families were not able to visit. Patients' needs were increased beyond the hospitals' capabilities to provide all of their services. To meet these demands, the staff from elective treatments was called in to care for these patients. There is a spike in demand for diagnostic services and clinical staff to administer them. Non-profit and military organizations have been deployed to help. Since health care ailments may be directed away from the hospitals, the need for home health workers will eventually skyrocket. Even after the current crisis settles down, there will be numerous public health issues and social needs. Care may have to be provided by those individuals without advanced clinical degrees. Inspiration from organizations like the Peace Corps or Teach for America could provide direction in establishing a new workforce.

Health care coverage is a major issue that needs to be addressed in America. With this pandemic, major changes are coming to the overall economy and society. A major crisis exposes what is broken and gives new leaders a chance to build something better. Hopefully, the health care system, which has been needing an overhaul for a long time, will work more efficiently for all. It is critical for people who are not on the frontlines to start looking at lessons learned from this pandemic. They must begin working on ways to manage the next crisis more efficiently, because future pandemics caused by airborne viruses are inevitable. East Asia has already had several this century. The basic operations of our health care system have to improve fundamentally. There needs to be a guarantee of universal health care, which is not just a safety net but is a matter of national security. COVID-19 has shown that our survival is inextricably connected to the health of strangers and visitors.

Travel is a luxury that not only Americans, but people worldwide have cherished. That pleasure has been stripped from everyone with the global spread of the coronavirus. Most of the airlines have been grounded.360 Some flights are starting back up and will require passengers and flight attendants to wear masks. Emirates airline is testing people for the virus before they can board flights. They are taking the passengers' temperature before boarding the flight to ensure that they are symptom free. Even when flights start back up, travel choices will be limited. Due to limited availability, flights might be crowded.

Several cruise ships were stuck at sea, and many ports around the world refused to let them dock. Passengers will have to accept that these events can happen again if there is a resurgence of the virus. Hygienic standards aboard cruise ships will be more stringent. They may be required to expand their onboard medical capabilities. They have faced challenges in the past and have always rebounded, due to a loyal customer base.

The cruise bookings for 2021 are already reported to be strong. Anyone who has booked vacations and gone through the trauma of cancelling and receiving refunds may be reluctant to book another trip so soon. The travel industry has never faced panic, change, and disruption at this level.

Many countries including the US have mandatory requirements for visitors to isolate for two weeks. While traveling, until this situation gets under control, you will have to think about your own health and the well-being of the people you will be visiting. You could inadvertently be a carrier of the coronavirus to your next destination. Travel will be extremely difficult the next few years with many health procedures for passengers' safety. Many families have been impacted by the loss of a job or business. Senior travelers may be braver and pursue traveling before they are physically not able to do so. The very rich will travel on private jets. There has been a tremendous increase in charter air travel during the pandemic.

There may be plenty of "deals" to entice people to travel again, from cheap flights to affordable hotel rooms. Rebound for this industry will be slow. Hotels have laid off thousands of employees due to traveling restrictions. And it will be difficult for people to feel safe staying at hotels after the pandemic. Hotels will offer guest safety with their cleaning standards. Rental homes through Airbnb may not be able to offer the same standards but seem to be popular. Despite this tragedy with entire countries closed to the outside world, most experts agree that people will travel again. Most individuals seek the excitement and positive impact of travel.

Over 11% of global CEOs fear their businesses won't survive the coronavirus pandemic.[361] The hospitality and restaurant sector has forecasted the most severe outlook. More than 40% of the CEOs expect their revenue to be down by 20% a year from now, 30% of leaders in aerospace and aviation, 19% in wholesale and retail sales, and 19% in education stated that their businesses were at risk for failure. Offices may operate on shifts and will rely heavily on teleworking. Businesses will have to increase their cyber security.

Until a vaccine is available, or an effective treatment is produced, social gatherings will have to be limited. This type of social interaction will cause real problems in big cities where numerous people use the subway or other public transportation. Concerts, conferences, summer camps, political rallies, large weddings, and major sporting events may well have to be suspended for at least a year. Dr. Fauci thinks that the baseball season may get the go ahead in the fall. Entertainment and social events may be restricted to potlucks, board games, and watching endless streaming shows on television or other mobile devices, instead of going to the movies or restaurants. Another spike in the numbers of infected individuals or people dying from the virus will bring a halt to all gatherings.

During the pandemic, 2.3 million incarcerated Americans have been housed in overcrowded facilities.[362] They are the most vulnerable to the infection. In response to the overcrowding, some local governments are suspending jail time for technical violations, reducing arrests for low-level offenses, and identifying at-risk prisoners who could serve the rest of their sentence at home. People serving misdemeanor sentences have also been released. Pretrial detainees are free until they have to return for trial. These are emergency tactics, not reforms. The pandemic has provided an opportunity to test and observe more, just policing and incarceration policies. It could reduce the overcrowding of our prisons and lead to permanent reform within our criminal justice system.

Vogue editor, Anna Wintour spoke about the impact of the pandemic on the fashion industry and its future. She wanted to take this opportunity to look at their lives and rethink their values. She wanted to really think about the waste, and the amount of money, consumption, and excess. She felt everyone had indulged in this fantasy, and they needed to rethink what the industry stood for. At some level, we all need to do this.

Many of these problems are surmountable. The US is still a scientific and biomedical powerhouse. This pandemic has also mobilized the experts from around the world to work together for a common cause. Not the politicians, but the health experts and the CDC will have to take charge in guiding people moving forward. In the words of Dr. Gupta, "America deserves briefings by the full Task Force. Briefings where health experts can speak, and questions can be asked about the most acute public health crisis of our lifetime."[363] There needs to be an absolute, unwavering faith that we can prevail. America and the world should never be caught short- handed again. The US needs to be more self-reliant. Essential items and medications should be manufactured in America. To reduce our reliance on China, the federal government announced at the end of July 2020 that it plans to give Eastman Kodak a $765 Million loan to start producing the chemical ingredients needed to make pharmaceuticals. The company plans to establish a new division, Kodak Pharmaceuticals, that will focus on the building blocks used to produce generic drugs. Kodak aims to be one of the 'greatest second acts' in American industry and is expected to create at least 350 new jobs.

We must demonstrate discipline, confront the facts, and make hard choices before the next disaster. Too much has been lost playing catch up, mainly in the loss of lives. It is difficult to comprehend that 102 years after the last major pandemic, with all the technical resources available now, the world's leaders could not isolate and eradicate another devastating virus effectively to avoid the massive loss of lives globally.

This virus has disproportionately killed people in low-income jobs. They did not have the privilege of working from home. It was also more devastating to the black community, Latino and Native Americans, and the elderly, especially if they had pre-existing health conditions. The older population has been through the Great Recession, the cold war, civil-rights movements, and the women's movement. They are living historians. We need to cherish and learn from them. Measures must be put in place now before a resurgence or worse, a new virus arrives. If more severe lockdowns are mandated, people will rebel like they have already done during this pandemic. People will become tired from social distancing and compliance will fail. Citizens will be unwilling to make individual sacrifices for the sake of everyone. The emotional climate is already filled with anger and frustration, as expressed by American citizens and global nationals.

Most citizens want to stop America from falling into a downward spiral, into the abyss. Uncooperative people may have to be forcibly quarantined or criminal charges imposed. This act will fracture our society even more. The people with wealth and means to take care of themselves will be in a position of being envied by the people who do not have these assets. We cannot even fantom a situation where there is survival of the fittest, and every man for himself.

Most of the companies will have to rethink their allocation of funds. A higher proportion will need to be dedicated to research and development. Things must work more efficiently. Looking for bigger shareholder returns or bonuses for the CEOs may have to be adjusted. In turn, the average person also must start saving. In an affluent country like the US, it is distressing that majority of people do not have enough savings to ride out one or two months of expenses, without getting a paycheck. It is estimated that 30% of Americans have zero savings. One-fifth of the population has savings to last six months. This pandemic should really be an eye opener for every family. People may be reluctant to spend money to eat out at restaurants or go shopping. Americans may now start saving money and pay off their mortgages.

A report in September provided some evidence that this came to fruition. America's "personal saving rate" which is the share of people's disposable income that gets saved or invested, has rarely exceeded 10 percent in the past 20 years.[364] However in the first few months of the coronavirus pandemic, it increased to more than three times that in April. The checking- account balances of Americans regardless of income level, rose, thanks to the government stimulus aid. Many people who were out of work were able to stay afloat because of the federal aid. With some businesses closing permanently and many low-income workers relying on another stimulus package, there were millions straining to make ends meet. More than 5,000 businesses closed in NY since March, according to Yelp. People were reporting that their monthly expenses had fallen by hundreds and in some cases, thousands of dollars during the pandemic. They were spending less on eating out, entertainment, new clothes, and extracurriculars for their kids. These activities were now thought to be dangerous, or unnecessary. Prior to the pandemic, lots of working people ate out nearly every day. The cost of this adds up very quickly. There was extra money in the bank but despite wanting to buy things, there was no reason to buy things and nothing to spend money on. People were not traveling, and so large amounts of cash were saved.

Fewer people may start a new business, and the ones that do survive, may downsize, or hire less workers and borrow less money. On the other hand, since spending was at an all-time low during the shutdown, people may be ready to go out and splurge, and spoil themselves. America has a consumer driven economy. However, there needs to be a balance between spending for needs, fewer social activities, and the necessity to save for difficult times. The US consumer index had fallen 30% since February. Many of the newly unemployed workers and small businesses could not or were not paying their rent or mortgage. In September, the Department of Health and Human Services and the Centers for Disease Control and Prevention issued an order to temporarily halt evictions through the end of the year.

The CDC said evictions threatened to increase the spread of coronavirus because they forced people to either move from one state to another, or into a group setting like shelters or share housing.[365]

People were already moving out of their condos in the city and moving into the country to have homes with space for a yard or a vegetable garden. 15,025 apartments were vacant in August in Manhattan, as people continue to leave the city due to the pandemic.[366] That represented about 5% of all apartments in the area. Vacancy rate is usually 1.5% to 2.5%. During the Great Depression, families relied on kitchen gardens and community victory gardens to grow food rather than buy it. Americans may well return to self-sustaining living if they have space.

Lifestyle decisions need to be made, from borrowing money, to having children, to living in crowded cities. After all, even without everyone getting tested, they are reporting one in five people living in New York and one in four living in Arizona as being infected. For infections, it is a disaster waiting to happen, with so many people living in such confined spaces. Because of their size, density, and exposure to foreign travelers, cities initially endured the worst of this pandemic. The greatest lesson of the outbreak may be that modern cities are inadequately designed to keep us safe, not only from coronaviruses, but from other forms of infectious disease and from environmental conditions, such as pollution (which contributes to illness) and overcrowding (which contributes to the spread of illness). Maybe we need to design cities with a greater awareness of all threats to our health.[367] The US is also facing demise of many major cities like Portland, San Francisco,

Seattle, Chicago, Washington D.C., Houston, Pittsburg, and Detroit due to an increased cost of living, and property taxes, crumbling infrastructure, increased homelessness, and crime rate.

On the 50th anniversary of Earth Day this year, March 22, 2020, Greta Thunberg, the 17-year-old Swedish girl, global-warming activist, compared the pandemic to the "climate crisis." She wanted to remind the people of the world that both these events needed to be addressed simultaneously.[368] She reiterated that at such difficult junctures, we all need to listen to the experts. In a crisis, people must put their differences aside, make decisions that are foreign to them at that moment, but may be necessary for the common well-being of all members in our society for the long run. In 2010, leaders from 196 countries gathered in Japan and agreed on a list of goals designed to save the Earth. The Aichi Biodiversity Targets laid out a 10-year plan to conserve the world's biodiversity, promote sustainability, and protect ecosystems. We reached the deadline in 2020, but the world collectively failed to fully achieve a single goal. "Humanity stands at a crossroads with regard to the legacy it leaves to future generations," the report warned.[369]

No one would have anticipated a benefit from this devastating pandemic. However, the planet is rejoicing, even if it is a brief respite.[370] India's capital, New Delhi, is one of the world's most polluted cities. During the shutdown and minimal road traffic, the skies above New Delhi turned blue. Many people could see the Himalayas for the first time. The air was outstandingly clean in China. In the canals of Venice, normally soiled by boat traffic, the water was so clear that fish were visible. In Seattle, New York, Los Angeles, Chicago and Atlanta, the fog pollution from the usual motorway traffic had lifted. The global air quality improved fast due to grounded flights, decreased highway traffic, and stalled factories. Even global carbon emissions fell due to the shutdown of economic activity and a drastic reduction in the use of fossil fuels. Policymakers have spent trillions of dollars and passed countless regulations, standards, and mandates to encourage use of clean energy. It took a pandemic-induced economic standstill to bring emissions down. It should be a sobering reminder of just how hard addressing climate change will be. Unfortunately, any climate benefits from the Covid-19 crisis are likely to be short term and negligible.

Countries like China have already prioritized human and economic welfare before the environment. China has opened its factories and given permission to more coal burning factories that were closed previously to make up for the economic losses. Covid-19 may chip away at public support for stronger climate action during times of economic hardship. Historically, there is an inverse relationship in the United States and Europe between public concern about the environment and economic concerns. Countries have a chance to choose a new path as societies begin to return to normal. As with climate change, if a single virus can destroy world economies in a matter of weeks, it shows that we are not thinking long term. The fact that it takes severe economic slowdowns like the Great Recession or Covid-19 to bring emissions down, serves as a reminder of just how strongly tied emissions remain to economic growth, and how hard it is to lower them.

Some governments can force their citizens to stay home. However, there is no global institution with the enforcement power to require nations to curb their emissions. Climate change will affect future generations the most. Only half of Americans believe climate change should be a top priority for the federal government. Why are we so bent on destroying the only planet we have for future generations? Taking action, even by countries less at-risk than others, can help due to the uncertainty from the impacts of climate change.

Memory researchers say that the memories from these last few months of isolation at home will become a blur over time.[371] That is good news as we do not want to relive this horrific tribulation. However, will humanity remember enough what has happened to make lasting changes? Sadly, from the past thousands of years, humanity has chosen to forget the past, hence repeating the same mistakes of war, famine, greed, pollution, and raping the planet to causing its demise.

Since we are living through this historic event, moments of each day may feel like an eternity. All conversations revolve around the virus. It is strange and tragic to hear the number of deaths daily, not only close to home, but all over the world. In 1890, psychologist William James wrote that emotional events have such a huge effect on our minds they "almost leave a scar upon the cerebral tissues."[372] Powerful emotions, both happy and sad, influence what we remember. What we end up remembering, may not be 100% accurate, even from once in a lifetime event. We remember certain details that are emotionally charged and obscure the rest. It is almost like focusing with a camera!

For many of us, who are just isolating at home, we will forget people, places, our moods, and the events will become a blur. We are not laying down emotional-laden memories. What is happening is something foreign. We fill our days with the same routines. Days and weeks blend one into the other. There will be memories of an absence of things we could not do, like attend funerals, celebrate birthdays and anniversaries, and canceled weddings or trips of a lifetime.

Those on the frontlines will remember it differently. They have witnessed the tragic loss of human life and lived through days of heightened emotions like grief, fear, and anxiety. They may end up with post-traumatic stress disorder (PTSD). Those people facing extreme stressors, whose loved ones got sick and died alone, who lost their jobs, businesses, livelihoods by the economic downturn, may continue to hold onto the feelings and memories, even if they are not accurate.

As humans, we try to make sense of the moment. We can recall with ease the first or last moments of an event. After times of crises, the US government and its people historically have tended to go back to the way it was before the event. Memories can be strengthened, weakened, or incorporated. Will it be different this time after the pandemic? The immediate problem is the virus. The long-term problem is the structure of our social, political, and economic systems.

America broke down; it was brought to its knees by an invisible enemy. It has the potential to be fixed and ready for the next assault, if the government and the citizens are willing to make the hard decisions, exert self-discipline and work for the good of all, and not just a few! Maybe remembering that we were all part of this pandemic will motivate everyone to do their part, however big or small. After analyzing health experts' solutions and not the uneducated politicians' "knee jerk" reactions in these healthcare matters, long term plans need to be implemented before the next crisis erupts.

The US is unhinged. By end of December 2020, over 19 million people have been diagnosed with the coronavirus. More than 326,800 Americans have lost their lives. It is predicted that up to 500,000 Americans will die by early 2021. More shocking is to listen to people being outraged at the simple request to wear a mask. Why is it so difficult to understand how dangerous it is to walk around unprotected for yourself and other citizens? If individuals do not want to protect their own health, please be respectful to the other individuals around you. You could very well be an asymptomatic carrier of COVID-19. Globally, young people continue to behave irresponsibly and are now dying. They continue to attend parties, congregate at beaches, bars, and restaurants. They are refusing outright or are very reluctant to social distance or wear masks. California and Mississippi were recording rates nearing 10% of overall cases under the age of 18.

More than 33 million world inhabitants have been infected. The number of deaths worldwide has exceeded one million. Some say the numbers fall short, and in fact, the infection rate may be ten times higher than previously thought. For every one individual who has tested positive, scientists believe that ten other people have been infected. Almost a million global citizens have died from the coronavirus. If the younger generation does not follow the guidelines or show resilience, humanity is doomed. All age groups are responsible for the fate of global society. We all have choices, make the right ones for the welfare of humanity.

Most people just want the pandemic to be over, so we go back to how it was earlier in the year. Americans want instant gratification. Even President Trump is not looking beyond the invention and distribution of the vaccine in dealing with these pandemic ramifications. Keeping the status-quo can prove to be more compelling than the need for urgent change. The world's chaos and our own mortality require that we make peace with this calamity. There are significant inequalities as to what is or what will be normal for different people in the future. We have an opportunity to rethink how we can be less vulnerable and equitable to everyone. Disasters reveal problems that already existed, and in doing so, create an opportunity to evaluate alternate, more efficient, and healthy ways of living. Tragedies can motivate us from the haze of complacency and force us to look for better solutions. We can squander this opportunity or utilize it to make lasting meaningful changes. The most important changes following past catastrophes went beyond the devastation itself. The questions to ponder are: What is a community for? How can it exist safely to survive calamities? What are its basic needs? How should we provide them? These are the questions we should be asking about our own world as we confront the coronavirus pandemic and what should follow. "Right now, with COVID-19, we are all putting our hopes in one thing, one cure, one vaccine and it speaks to how narrow our vision of society has become," says David Rosner, Columbia University public-health historian.[373] These are uncertain times not only for the individual, but also for the world.

"Carefully watch your thoughts, for they become your words. Manage and watch your words, for they will become your actions. Consider and judge your actions, for they will become your habits. Acknowledge and watch your habits for they shall become your values. Understand and embrace your values, for they become your destiny."[374]

Mahatma Gandhi

Acknowledgements

First, I need to thank my parents for instilling in me a sense of responsibility and tenacity to undertake the challenge of writing this book. However, it would never have come to fruition if my close friend Robert Koeneman, had not insisted that I write it. The book is mainly his vision to make people think and make the best decisions for humanity to move forward. His concerns about humans destroying themselves gave rise to ideas for this book, and his constant encouragement helped me complete the task. He spent endless hours helping me navigate the computer glitches and educated me in the art of using a computer and not treating it like a typewriter! His belief that I could help people understand different viewpoints, spurred me on to gather ideas and to present them in the book.

Thank you, Hari Zwander, for introducing me to the book, *The Alchemist by Paulo Coelho.* After reading this book, I started thinking that maybe I could put some ideas and concerns down on paper, which might help people struggling with issues that are so troubling in the current era.

Michele Gottlieb, a librarian, and a French professor at the College of Central Florida, threw me a lifeline after reading this book. She understood and was enthusiastic about the American cultural issues and associated problems that I wanted to analyze. Her constant encouragement and vision for this book gave me confidence to continue, and with her help, the manuscript became more fluid and concise. With all her energy and enthusiasm, she inspired me to work harder, persevere, and enhance the book's quality. She became the wind beneath my wings and kept me motivated. I owe her immense gratitude for all her help.

Next, I have a deep appreciation for many friends who read the book and gave their input and editing advice. Dennis Jenkins, who worked as a contractor to NASA for 33 years and was involved in the Air and Space Museums, both in California and Kennedy Space Center in Florida, has authored many books. He took time away from his writing to give me much needed input and direction. He made me understand the need to edit and continue reediting.

Mark George, a former colleague from my time in Valdosta, was very gracious to read the book and spend time giving me feedback on what improvements were needed to engage the reader. Jay Hood, a very successful businessman and an avid reader, immediately understood the significance of the material in the book and was very encouraging in wanting to get the book published. He echoed my sentiments that this book had the potential to make readers think and obtain help for those looking for direction. Donald Pakosh, another businessman, was also very enthusiastic in wanting to help get the book published. Paul Miller, a retired teacher originally from Barbados, immigrated to Manchester, U.K., and now living in California, read the book over a weekend and gave me confidence that I had a good roadmap to help people heal.

Susie Wenstrome, a retired lawyer, spent time pointing out areas that needed improvement and provided redirection in specific chapters. Thank you to Judy Toscano, Jennifer Brand, Gloria Ragonetti, Angela Paporello, Nancy Bray and Kris Kalidindi, who read the book and provided feedback. When I was beginning to write, some other individuals also helped with their suggestions: Lori Rohm, Valerie Robinson, Claire Brew, and her sister Susan Rehwald.

Finally, I want to thank my partner of 30 years, Stephen Ryals, who remains a constant source of support, and I appreciate all he does to help, encourage, and believe in me.

Endnotes

Introduction

[1] "Pop Culture Dictionary," Dictionary, updated 2020, accessed September 9, 2020, https://www.dictionary.com/e/pop-culture/cancel-culture/.

[2] John Stossel, "Cancel Culture Is Out of Control," Reason, published July 8, 2020, accessed September 9, 2020, https://reason.com/2020/07/08/cancel-culture-is-out-of-control/.

A Professional Journey

[3] Kenneth Pletcher, "Aksai-Chin Plateau Region, Asia," Encyclopedia Britannica, accessed September 2, 2019, https://www.britannica.com/place/Aksai-Chin.

[4] "2020 China-India Skirmishes," *Wikipedia*, updated September 8, 2020, accessed September 9, 2020, https://en.wikipedia.org/wiki/2020_China%E2%80%93India_skirmishes#:accessed.

[5] "Karen Carpenter," *Wikipedia,* last modified September 11, 2019, accessed September 2, 2019, https://en.wikipedia.org/wiki/Karen_Carpenter.

[6] Akhilesh Pillalamarri, "The Origin of Hindu-Muslim Conflict in South Asia," *The Diplomat*, published March 16, 2019, accessed July 27, 2020, https://thediplomat.com/2019/03/the-origins-of-hindu-muslim-conflict-in-south-asia/.

[7] "Shirley Ardell Mason," *Wikepida*, last modified September 8, 2019, accessed September 10, 2019 https://en.wikipedia.org/wiki/Shirley_Ardell_Mason.

[8] 18 "Healing Emotional Trauma to Release Your Creativity," *The Creative Mind*, accessed September 2, 2019, http:// thecreativemind.net/5023/healing-emotional-trauma-to-release-your-creativity/.

[9] Nicole Spector, "Why Physicians Are Leaving Their Practices to Pursue Other Careers," *NBC News*, published August 18, 2018, accessed September 2, 2020, https://www.nbcnews.com/business/business-news/doctor-out-why-physicians-are-leaving-their-practices-pursue-other-n900921.

[10] "The Complexities of Physician Supply and Demand: Projections from 2013 – 2015," *HIS (Information Handling Services)*, published March 2015, accessed September 2, 2019, https://www.aamc.org/download/426246/data/ihsworkforcereport.pdf.

[11] "How Doctors Feel About Electronic Health Records," *Stanford Medicine & The Harris Poll*, published 2018, accessed September 2, 2019, https://med.stanford.edu/content/dam/sm/ehr/documents/EHR-Poll-Presentation.pdf.

[12] Sandra Vander Schaaff, "There's a Shortage of Child Psychiatrists and Kids Are Hurting," *The Washington Post*, published October 30, 2016, accessed September 2, 2019, https://www.washingtonpost.com/national/health-science/theres-a-shortage-of-child-psychiatrists-and-kids-are-hurting/2016/10/28/37fd19f0-63b6-11e6-be4e-23fc4d4d12b4_story.html.

[13] "Powerful Advice from a Dying Twenty-four Year Old," *Power of Positivity*, accessed September 3, 2019, https://www.powerofpositivity.com/powerful-advice-dying-24-year-old/.

[14] Steve Jobs, "Steve Jobs Quotes," *BrainyQuote*, updated 2020, accessed December 1, 2020, https://www.brainyquote.com/quotes/steve_jobs_416859
.

The Biochemistry of Emotions

[15] Terri Fisher, "Study Debunks Stereotype That Men Think About Sex All Day Long," *Ohio State University News*,

published November 27, 2011, accessed September 3, 2019, https://news.osu.edu/study-debunks-stereotype-that-en-think-about-sex-all-day-long/.

16 D. E. Berlyne et al., "Thought," *Encyclopedia Britannica*, accessed September 3, 2019, https://www.britannica.com/topic/thought.

17 Joel Brown, "Hundred Dalai Lama Quotes That Will Change Your Life," *Addicted to Success*, published November 6, 2016, accessed September 3, 2019, https://addicted2success.com/quotes/100-dalai-lama-quotes-that-will-change-your-life/.

18 Dr. Arthur Arun, "Science: Human Body & Mind, The Science of Flirting," *BBC*, archived November 6, 2014, accessed September 4, 2019, https://www.bbc.co.uk/science/hottopics/love/flirting.shtml.

19 Helen Fisher, "Science: Human Body & Mind, The Science of Love," *BBC*, archived September 17, 2014, accessed September 4, 2019, https://www.bbc.co.uk/science/hottopics/love/index.shtml.

20 Melanie Greenberg, Ph.D., "The Science of Love and Attachment: How Understanding Your Brain Chemicals Can Help You Build Everlasting Love," *Psychology Today*,

published March 30, 2016, accessed September 4, 2019, https://www.psychologytoday.com/us/blog/the-mindful-self-express/201603/the-science-love-and-attachment.

[21] "Me Too Movement," *Wikipedia*, last modified September 22, 2019, accessed September 24, 2019, https://en.wikipedia.org/wiki/Me_Too_movement.

[22] Greenberg, Ph.D., The Science of Love and Attachment.

[23] Robert J. Sternberg and Karin Weis, eds., "The New Psychology of Love," reprint ed., (New Haven, CT: Yale University Press, 2008), 171-183.

[24] Robert J. Sternberg and Karin Weis, eds., "The New Psychology of Love," reprint ed., (New Haven, CT: Yale University Press, 2008), 171-183.

[25] Robert J. Sternberg and Karin Weis, eds., "The New Psychology of Love," reprint ed., (New Haven, CT: Yale University Press, 2008), 171-183.

[26] Dr. Arun, Science: Human Body & Mind, The Science of Flirting.

[27] Ziad K. Abdelnour, "Ziad K. Abdelnour Quotes," AZ Quotes, accessed September 5, 2019, https://

www.azquotes.com/author/27727-Ziad_K_Abdelnour.

[28] Samantha Bruce-Benjamin, "Samantha Bruce-Benjamin Quotes," Goodreads, updated 2020, accessed December 1, 2020, https://www.goodreads.com/quotes/351917-it-is-a-dull-sensation-your-heart-breaking-like-the.

[29] Meghan Laslocky, "This is Your Brain on Heartbreak," Greater Good Magazine: Science-Based Insights for a Meaningful Life, published February 15, 2013, accessed September 5, 2019, https://greatergood.berkeley.edu/article/item/this_is_your_brain_on_heartbreak.

[30] "Health Threats from High Blood Pressure," American Heart Association, Inc., last modified October 31, 2016, accessed September 6, 2019, https://www.heart.org/en/health-topics/high-blood-pressure/health-threats-from-high-_blood-pressure.

[31] "Broken Heart Syndrome," Mayo Clinic, last modified November 5, 2016, accessed September 6, 2019, https:// www.mayoclinic.org/diseases-conditions/broken-heart-syndrome/symptoms-causes/syc-20354617.

[32] J. M. Lawrence, "J. M. Lawrence Quote," Daily Inspirational Quotes, updated 2020, accessed December 1, 2020, https://www.dailyinspirationalquotes.in/2019/04/its-not-

what-we-have-in-life-but-who-we-have-in-our-life-that-matters-j-m-lawrence/.

33 Steve Duck, "Towards a Social Psychology of Loneliness: Daniel Perlman and Letitia Anne Peplau," in Personal Relationships in Disorder, ed. Robin Gilmour, (Ann Arbor: University of Michigan, 1981), 31-56, digitized July16, 2009, accessed September 6, 2019, https://pdfs.semanticscholar.org/52d9/6cedd5fc0a7658e6e0a8a 17d0dcab428850b.pdf.

34 Daniel Russell, Letitia Peplau and Mary Lund Ferguson, "Developing a Measure of Loneliness," Journal of Personality Assessment 42, no. 3 (1978): 290-294, published online June 10, 2010, accessed September 7, 2019, https://www.tandfonline.com/doi/abs/10.1207/s15327752jpa42 03_11.

35 Jason Daley, "The UK Now Has a Minister for Loneliness. Here's Why It Matters," Smithsonian, published January 19, 2018, accessed September 7, 2019, https://www.smithsonianmag.com/smart-news/minister-loneliness- appointed-united-kingdom-180967883/.

36 Kasley Killam, "To Combat Loneliness, Promote Social Health," Scientific American, published January 23, 2018, accessed September 7, 2019,

 https://www.scientificamerican.com/article/to-combat-loneliness-promote- social-health1/.

[37] Ye Luo, Ph.D., Louise Hawkley, Ph.D. and John Cacioppo, Ph.D., "Loneliness, Health, and Mortality in Old Age: A National Longitudinal Study," Social Science and Medicine (Soc Sci Med.) 74 no. 6 (March 2012): 907-914, published online January 25, 2012, accessed September 8, 2019, https://www.ncbi.nlm.nih.gov/pmc/articles/ PMC3303190/.

[38] Ye Luo, Ph.D., Louise Hawkley, Ph.D. and John Cacioppo, Ph.D., "Loneliness, Health, and Mortality in Old Age: A National Longitudinal Study."

[39] CDC, "Depression Evaluation Measures | Workplace Health," CDC, reviewed April 1, 2016, accessed July 27, 2020, https://www.cdc.gov/workplacehealthpromotion/health-strategies/depression/ evaluation-measures/index.html.

How to Deal with Loneliness

[40] Norman Cousins, "Norman Cousins Quotes," Goodreads, updated 2020, accessed December 1, 2020, https://www.goodreads.com/quotes/684700-the-tragedy-of-life-is-not-death-but-what-we#:~:text=Quote.

41 Doe Zantamata, "Friendship Quotes," Daily Inspirational Quotes, accessed September 8, 2019, https://www.dailyinspirationalquotes.in/2016/06/good-friends-help-find-important-things-lost-smile-hope-courage-doe-zantamata/.

42 Claude Fischer Ph.D., "Understanding How Personal Networks Change," *National Institutes of Health*, accessed September 8, 2019, http://grantome.com/grant/NIH/R01-AG041955-02.

43 Dr. Sanjay Gupta, "Just Say Hello: The Powerful New Way to Combat Loneliness," *Oprah*, published February 18, 2014, accessed September 8, 2019, http://www.oprah.com/health/just-say-hello-fight-loneliness/all.

44 Michele Baird, "Dating Sites Reviews: SugarDaddie Reviews," *Lovenet-jp*, published January 29, 2019, accessed September 9, 2019, http://lovenet-jp.com/sugardaddie-com-review/.

45 "Red Thread of Fate," *Wikipedia*, edited November 19, 2020, accessed December 1, 2020, https://en.wikipedia.org/wiki/Red_thread_of_fate.

For a Better Marriage, Act Like a Single Person

[46] Ibn Taymiyyah, "Find and Share Quotes with Friends," *Goodreads*, accessed September 9, 2019, https://www.goodreads.com/quotes/646901-don-t-depend-too-much-on-anyone-in-this-world-because.

[47] Stephanie Coontz, "For a Better Marriage, Act Like a Single Person," *The New York Times*, published February 10, 2018, accessed September 9, 2019, https://www.nytimes.com/2018/02/10/opinion /sunday/for-a-better-marriage-act-like-a-single-person.html.

[48] Stephanie Coontz, "For a Better Marriage, Act like a Single Person."

[49] Ashley Mateo, "The Surprising Benefits of Being Single," *The Oprah Magazine*, published June 10, 2019, accessed September 6, 2019, https://www.oprahmag.com/life/relationships-love/a27790346/benefits-of-being-single/.

[50] Julian Holt-Lunstad, Timothy B. Smith and J. Bradley Layton, "Social Relationships and Mortality Risk: A Meta-analytic Review," *PLOS/Medicine (Public Library of Science)*, published July 27, 2010, accessed September 10, 2019,

https://journals.plos.org/plosmedicine/article?id=10.1371/journ al.pmed.1000316.

51 Harper Lee, "Find and Share Quotes with Friends," *Goodreads,* accessed September 10, 2019, https:// www.goodreads.com/quotes/138836-you-can-choose-your- friends-but-you-sho-can-t-choose.

52 Cecilia Dey, "Looking at Things from a Different Angle," *Picture This,* published April 8, 2014, accessed November 3, 2019, https://ceciliadeyprevails.wordpress.com/2014/04/08/family-is- not-about-blood-its-about-who-is-willing-to-hold-your-hand- when-you-need-it-the-most/.

53 Elyakim Kislev, "The Impacts of Friendship on Single and Married People," *Psychology Today*, posted April 7, 2019, accessed September 11, 2019, https://www.psychologytoday.com/us/blog/happy- singlehood/201904/the- impact-friendships-single-and- married-people.

54 William Chopik and Andy Henion, "Are Friends Better for Us Than Family," *Michigan State University Today*, published June 6, 2017, accessed September 11, 2019, https://msutoday.msu.edu/news/2017/are-friends-better-for- us- than-family/.

[55] Pure Love Quotes, "Quote by Anonymous," *Pure Love Quotes*, published 2019, accessed November 3, 2019, https://www.purelovequotes.com/author/anonymous/one-smile-can-start-a-friendship-one-word-can/.

Happiness

[56] Ralph Marston, "Ralph Marston, Happiness is a choice...," *AZ Quotes*, accessed September 11, 2019, https://www.azquotes.com/quote/824585.

[57] Leah Fessier, "This CEO Plans to Get a Woman Elected Whether You Like It or Not," *Quartz at Work*, published February 6, 2018, accessed September 12, 2019, https://qz.com/work/1176111/emilys-list-ceo-stephanie-schriock- will-get-a-woman-elected-as-us-president-whether-you-like-it-or-not/.

[58] Unknown author, "The Quote Archive," *Tiny Buddha*, accessed September 12, 2019, https://tinybuddha.com/wisdom-quotes/the-happiest-people-dont-have-the-best-of-everything-they-just-make-the-best-of-everything-they- have/.

[59] "The Science of Well-being: Yale's Most Popular Course Ever Available by Coursera," *Yale News*, published February 20, 2019, accessed September 12, 2019,

https://news.yale.edu/2018/02/20/yales-most-popular-class-ever- be-available-coursera.

60 Brandon A. Webber, "Yale's Most Popular Course Is Now Available Online -for Free," *BIGTHINK*, published April 12, 2018, accessed September 12, 2019, https://bigthink.com/brandon-weber/the-famous-yale-class-known-as- psyc-157-or-psychology-and-the-good-life-is-now-available-to-the-world.

61 Brandon A. Webber, "Yale's Most Popular Course Is Now Available Online -for Free."

62 Ricky Gervais, "Ricky Gervais Quotes," *Brainy Quote*, accessed September 14, 2019, https://www.brainyquote.com/quotes/ricky_gervais_201998.

63 Dan Billefsky, "Albert Einstein's Theory of Happiness Fetches $1.56 Million," *The New York Times*, accessed September 14, 2019, https://www.nytimes.com/2017/10/25/world/middleeast/einstein-theory-of-happiness.html? auth=login-email&login=email.

64 "Nobel Prize in Physics in 1921," *Nobel Prize*, accessed September 14, 2019, https://www.nobelprize.org/prizes/ physics/1921/summary/.

65 Dan Billefsky, "Albert Einstein's Theory of Happiness Fetches $1.56 Million."

66 Tara Parker-Pope, "The Power of Positive People," *The New York Times*, accessed September 14, 2019, https://www.nytimes.com/2018/07/10/well/the-power-of-positive-people.html.

67 Dan Buettner, "Blue Zones," *Blue Zones*, accessed September 14, 2019, https://www.bluezones.com/dan-buettner/.

68 Ibid.

69 Mark Stibich, "Okinawan Longevity and Healthy Aging in Blue Zones," *Very Well Health*, accessed September 14, 2019, https://www.verywellhealth.com/the-okinawans-key-to-healthy-aging-2223603.

70 Blue Zones, "Moai, This Tradition is Why Okinawan People Live Longer, Better," *Blue Zones,* accessed September 14, 2019, https://www.bluezones.com/2018/08/moai-this-tradition-is-why-okinawan-people-live-longer- better/.

71 Blue Zones, "Moai, This Tradition is Why Okinawan People Live Longer, Better," *Blue Zones,* accessed September 14, 2019, https://www.bluezones.com/2018/08/moai-this-

tradition-is-why-okinawan-people-live-longer- better/.

72 Buettner, "Blue Zones."

73 Dan Buettner.

74 Travis Bradberry, "Travis Bradberry Quotes," *BrainyQuote*, updated 2020, accessed December 1, 2020, https://www.brainyquote.com/quotes/travis_bradberry_734896.

75 John Templeton, "Happiness Comes from Spiritual Wealth…" *AZ Quotes*, published 2019, accessed November 3, 2019, https://www.azquotes.com/quote/520605.

Laughter

76 Asad Meah, "35 Inspirational Quotes on Laughter," *Awaken the Greatness Within*, accessed September 20,2019, https://www.awakenthegreatnesswithin.com/35-inspirational-quotes-on-laughter/.

77 "Bangalore, India's Laughter City," *Laughter Yoga University,* accessed September 18, 2019, https://laughteryoga.org/bangalore-indias-laughter-city/.

78 "Laughter is the Best Medicine" – *Help Guide*, accessed July 26, 2020,

https://www.helpguide.org/articles/mental-health/laughter-is-the-best-medicine.htm.

[79] S. Romundstad et al. "A 15-Year Follow-up Study of Sense of Humor and Causes of Mortality: The Nord- Trondelag Health Study," *PubMed.gov, US National Library of Medicine*, accessed September 18, 2019, https://www.ncbi.nlm.nih.gov/pubmed/26569539.

Negative Emotions

[80] Samantha Gluck, "Depression Quotes and Sayings about Depression," *Healthy Place for Your Mental Health*, accessed September 20, 2019, https://www.healthyplace.com/insight/quotes/depression-quotes-and-sayings-about- depression.

[81] "Morbidity and Mortality Weekly Report, Vol. 67, No.8, Youth Risk Behavior Surveillance – United States, 2017," *Center for Disease Control and Prevention*, June 15, 2018, accessed September 20, 2019, https://www.cdc.gov/healthyyouth/data/yrbs/pdf/2017/ss6708.pdf.

[82] "Men's Health Week 2019: By Numbers," *Men's Health Forum*, accessed September 20, 2019, https://www.menshealthforum.org.uk/mens-health-week-2019-numbers.

[83] "Tackling the Growing Crisis of Lonely Men," *Age UK*, June 2018, accessed September 20, 2019, https://www.ageuk.org.uk/our-impact/policy-research/loneliness-research-and-resources/tackling-growing-crisis-lonely-men/.

[84] "Why Mentor," *Mentor, The National Mentor Partnership*, accessed September 20, 2019, https://www.mentoring.org/why-mentoring/mentoring-impact/?

[85] "No matter how educated, rich, or cool you believe you are...," *Simple Reminders*, accessed September 20, 2019, https://gomcgill.com/no-matter-how-educated-talented-rich-or-cool-you-believe-you-are-how-you-3/.

[86] Shelby Lin Erdman, "Drug Overdose Deaths Jump in 2019 to nearly 71,000, a Record High, CDC Says," *CNN*, published July 16, 2020, accessed August 12, 2020, https://www.cnn.com/2020/07/15/health/drug-overdose-deaths-2019/index.html.

[87] Dr. Mike Ronsisvalle, "Ronsisvalle: Societal Shift Needed to Stop School Shootings," *Special to Florida Today*, published February 20, 2018, accessed September 20, 2019, https://www.floridatoday.com/story/life/wellness/2018/02/20/ronsisvalle-societal-shift-needed-stop-school-shootings/354603002/.

88 Eli Watkins, "Marco Rubio Stands by Taking NRA Contributions," *CNN*, published February 22, 2018, accessed July 26, 2020, https://www.cnn.com/2018/02/21/politics/rubio-nra-money-cameron-kasky/index.html.

89 Bill O'Reilly, "Bill O'Reilly Quotes," *BrainyQuote*, updated 2020, accessed December 1, 2020, https://www.brainyquote.com/quotes/bill_oreilly_593039.

90 Dr. Mike Ronsisvalle, "Societal Shift Needed."

91 Ibid.

92 Dr. Patricia Conrod and Scientists at CHU Saint-Justine & Université de Montréal, "Increases in Social Media Use and Television Viewing Associated with Increases in Teen Depression," *Eurek Alert!*, published July 15, 2019, accessed September 21, 2019, https://www.eurekalert.org/pub_releases/2019-07/uom-iis071119.php.

93 Dr. Jennifer B. Johnson, PhD and Andrew Joy, "Media Contagion is Factor in Mass Shootings, Study Says," *American Psychological Association*, August 4, 2016, accessed September 21, 2019, https://www.apa.org/news/press/releases/2016/08/media-contagion.

94 Curt Devine et al., "What We Know about Jacksonville Shooting Suspect David Katz," *CNN News*, August 28, 2018, accessed September 21, 2019, https://www.cnn.com/2018/08/27/us/jacksonville-madden-tournament-suspect/ index.html.

95 "Columbine High School Massacre," *Wikepedia*, last modified September 21, 2019, accessed September 21, 2019, https://en.wikipedia.org/wiki/Columbine_High_School_massacre.

96 "2011 Norway Attacks," *Wikepedia*, last modified September 16, 2019, accessed September 21, 2019, https://en.wikipedia.org/wiki/2011_Norway_attacks.

97 "Sandy Hook Elementary School Shooting," *Wikepedia*, last modified September 21, 2019, accessed September 21, 2019, https://en.wikipedia.org/wiki/Sandy_Hook_Elementary_School_shooting.

98 "Active Shooter Video Game Pulled from Platform after Outcry," *NBC News*, published May 30, 2018, accessed September 21, 2019, https://www.nbcnews.com/news/us-news/active-shooter-video-game-prompts-outrage-amid- spate-school-shootings-n878156.

[99] "Moral Combat: Why the War on Violent Video Games is Wrong," *Amazon Prime Books*, accessed September 21, 2019, https://www.amazon.com/Moral-Combat-Violent-Video-Games/dp/1942952988.

Changing the Culture

[100] Albert Einstein, "Albert Einstein > Quotes," *Goodreads*, accessed September 21, 2019, https://www.goodreads.com/quotes/8144295-the-world-will-not-be-destroyed-by-those-who-do.

[101] Dr. Mike Ronsisvalle, "Ronsisvalle: Selfie Culture Needs to Find Purpose," *Florida Today*, published January 23, 2018, accessed October 5, 2019, https://www.floridatoday.com/story/life/wellness/2018/01/23/ronsisvalle-selfie-culture-needs-find-purpose/1057425001/.

[102] Socrates, "Socrates Quotes," *Goodreads*, updated 2020, accessed December 1, 2020, https://www.goodreads.com/quotes/63219-the-children-now-love-luxury-they-have-bad-manners-contempt.

[103] Zakaria, "Examining Free Speech Suppression on American College Campuses," *CNN Transcripts*, aired September 9, 2018, accessed Fareed October 5, 2019,

http://transcripts.cnn.com/TRANSCRIPTS/1809/09/fzgps.01.html.

104 Greg Lukianoff and Jonathan Haidt, "The Coddling of the American Mind: How Good Intentions and Bad Ideas Are Setting Up a Generation for Failure," *The Coddling*, accessed October 5, 2019, https://www.thecoddling.com/.

105 Lukianoff and Haidt, *The Coddling of the American Mind.*

106 Joann Black, "Coddled Kids: How 'Safetyism' Created an Epidemic of Anxiety and Fragility," *NZ Listener*, published January 22, 2019, accessed October 5, 2019, https://www.noted.co.nz/currently/currently-social-issues/coddled-generation-safetyism-created-epidemic-anxiety-fragility.

107 Lukianoff and Haidt, *The Coddling of the American Mind.*

108 Glenn C. Altschuler, "Coddling of the American Mind: Parents Raising Children to be Fragile," *The Philadelphia Inquirer*, published September 28, 2018, accessed October 6, 2019, https://www.inquirer.com/philly/entertainment/arts/coddling-of-the-american-mind-parents-raising-children-to-be-fragile-

20180928.html.

109 "Media Violence," *American Academy of Pediatrics News & Journals* 124, no. 5 (November 2009), accessed October 6, 2019, https://pediatrics.aappublications.org/content/124/5/1495.

110 Cris Rowan, "Ten Reasons Why Handheld Devices Should Be Banned for Children under the Age of 12," *HuffPost*, updated December 6, 2017, accessed July 15, 2020, https://www.huffpost.com/entry/10-reasons-why-handheld-devices-should-be-banned_b_4899218.

111 Cris Rowan, "Ten Reasons Why Children under the Age of Twelve Should Not Play Violent Video Games," *Moving to Learn*, published July 31, 2018, accessed October 6, 2019, http://movingtolearn.ca/2018/ten-reasons-why-children-under-the-age-of-12-should-not-play-violent-video-games.

112 "Deloitte: Global Mobile Consumer Survey," *Deloitte*, published 2019, accessed October 6, 2019, https://www2.deloitte.com/us/en/pages/technology-media-and-telecommunications/articles/global-mobile-consumer-survey-us-edition.html.

113 Serenitie Wang and Katie Hunt, "Why 'Tents of Love' Are Popping Up in Chinese Colleges," *CNN*, published

September 12, 2016, accessed October 10, 2019, https://www.cnn.com/2016/09/12/asia/china-college-parents-tents-of-love/index.html.

[114] Bill Chappell and Merit Kennedy, "US Charges Dozens of Parents, Coaches in Massive College Admissions Scandal," *NPR*, published March 12, 2019, accessed October 10, 2019, https://www.npr.org/2019/03/12/702539140/u-s-accuses-actresses-others-of-fraud-in-wide-college-admissions-scandal.

[115] Trent Hamm, "Breaking Away From Financial Dependence on Your Parents," *The Simple Dollar*, updated July 17, 2019, accessed October 12, 2019, https://www.thesimpledollar.com/breaking-away-from-financial-dependence-on-your-parents/.

[116] Alfie Kohn, "Why Incentive Plans Cannot Work," *Harvard Business Review*, published online September – October 1993, accessed October 12, 2019, https://hbr.org/1993/09/why-incentive-plans-cannot-work.

[117] Vanessa LoBue, Ph.D., "Violent Media and Aggressive Behavior in Children: Does Watching Violence on TV, in the Movies, or Video Games Promote Aggression?," *Psychology Today*, posted January 8, 2018, accessed October 12, 2019, https://www.psychologytoday.com/us/blog/the-baby-

scientist/201801/violent-m%C3%A9dia-and-aggressive-behavior-in-children.

[118] Michele Ybarra, MPH, Ph.D., "Is Sex in the Media Related to Sexual Behavior Among Teens?," Psychology Today, posted on June 28, 2016, accessed October12,2019 https://www.psychologytoday.com/us/blog/connected/201606/is-sex-in-the-media-related-sexual-behavior-among teens.

[119]https://www.bobdesautels.com/blog/2019/2/28/the-great-revolution-of-our-generation-is-the-discovery-that-human-beings-by-changing-the-inner-attitudes-of-their-minds-can-change-the-outer-aspects-of-their-lives-william-james#:~:text=3%20BlogsContact, accessed December 6, 2020.

Problems in Society Today: Do-gooders, Parenting & Discipline

[120] Cameron Jenkins and Lulu Garcia-Navarro, "The American Academy of Pediatrics on Spanking Children: Don't Do It, Ever," NPR, published November 11, 2018, accessed October 13, 2019, https://www.npr.org/2018/11/11/666646403/the-american-academy-of-pediatrics-on-spanking-children-dont-do-it-ever.

Problems in Society Today: Teachers & Student Discipline

Problems in Society Today: Disruptive College Campuses

[121] Lukianoff and Haidt, The Coddling of the American Mind.

[122] Park and Kyung Lah, "Berkeley Protests of Yiannopoulos Caused $100,000 in Damage," CNN, published Madison February 2, 2017, accessed October 15, 2017, https://www.cnn.com/2017/02/01/us/milo-yiannopoulos-berkeley/index.html.

Problems in Society Today: Difficult Working Conditions & Teacher Shortages

[123] Boyce, "The Teacher Shortage Is Real, and about to Get Much Worse," FEE (Foundation for Economic Education), published September 19, 2019, Paul accessed October 15, 2019 https://fee.org/articles/the-teacher-shortage-is-real-and-about-to-get-much-worse-heres-why/.

[124] Lauren Camera, "The Teacher Shortage Crisis Is Here," US News, published September 14, 2016, accessed October 15, 2019,

https://www.usnews.com/news/articles/2016-09-14/the-teacher-shortage-crisis-is-here.

[125] Lauren Camera, "The Teacher Shortage Crisis Is Here."

[126] Lauren Camera, "The Teacher Shortage Crisis Is Here."

Problems in Society Today: School Discipline & No-tolerance Policy

[127] Derek Black, "Georgia Supreme Court Places Limit on Zero Tolerance Discipline," Law Professor Blog Network, published September 5, 2017, accessed October 18, 2019, https://lawprofessors.typepad.com/education_law/2017/09/georgia-supreme-court-strikes-down-schools-zero-tolerancediscipline.html#:~:text=Georgia.

[128] Child Trends and EMT Associates, Inc., "Georgia Compilation of School Discipline Laws and Regulations," Safe Supportive Learning, U.S. Department of Education, published January 31, 2020, accessed February 2, 2020, https://safesupportivelearning.ed.gov/sites/default/files/disciplinecompendium/Georgia%20School%20Discipline%20Laws%20and%20Regulations.pdf.

[129] Pascal D. Forgione, Jr., Ph.D., "Zero Tolerance Policy," National Center for Education Statistics, published March 18, 1998, accessed October 18, 2019, https://nces.ed.gov/pressrelease/violence.asp.

Problems in Society Today: Nikolas Cruz, the High School Shooter from Parkland, Florida

[130] "Stoneman Douglas High School Shooting," Wikipedia, updated October 18, 2019, accessed October 18, 2019, https://en.wikipedia.org/wiki/Stoneman_Douglas_High_School _shooting.

[131] "Baker Act," University of Florida Health, updated October 18, 2019, accessed October 18, 2019, https:// ufhealth.org/baker-act.

[132] Brittany Wallman and Paula McMahon, "Here's What Broward Schools Knew About Parkland Shooter – Details Revealed by Mistake," South Florida Sun Sentinel, published August 3, 2018, accessed October 18, 2019, https://www.sunsentinel.com/local/broward/parkland/florida-school-shooting/fl-florida-school-shooting-consultant-report-full-20180803-story.html.

Problems in Society Today: Mental Health Issues & Young Adults

[133] Amanda Jackson, "A Judge Sides with Parents and Rules Their 30-Year-Old Son Must Move Out," CNN, published May 23, 2018, accessed October 19, 2019, https://www.cnn.com/2018/05/22/us/judge-rules-son-must-move-out-new-york-trnd/index.html.

Problems in Society Today: Gun Violence vs. Gun Control

[134] Giffords Law Center, "Waiting Periods," *Giffords Law Center to Prevent Gun Violence*, published 2018, updated 2019, accessed October 19, 2019, https://lawcenter.giffords.org/gun-laws/policy-areas/gun-sales/waiting-periods/.

[135] Dr. Mike Ronsisvalle, "Response to the South Florida School Shooting," *Florida Counseling Centers*, published February 26, 2018, accessed October 20, 2019, http://www.floridacounselingcenters.com/2018/02/26/response-to-the-south-florida-school-shooting/.

[136] Eric Levenson, Elise Hammond and Veronica Rocha, "CNN Hosts a Town Hall on Gun Violence," *CNN*, published August 7, 2019, accessed October 20, 2019,

https://www.cnn.com/us/live-news/cnn-town-hall-guns-august-2019/index.html.

[137] Faith Karimi and Allen Kim, "Texas Loosend Firearm Laws Hours After the State's Latest Mass Shooting Left Seven Dead," *CNN*, published September 1, 2019, accessed October 20, 2019, https://www.cnn.com/2019/09/01/us/texas-new-gun-laws-trnd/index.html.

Problems in Society Today: Corporate Greed vs. Worker & Consumer Benefits

[138] Adam Hayes, "Golden Parachute," *Investopedia*, updated August 13, 2019, accessed October 20,2019,https://www.investopedia.com/terms/g/goldenparachute.asp.

[139] Jeffrey Sonnenfeld, "Why Bob Iger Deserves His $66 Million Pay Package," *Fortune*, published May 4, 2019, accessed October 24, 2019, https://fortune.com/2019/05/04/bob-iger-abigail-disney-stock.

[140] Disneyland Corporation, "Theme Park Tickets," *Disneyland*, published September 26, 2019, accessed October 24, 2019, https://disneyland.disney.go.com/tickets/.

[141] Steven Greenhouse, "American Unions Have Been Decimated. No Wonder Inequality Is Booming." *The Guardian*, published August 15, 2019, accessed October 25, 2019, https://www.theguardian.com/commentisfree/2019/aug/15/valuing-corporations-over-workers-has-led-to-americas-income-inequality-problem.

[142] Justin Fox, "A Brief History of Co-determination, Which Elizabeth Warren Now Wants to Bring to the U.S. Corporations," *Bloomberg*, published August 24, 2018, accessed October 25, 2019, https://www.bloomberg.com/opinion/articles/2018-08-24/why-german-corporate-boards-include-workers-for-co-determination.

[143] Worker Participation-EU, "Board Level Representation," *ETUI (European Trade Union Institute)*, published 2016, accessed October 25, 2019, http://www.worker-participation.eu/National-Industrial-Relations/Countries/Germany/Board-level-Representation.

Problems in Society Today: Financial Crisis of Student Debt

[144] Zack Friedman, "Student Loan Debt Statistics in 2019: A $1.5 Trillion Crisis," *Forbes*, published February 25, 2019, accessed October 24, 2019,

https://www.forbes.com/sites/zackfriedman/2019/02/25/student-loan-debt-statistics-2019/#a576814133fb.

145 Richard J. Murphy, Judith Scott-Clayton and Gillian Wyness, "Lessons from Free College in England," *Brookings*, published April 27, 2017, accessed October 25, 2019, https://www.brookings.edu/research/lessons-from- the-end-of-free-college-in-england/.

146 Jessica Dickler, "Tuition-free College is Now a Reality in Nearly Twenty States," *CNBC*, published March 12, 2019, updated September 5, 2019, accessed October 25, 2019, https://www.cnbc.com/2019/03/12/free-college-now-a-reality-in-these-states.html.

147 Kaplan, "What is the Real Cost of Medical School?," *Kaplan*, published September 26, 2019, accessed October 25, 2019, https://www.kaptest.com/study/mcat/whats-the-real-cost-of-medical-school/.

148 Katie Lobosco, "Why Colleges with Big Endowments Still Charge Tuition," *Money.CNN*, published November 4, 2016, accessed May 25, 2020, https://money.cnn.com/2016/11/04/pf/college/endowments-financial-aid/index.html.

[149] Katie Lobosco, "Why Colleges with Big Endowments Still Charge Tuition."

[150] Katie Lobosco, "Why Colleges with Big Endowments Still Charge Tuition".

[151] Sarah Chamberlain, "Addressing the Skilled Labor Shortage in America," *Forbes*, published August 21, 2019, accessed July 29, 2020, https://www.forbes.com/sites/sarahchamberlain/2019/08/21/addressing-the-skilled-labor-shortage-in-america/?sh=4de92b7d181d.

[152] Emily Cochrane, "Bernie Sanders Unveils Education Plan to Eliminate Student Loan Debt," *The New York Times*, published June 24, 2019, accessed October 25, 2019, https://www.nytimes.com/2019/06/24/us/politics/bernie-sanders-student-debt.html.

Problems in Society Today: Misplaced Societal Values

[153] Annie Pei, "The Fortnite World Cup Has Kicked Off in New York City, and a $30 Million Prize Pool Is on the Line," *CNBC*, published July 27, 2019, accessed October 29, 2019, https://www.cnbc.com/2019/07/26/fortnites-30-million-world-cup-kicks-off.html.

154 Alex Fitzpatrick, "Here Are All the 2019 Nobel Prize Winners," *Time*, published October 14, 2019, accessed October 29, 2019, https://time.com/5694094/nobel-prize-winners-2019/.

155 Spotrac, "NFL Salary Rankings," *Spotrac*, published 2020, accessed October 29, 2020, https://www.spotrac.com/nfl/rankings/cash/.

Problems in Society Today: Climate Change & Our Responsibility to the Planet

156 OpenMind. "Svante Arrhenius, the Man Who Foresaw Climate Change," *OpenMind*, published February 19, 2019, accessed October 29, 2019, https://www.bbvaopenmind.com/en/science/leading-figures/svante-arrhenius-the-man-who-foresaw-climate-change/.

157 OpenMind, "Svante Arrhenius, the Man Who Foresaw Climate Change."

158 OpenMind, "Svante Arrhenius, the Man Who Foresaw Climate Change."

159 CBS News, "Newspaper Clipping from 1912 Mentions Link between Burning Coal and a Warmer Planet," *CBS News*, published August 14, 2018, accessed October 29,

2019, https://www.cbsnews.com/news/newspaper-clipping-from-1912-mentions-link-between-burning-coal-and-a-warmer-planet.

[160] Wikipedia, "Effect of Global Warming on Humans," *Wikipedia*, updated October 24, 2019, accessed October 29, 2019, https://en.m.wikipedia.org/wiki/Effects_of_global_warming_on_humans.

[161] Jeff Brady, "Teen Climate Activist Greta Thunberg Arrives in New York after Sailing the Atlantic," *NPR*, published August 28, 2019, accessed October 30, 2019, https://www.npr.org/2019/08/28/754818342/teen-climate-activist-greta-thunberg-arrives-in-new-york-after-sailing-the-atlan.

[162] Somini Sengupta and Lisa Friedman, "At U.N. Climate Summit, Few Commitments and U.S. Silence," *New York Times*, published September 24, 2019, accessed October 30, 2019, https://www.nytimes.com/2019/09/23/climate/climate-summit-global-warming.html.

[163] Wikipedia, "Greta Thunberg," *Wikipedia*, updated November 1, 2019, accessed November 2, 2019, https://en.wikipedia.org/wiki/Greta_Thunberg.

164 Stephen Leahy, "By 2050, Many U.S. Cities Will Have Weather Like They've Never Seen," *National Geographic*, published July 10, 2019, accessed October 30, 2019, https://www.nationalgeographic.com/environment/2019/07/maj or-us-cities-will-face-unprecedente-climates-2050/.

165 Christina Nunez, "Climate 101: Deforestation," *National Geographic*, published February 7, 2019, accessed October 30, 2019, https://www.nationalgeographic.com/environment/global-warming/deforestation/.

166 Leslie Taylor, "Rainforest Facts – The Disappearing Rainforests," Raintree, updated 2019, accessed October 30, 2019, http://www.rain-tree.com/facts.htm.

167 Reuters Staff, "Deforestation in Brazil's Amazon Surges, Bolsonaro Readies Troops," *Reuters,* published May 8, 2020, accessed July 29, 2020, https://www.reuters.com/article/us-brazil-environment/deforestation-in-brazils-amazon-surges-bolsonaro-readies-troops-idUSKBN22K1U1.

168 Francesco Bessetti, "Sir David Attenborough Gives us the Facts on Climate Change," *Foresight, the CMCC Observatory on Climate Policies and Futures*, published May

2019, accessed November 2, 2019, https://www.climateforesight.eu/future-hearth/sir-david-attenborough-gives-us-the-facts-on-climate-change/.

[169] Francesco Bessetti, "Sir David Attenborough Gives us the Facts on Climate Change."

Problems in Society Today: Looking Back Instead of Moving Forward

[170] History Editors, "Slavery in America," *History*, updated 2020, accessed July 19, 2020, https://www.history.com/topics/black-history/slavery.

[171] Tim Pulliam, "Why This Descendant of Slaves Says He Is Against Reparations," *abc11*, published August 1, 2019, accessed July 30, 2020, https://abc11.com/reparations-definition-bill-slavery/5433156/.

Solutions: Mentoring Our Children

[172] David Boroff, "Stepmother, Daughter Busted for Beating Woman during Road Rage Incident Caught on Video: 'It was the Longest Red Light of My Life,'" *New York Daily News*, published September 22, 2017, accessed November 5, 2019,

https://www.nydailynews.com/news/crime/mother-daughter-busted-road-rage-incident-caught- video-article-1.3513819.

Solutions: Anger Management

173 Barack Obama, "Obama Quotes," *AZ Quotes*, updated 2020, accessed December 1, 2020, https://www.azquotes.com/author/11023-Barack_Obama/tag/passion.

174 Kate Conger and Nicholas Bogel-Burroughs, "Fact Check: How Violent Are the Portland Protests," *New York Times*, published July 28, 2020, accessed August 23, 2020, https://www.nytimes.com/2020/07/28/us/portland-protests-fact-check.html.

175 Lauren Dake and Rebecca Ellis, "As Portland's Mayor faces Calls to Resign, He Find an Unlikely Ally," *OPB*, published June 15, 2020, accessed September 18, 2020, https://www.opb.org/news/article/portland-oregon-mayor-ted-wheeler-jo-ann-hardesty/·

176 "Reno Friends Quaker Meeting: Silent Protests vs. Speaking Our Truth," *Renofriends*, published September 28, 2020, accessed September 30, 2020, https://www.renofriends.org/silent-protest-vs-speaking-our-truth/.

[177] Julie Bort, "George Floyd's GoFundMe Accounts Have Raised over $13.7 Million for His Family…and Still Counting," *MSN*, published June 8, 2020, accessed July 18, 2020 https://www.msn.com/en-us/money/personalfinance/george-floyd-s-gofundme-accounts-have-raised-over-13-7-million-for-his-family-and-counting/ar-BB14TCc4.

[178] Doug Smith et al., "Two L.A. County Sheriff's Deputies Shot in 'Ambush' Attack Recovering after Surgery," *Los Angeles Times*, updated September 13, 2020, accessed September 14, 2020, https://www.latimes.com/california/story/2020-09-12/l-a-sheriffs-deputy-shot-in-compton-near-blue-line-station.

[179] David Lubetzky, "David Lubetzky Quotes," *9 Quotes*, updated 2020, accessed December 1, 2020, https://www.9quotes.com/quote/daniel-lubetzky-651762.

[180] Reverend Martin Luther King, Jr., "King's March 8, 1956 Speech in Selma, Alabama," *Endnotes*, updated 2020, accessed September 15, 2020, https://www.enotes.com/homework-help/our-lives-begin-end-day-we-become-silent-about-343191.

[181] ***Author Unknown,*** Unable to locate source of quote.

[182] Simon Briggs and Charlie Eccleshare, "Serena Williams Unleashes Furious Rant at Umpire as She Loses U.S. Open Final to Naomi Osaka," *The Telegraph UK*, published September 9, 2018, accessed November 5, 2019, https://www.telegraph.co.uk/tennis/2018/09/08/serena-williams-vs-naomi-osaka-us-open-2018-final-live-score/.

[183] Simon Briggs and Charlie Eccleshare, "Serena Williams Unleashes Furious Rant at Umpire as She Loses U.S. Open Final to Naomi Osaka."

Solutions: Teaching Respect & Dignity

[184] Michael Lewis, "Joining the Military after High School – Benefits and Risks," *Money Crashers*, updated 2019, accessed November 5, 2019, https://www.moneycrashers.com/joining-military-benefits-risks/.

[185] Tammy Duckworth Senate Office, "Duckworth Joins Reed, Coons, Larson & Colleagues in Introducing Bill to Expand and Promote Opportunities for National Service," *Tammy Duckworth Senate Office*, published April 3, 2019, accessed November 5, 2019, https://www.duckworth.senate.gov/news/press-releases/duckworth-joins-reed-coons-larson-and-colleagues-in-

introducing-bill-to-expand-and-promote-opportunities-for-national-service.

[186] Tammy Duckworth Senate Office, "Duckworth Joins Reed, Coons, Larson & Colleagues in Introducing Bill to Expand and Promote Opportunities for National Service."

Solutions: Understanding Religious Controversies

[187] Alissa Zhu, "Megachurch Pastor Tells Church to Stop Going to Yoga Because of Its Demonic Roots," *Springfield News*, published November 12, 2018, updated November 13, 2018, accessed November 5, 2019, https://www.king5.com/article/news/nation-now/megachurch-pastor-tells-church-to-stop-going-to-yoga-because-of-its-demonic-roots/.

[188] Dr. Ishwar V. Basavaraddi, "Yoga: Its Origin, History and Development," *Ministry of External Affairs, Government of India*, published April 23, 2015, accessed November 5, 2019, https://mea.gov.in/in-focus-article.htm?25096/Yoga+Its+Origin+History+and+Development.

[189] Dr. Thomas G. Plante, "Separating Facts from Clergy Abuse from Fiction," *Illuminate of Santa Clara University*, published August 30, 2018, accessed November 7, 2019,

https://www.scu.edu/illuminate/thought- leaders/thomas-plante/separating-facts-about-clergy-abuse-from-fiction.html.

[190] ThoughtCo., "Understanding Celibacy," *ThoughtCo.*, published 2019, accessed November 7, 2019, https://www.thoughtco.com/celibacy-abstinence-chastity-difference-4156422.

[191] Barbara Latza Nadeau, "The Secret Sex Life of Nuns," *Daily Beast*, published May 15, 2019, accessed November 7, 2019, https://www.thedailybeast.com/the-secret-sex-lives-of-nuns.

[192] Francis X. Rocca, "Pope Opens Debate on Celibacy Requirement for Catholic Priests," *The Wall Street Journal*, published November 7, 2019, accessed November 7, 2019, https://www.wsj.com/articles/pope-opens-debate-on-celibacy-requirement-for-catholic-priests-11570352167.

[193] Barbara Latza Nadeau, "The Secret Sex Life of Nuns."

Solutions: Understanding Euthanasia

[194] World Population Review, "Right to Die States 2019," *World Population Review*, updated August 27, 2019, accessed November 8, 2019,

http://worldpopulationreview.com/states/right-to-die-states/.

[195] Joseph Shamie, "Assisted Suicide: Human Right or Homicide?," *Yale Global Online*, published August 9, 2018, accessed November 8, 2019, https://yaleglobal.yale.edu/content/assisted-suicide-human-right-or-homicide.

Solutions: Understanding a Woman's Right to Abortion

[196] Holly Yan, "These Six States Have Only 1 Abortion Clinic Left. Missouri Could Become the First with Zero,"*CNN*, published June 21, 2019, accessed November 8, 2019, https://www.cnn.com/2019/05/29/health/six-states- with-1-abortion-clinic-map-trnd/index.html.

[197] Anna North, "Missouri Could Lose Its Last Abortion Clinic. Its Fate Will Be Decided This Week," *Vox*, published October 28, 2019, accessed November 8, 2019, https://www.vox.com/identities/2019/10/28/20932235/planned-parenthood-missouri-abortion-clinic-roe-wade.

[198] Anna North, "Missouri Could Lose Its Last Abortion Clinic. Its Fate Will Be Decided This Week."

199 Darla Cameron and Kim Soffen, "For Every Woman in Political office, There Are Three Men," *The Washington Post*, updated February 7, 2018, accessed November 8, 2019, https://www.washingtonpost.com/graphics/2018/politics/wome n-running-for-office/.

200 Planned Parenthood, "What Are TRAP Laws?" *Planned Parenthood*, updated 2019, accessed November 8, 2019,https://www.plannedparenthoodaction.org/issues/abortion /trap-laws.

201 Center for Reproductive Rights, "Targeted Regulation of Abortion Providers (TRAP)," *Reproductive Rights*, published August 28, 2015, accessed November 9, 2019, https://reproductiverights.org/document/targeted-regulation-abortion-providers-trap.

202 Gretchen Livingston and Deja Thomas, "Why is the Teen Birth Rate Falling?" *Pew Research Center*, published August 2, 2019, accessed November 8, 2019, https://www.pewresearch.org/fact-tank/2019/08/02/why-is-the-teen-birth-rate-falling/.

203 Pew Research Center, "Millennials Less Likely to Be Married than Previous Generations at the Same Age," *Pew Research Center*, published February 13, 2019, accessed November 8, 2019,

https://www.pewsocialtrends.org/essay/millennial-life-how-young-adulthood-today-compares-with-prior-generations/psdt_02-14-19_generations-00-06/.

204 Reproductive Health Access Project, "Honoring Dr. Linda Prine," *Reproductive Health Access Project*, published October 18 2016, accessed November 10, 2019, https://www.reproductiveaccess.org/2016/10/honoring-dr-linda- prine-linda-prine-webthis-fall-linda-prine-our-medical-director-is-receiving-two-major-awards-that-recognize-her-achievements-as-a-teacher-mentor-and-advocate-on-october-31st/.

205 Wikipedia, "Dr. Linda Prine," *Wikipedia*, updated September 25, 2019, accessed November 10, 2019, https://en.wikipedia.org/wiki/Linda_Prine#Activism.

206 Louisiana Department of Health, "Women's Right to Know: Methods and Medical Risks of Abortion,"*Louisiana Department of Health*, published 2019, accessed November 10, 2019, http://ldh.la.gov/index.cfm/page/1036.

207 Harry McGee, "Day on Which Abortion Services Become Legal Described as 'Historic Day' for Ireland," *The Irish Times*, published January 2, 2019, accessed November 10, 2019,

https://www.irishtimes.com/news/politics/day-on-which-abortion-services-become-legal-described-as-historic-day-for-ireland-1.3745449.

[208] Anonymous, "Everyone makes mistakes...," *Pinterest*, updated 2020, accessed December 1, 2020, https://www.pinterest.com/pin/316940892500095871/?autologin=true

Solutions: Adoption

[209] U.S. Department of Health and Human Services, Administration for Children and Families, "Adoption and Foster Care Analysis and Reporting System (AFCARS)," *Administration for Children and Families,* published August 22, 2019, accessed November 10, 2019, https://www.acf.hhs.gov/sites/default/files/cb/afcarsreport26.pdf.

[210] U.S. Department, "Who Can Adodpt," U.S. Department of State, Bureau of Consular Affairs, updated September 12, 2018, accessed November 10, 2019, https://travel.state.gov/content/travel/en/Intercountry-Adoption/Adoption-Process/before-you-adopt/who-can-adopt.html.

211 American Adoptions, "Comparing the Costs of Domestic, International and Foster Care Adoption," *American Adoptions*, updated 2019, accessed November 10, 2019, https://www.americanadoptions.com/adopt/the_costs_of_adopti ng.

212 Advanced Fertility Center of Chicago, "Cost of Fertility Treatment for Women and Men – National Averages, Ranges, and Our Prices," *Advanced Fertility Center of Chicago*, updated 2019, accessed November 10, 2019,https://www.advancedfertility.com/fertility-treatment-costs.htm.

Solutions: Birth Control

213 Child Stats Government, "Number of Children (In Millions) Ages 0-17 in the United States by Age 2018, *ChildStats.Gov*, published 2018, accessed November 2019 https://www.childstats.gov/americaschildren/tables/pop1.asp.

214 Kaiser Family Foundation, "Medicaid's Role for Women, Who is Eligible for Coverage," Kaiser Family Foundation, published March 2019, accessed November 12, 2019, http://files.kff.org/attachment/Fact-Sheet-Medicaids-Role-for-Women.

215 Jenna Walls, Kathy Gifford, Usha Ranji and al., "Medicaid Coverage of Family Planning Benefits – Results from a State Survey," *Kaiser Family Foundation*, published September 15, 2016, accessed November 12, 2019, https://www.kff.org/report-section/medicaid-coverage-of-family-planning-benefits-results-from-a-state-survey-sterilization-procedures/.

Problems & Solutions: Overpopulation

216 Matt Rosenberg, "Current World Population and Future Projections," *ThoughtCo.*, published July 19, 2019, accessed November 12, 2019, https://www.thoughtco.com/current-world-population-1435270.

217 United Nations Department of Economics and Social Affairs, "Growing at a Slower Pace, World Population Is Expected to Reach 9.7 Billion in 2050 and Could Peak at 11 Billion around 2100," *United Nations*, published June 17, 2019, accessed September 4, 2020, https://www.un.org/development/desa/en/news/population/world-population-prospects-2019.html.

218 United Nations, "Shaping Our Future Together: Population," *United Nations*, published 2019, accessed November 15, 2019, https://www.un.org/en/sections/issues-depth/population/index.html.

[219] Wendy Connett, "Understanding China's Former One Child Policy," *Investopedia*, published July 7, 2019, accessed November 15, 2019, https://www.investopedia.com/articles/investing/120114/understanding-chinas-one-child-policy.asp.

[220] Stuart Gietel-Basten, Xuehui Han, and Yuan Cheng, *"Assessing the Impact of the 'One-Child Policy' in China: A Synthetic Control Approach," PloS ONE* 14 (11): 1-2. doi: 10.1371/jounal.pone.0220170.

[221] Stuart Gietel-Basten, Xuehui Han, and Yuan Cheng, *"Assessing the Impact of the 'One-Child Policy' in China: A Synthetic Control Approach,"* 3.

[222] Stuart Gietel-Basten, Xuehui Han, and Yuan Cheng, 3-4.

[223] Stuart Gietel-Basten, Xuehui Han, and Yuan Cheng, 4.

[224] Wendy Connett, "Understanding China's Former One Child Policy."

[225] Stephen Covey, "Moral Authority…," *Brainy Quote*, updated 2019, accessed November 15, 2019, https://www.brainyquote.com/topics/respect-quotes.

Child Development & Parenting

226 JoAnn Deak, PhD, "Children Need a Wide Variety of Learning Experiences to Develop Female and Male Gender-related Skills," *Living Better*, published November 23, 2019, accessed January 4, 2020, http://www.livingbetter.org/livingbetter/articles/gender.html.

227 Kristie Rivers, MD, FAAP, Board Certified Pediatrician, "Differences in Development Between Boys and Girls," *Bundoo*, reviewed January 2019, accessed January 4, 2020, https://www.bundoo.com/articles/differences-in-development-between-boys-and-girls/.

228 Enrico Gnaulati, "Why Girls Tend to Get Better Grades Than Boys Do," *The Atlantic*, published September 18, 2014, accessed January 4, 2020, https://www.theatlantic.com/education/archive/2014/09/why-girls-get-better-grades-than-boys-do/380318/

229 Mark Hugo Lopez and Ana Gonzalez-Barrera, "Women's College Enrollment Gains Leave Men Behind," *Pew Research Center*, published March 6, 2014, accessed January 4, 2020, https://www.pewresearch.org/fact-tank/2014/03/06/womens-college-enrollment-gains-leave-men-behind/.

[230] Mark Hugo Lopez and Ana Gonzalez-Barrera, "Women's College Enrollment Gains Leave Men Behind."

[231] Melissa Dahl, "7 Insights From Social Science on Raising a Boy," *The Cut*, published March 5, 2018, accessed January 12, 2020, https://www.thecut.com/2018/03/7-insights-from-social-science-on-raising-a-boy.html.

[232] JoAnn Deak, PhD, "Meet JoAnn Deak, PhD," *Kids in the House*, updated 2020, accessed January 12, 2020, https://www.kidsinthehouse.com/all-parents/experts/introductions/meet-joann-deak-phd.

[233] Rhaina Cohen, "Guys: We Have a Problem: How American Masculinity Creates Lonely Men," *NPR*, published October 14, 2019, accessed January 12, 2020, https://www.npr.org/2018/03/19/594719471/guys-we-have-a-problem-how-american-masculinity-creates-lonely-men.

[234] Peaceful Parent Institute, "Peaceful Parenting Basic Principles," *Peaceful Parenting*, updated 2020, accessed January 12, 2020, https://www.peacefulparent.com/peaceful-parenting-basic-principles/.

[235] Nancy Shute, "Tweeners Trust Kids More than Adults When Judging Risks," *NPR*, published March 31, 2015, accessed January 12, 2020, https://www.npr.org/sections/health-

shots/2015/03/31/395738320/tweeners-trust-peers-more-than-adults-when-judging-risks.

236 JoAnn Deak, PhD, "Meet JoAnn Deak, PhD."

237 Dorian Fortuna, PhD, "Male Aggression: Why Are Men More Violent?" *Psychology Today*, published September 22, 2014, accessed January 20, 2020, https://www.psychologytoday.com/us/blog/homo-aggressivus/201409/male-aggression.

238 Michael Reichert, PhD, "How to Raise Boys to Become Good Men," *Dr. Robyn Silverman Podcast*, published 2017, accessed January 12, 2020, https://drrobynsilverman.com/how-to-raise-boys-to-become-good-men-with-michael-reichert-phd/.

239 Will Leitch, "How to Raise a Boy – I'm Not Sure What to Think About What My Dad Tried to Teach Me. So, What Should I Teach My Sons?" *The Cut*, published March 5, 2018, accessed January 12, 2020, https://www.thecut.com/2018/03/will-leitch-on-raising-sons-in-2018.html.

240 Kathryn Shulten, "What Does It Take to Be a Real Man?" *The Learning Network*, published September 10, 2015, accessed January 18, 2020,

https://learning.blogs.nytimes.com/2015/09/10/what-does-it-mean-to-be-a-real-man/.

[241] Kathryn Shulten, "What Does It Take to Be a Real Man?"

[242] Ibid.

[243] Ibid.

[244] Ibid.

[245] Ibid.

[246] Ibid.

[247] Ibid.

[248] Ibid.

Raising Boys & Girls: Gender Biases

[249] Laurie Abraham, "What I Learned from Being Raised as a Daughter Like a Son," The Cut, published March 8, 2018, accessed January 20, 2020, https://www.thecut.com/2018/03/what-i-learned-being-a-girl-raised-like-a-boy.html.

[250] Laurie Abraham, "What I Learned from Being Raised as a Daughter Like a Son."

[251] Lisa Collier Cool, "Surprising Differences Between the Male and Female Brains," Women's Brain Health, published April 4, 2013, accessed January 20, 2020, https://womensbrainhealth.org/think-twice/surprising-differences-between-the-male-female-brain.

[252] Lisa Collier Cool, "Surprising Differences Between the Male and Female Brains."

[253] Alison Cashin, "New Report Finds Young People Troubled by Romantic Relationships and Widespread Sexual Harassment," *Harvard University: Making Caring Common Project*, published May 17, 2017, accessed January 21,2020, https://mcc.gse.harvard.edu/whats-new/2018/8/26/press-release-the-talk.

[254] Alison Cashin, "New Report Finds Young People Troubled by Romantic Relationships and Widespread Sexual Harassment."

[255] Alison Cashin, "New Report Finds Young People Troubled by Romantic Relationships and Widespread Sexual Harassment."

How to Raise Confident Children

256 Jacquelyn Smith, "A Psychologist Says That Parents Should Do These 18 Things to Raise a More Confident Child," *Business Insider*, published November 9, 2016, accessed January 21, 2020, https://www.businessinsider.com/psychologist-explains-how-to-raise-a-more-confident-child-2016-11.

Last Thoughts to Ponder

257 John Naisbitt, "The most exciting breakthroughs of the 21st century…," *Quote Fancy*, published 2020, accessed May 25, 2020, https://quotefancy.com/quote/1340364/John-Naisbitt-The-most-exciting-breakthroughs-of-the-21st-century-will-not-occur-because.

258 Ralph Waldo Emerson, "Success," *Word Press*, updated 2020, accessed May 29, 2020, *Ralph Waldo Emerson Images,* https://ralphwaldoemersonimages.wordpress.com/emerson-ephemera/ success/.

The Coronavirus: COVID-19 Pandemic of 2020

259 John Hopkins Medical Center, "COVID-19 United States Cases by County Level Tracking Map," *John Hopkins*

Medical Center, updated daily, accessed August 8, 2020, https://www.google.com/search?q=COVID-.

260 Roosa Tikkanen and Melinda K. Abrams, "U.S. Health Care from a Global Perspective, 2019: Higher Spending, Worse Outcomes," *The Commonwealth Fund*, published January 30, 2020, accessed August 9, 2020, https://www.commonwealthfund.org/publications/issue-briefs/2020/jan/us-health-care-global-perspective-2019.

261 Centers for Disease Control and Prevention, "History of 1918 Flu Pandemic," *CDC*, updated March 21, 2018, accessed June 2, 2020, https://www.cdc.gov/flu/pandemic-resources/1918-commemoration/1918-pandemic- history.htm#.

262 Evan Andrews, "Why Was It Called the 'Spanish Flu?'," *History*, updated March 27, 2020, accessed June 2, 2020, https://www.history.com/news/why-was-it-called-the-spanish- flu#.

263 Dave Roos, "Why the Second Wave of the 1918 Spanish Flu Was So Deadly," *History*, updated April 29, 2020, accessed June 2, 2020, https://www.history.com/news/spanish-flu-second-wave-resurgence.

264 Paul Rogers, "Coronavirus: Bill Gates Predicted Pandemic in 2015," *The Mercury News*, published March 27,

2020, accessed June 4, 2020,
https://www.mercurynews.com/2020/03/25/coronavirus-bill-gates-predicted- pandemic-in-2015/.

[265] Dominic Rushe, "US Jobs Report: Record-breaking Streak Continues as 225,000 Added in January,"*Exec Review*, published February 7, 2020, accessed June 4, 2020, http://www.execreview.com/2020/02/us-jobs- report-record-breaking-streak-continues-as-225000-added-in-january.

[266] Dominic Rushe, "US Jobs Report: Record-breaking Streak Continues as 225,000 Added in January".

[267] Andrew Soergel, "1 in 4 Americans Has Lost Job or Income Due to Coronavirus," *US News*, published April 8, 2020, accessed June 4, 2020, https://www.usnews.com/news/economy/articles/2020-04-08/1-in-4-americans-has- lost-job-or-income-to-coronavirus-survey.

[268] Bureau of Labor Statistics (BLS), "News Release: The Employment Situation – March 2020," *Bureau of Labor Statistics*, published April 3, 2020, accessed June 4, 2020, https://www.bls.gov/news.release/archives/empsit_04032020.pdf.

269 Eric Morath and Sarah Chaney, "US Jobless Claims Top 20 Million Since Start of Shutdowns," *Wall Street Journal*, published April 16, 2020, accessed June 4, 2020, https://www.wsj.com/articles/u-s-unemployment-claims-likely-continued-at-record-levels-11587029401.

270 Bureau of Labor Statistics, "TED: The Economics Daily, Employment and Unemployment Summary for July 2020," *BLS*, updated July 2020, accessed August 8, 2020, https://www.bls.gov/opub/ted/2020/unemployment-rate-16-point-1-percent-in-massachusetts-4-point-5-percent-in-utah-in-july-2020.htm#.

271 Aaron Kandola, "Coronavirus Cause: Origin and How It Spreads," *Medical News Today*, published March 17, 2020, accessed June 4, 2020, https://www.medicalnewstoday.com/articles/coronavirus-causes.

272 Eliza Barclay, "The Conspiracy Theories About the Origins of the Coronavirus, Debunked," *VOX*, updated March 12, 2020, accessed June 4, 2020, https://www.vox.com/2020/3/4/21156607/how-did-the-coronavirus-get- started-china-wuhan-lab.

273 Robert Kuznia and Drew Griffin, "How Did Coronavirus Break Out? Theories Abound as Researchers Race

to Solve Genetic Detective Story," *News 4 Jax*, updated April 7, 2020, accessed June 4, 2020, https://www.news4jax.com/news/local/2020/04/07/how-did-coronavirus-break-out-theories-abound-as-researchers-race-to-solve-genetic-detective-story/.

274 James Griffiths and Steven Jiang, "Wuhan Officials Have Revised the City's Coronavirus Death Toll Up by 50%," *CNN*, updated April 17, 2020, accessed June 4, 2020, https://www.cnn.com/2020/04/17/asia/china-wuhan-coronavirus-death-toll-intl-hnk/index.html.

275 Nectar Gan, Caitlin Hu, and Ivan Watson, "Beijing Tightens Grip Over Coronavirus Research: Amid US-China Row on Virus Origin," *CNN*, updated April 16, 2020, accessed June 6, 2020, https://www.cnn.com/2020/04/12/asia/china-coronavirus-research-restrictions-intl-hnk/index.html.

276 Robert Farley, "The Facts on Trump's Travel Restrictions," *Fact Check*, published March 6, 2020, accessed June 6, 2020, https://www.factcheck.org/2020/03/the-facts-on-trumps-travel-restrictions/.

277 Sarah Moon, "A Seemingly Healthy Woman's Sudden Death Is Now the First Known US Coronavirus Fatality," *CNN*, published April 24, 2020, accessed June 6, 2020,

https://www.cnn.com/2020/04/23/us/california-woman-first-coronavirus-death/index.html.

278 Jamie Ducharme, "The World Health Organization Declares COVID-19 a 'Pandemic.' Here's What That Means," *TIME*, published March 11, 2020, accessed June 7, 2020, https://time.com/5791661/who-coronavirus-pandemic-declaration/.

279 The New York Times, "White House Projects Grim Toll from Coronavirus," *The New York Times*, updated April 7, 2020, accessed June 7, 2020, https://www.nytimes.com/2020/03/31/world/coronavirus-live-news-updates.html.

280 Stephanie Hegarty, "The Chinese Doctor Who Tried to Warn Others About Coronavirus," *BBC*, published February 6, 2020, accessed June 6, 2020, https://www.bbc.com/news/world-asia-china-51364382.

281 Jennifer Couzin-Frankel, "From 'Brain Fog' to Heart Damage, COVID-19's Lingering Problems Alarm Scientists," *Science Magazine*, published July 31, 2020, accessed August 15, 2020, https://www.sciencemag.org/news/2020/07/brain-fog-heart-damage-covid-19-s-lingering-problems-alarm-scientists.

[282] Brianna Sacks, "COVID Is Making Younger, Healthy People Debilitatingly Sick for Months. Now They are Fighting for Recognition," *BuzzFeed News*, published August 21, 2020 accessed August 22, 2020, https://www.buzzfeednews.com/article/briannasacks/covid-long-haulers-who-coronavirus.

[283] Bing.com, "COVID-19 Tracker," *Bing,* updated April 15, 2020, accessed June 6, 2020, https://www.bing.com/covid/local/unitedstates.

[284] Jennifer Nessel, "CDC: 2018-2019: Flu Season the Longest in a Decade*,"* *Pharmacy Times*, published June 30, 2019, accessed June 6, 2020, https://www.pharmacytimes.com/resource-centers/flu/cdc-20182019-flu-season- the-longest-in-a-decade.

[285] Alex Abad-Santos, "Performative Masculinity Is Making American Men Sick," *VOX*, published August 10, 2020, accessed August 15, 2020, https://www.vox.com/the-goods/21356150/american-men-wont-wear-masks-covid-19.

[286] Christie Aschwanden, "How 'Superspreading' Events Drive Most COVID-19 Spread," *Scientific American*, published June 23, 2020, accessed August 15, 2020, https://www.scientificamerican.com/article/how-superspreading-events-drive-most-covid-19-spread1/.

287 Christina Maxouris, "Large Gatherings Are Fueling Rising Covid-19 Cases, but They Keep Happening," *CNN*, published July 29, 2020 accessed August 15, 2020, https://www.cnn.com/2020/07/29/us/coronavirus-americans-gatherings/index.html.

288 Caitlin O'Kane, "More Than 100 Coronavirus Cases in 8 States Linked to Massive Sturgis Motorcycle Rally in North Dakota," *CBS News*, published August 26, 2020, accessed August 26, 2020, https://www.cbsnews.com/news/coronavirus-sturgis-motorcycle-rally-south-dakota-over-100-cases-8-states/.

289 Emma Whitford, "August Wave of Campus Reopening Reversals," *Inside Higher Ed*, published August 12, 2020, accessed August 16, 2020, https://www.insidehighered.com/news/2020/08/12/colleges-walk-back-fall-reopening-plans-and-opt-online-only-instruction.

290 Matthias Gafni, "They Defied Health Rules for a San Francisco Wedding. The Virus Didn't Spare Them," San Francisco Chronicle, published July 26, 2020, updated: July 28, 2020, accessed August 16, 2020, https://www.sfchronicle.com/bayarea/article/They-defied-health-rules-for-a-storybook-San-15434220.php.

[291] Lauren Edmonds, "Divorce Rates Soar in America by 34% During the COVID-19 Pandemic with Marriages Crumbling Three Weeks into Quarantine and Newlywed Separations Doubling to 20%," Daily Mail Co. UK, published August 28, 2020, accessed August 30, 2020, https://www.dailymail.co.uk/news/article-8674001/Divorce-rates-America-soar-34-percent-COVID-19-pandemic.html.

[292] Reese Dunklin and Michael Rezendes, "AP: Catholic Church Lobbied for Taxpayer Funds, Got $1.4B," AP, published July 10, 2020, accessed September 14, 2020, https://apnews.com/article/dab8261c68c93f24c0bfc1876518b3f6.

[293] Christie Aschwanden, "How 'Superspreading' Events Drive Most COVID-19 Spread."

[294] Alana Abramson, "Democrats Pushed for Robust Oversight of $2.2 Trillion Aid Package. It Hasn't Happened Yet," TIME, published April 17, 2020 accessed August 17, 2020, https://time.com/5823510/coronavirus-stimulus-oversight/.

[295] July 15, 2020 Alexander Bolton, "Battle Brewing on Coronavirus Relief Oversight," The Hill, published July 15, 2020,accessed September 14, 2020,

https://thehill.com/homenews/senate/507380-battle-brewing-on-coronavirus-relief-oversight.

296 Peter Whoriskey et al., "Public Companies receive $1 Billion in Stimulus Funds Meant for Small Business," Seattle Times, originally published in The Washington Post, published May 1, 2020, accessed August 14, 2020, https://www.seattletimes.com/business/public-companies-received-1-billion-in-stimulus-funds-meant-for-small-businesses/.

297 Peter Whoriskey et al., "Public Companies receive $1 Billion in Stimulus Funds Meant for Small Business".

298 Alicia Wallace, "Walmart CEO Says We're in the Hair Color Phase of Panic Buying," CNN, published April 11, 2020, accessed June 7, 2020, https://www.cnn.com/2020/04/11/business/panic-buying-walmart-hair-color- coronavirus/index.html.

299 Daniella Diaz, Geneva Sands, and Cristina Alesci, "Protective Equipment Costs Increase Over 1000% Amid Competition and Surge in Demand," CNN, published April 16, 2020, accessed June 7, 2020, https://www.cnn.com/2020/04/16/politics/ppe-price-costs-rising-economy-personal-protective-equipment/index.html.

[300] Daniella Diaz, Geneva Sands, and Cristina Alesci, "Protective Equipment Costs Increase Over 1000% Amid Competition and Surge in Demand," CNN, published April 16, 2020, accessed June 7, 2020, https://www.cnn.com/2020/04/16/politics/ppe-price-costs-rising-economy-personal-protective-equipment/index.html.

[301] Brian P. Dunleavy, "More Than 9K Health Workers Sickened with COVID-19," *UPI Health News*, published April 14, 2020, accessed June 7, 2020, https://www.upi.com/Health_News/2020/04/14/More-than-9K-health-workers-sickened-with-COVID-19/1181586890028/.

[302] Danielle Renwick and Shoshana Dubnow, "More Than 900 Healthcare Workers Have Died of COVID-19 and the Toll Is Rising," *The Guardian*, published August 11, 2020, accessed August 13, 2020, https://www.theguardian.com/us-news/2020/aug/11/covid-19-healthcare-workers-nearly-900-have died#.

[303] Russell Redman, "FCW: Over 11,500 Grocery Workers Affected in First 100 Days of Pandemic," Supermarket News, published June 26, 2020, accessed August 13, 2020, https://www.supermarketnews.com/issues-trends/ufcw-over-11500-grocery-workers-affected-first-100-days-pandemic.

304 Seema Mehta, "As Coronavirus Restriction Protests Take Place Across the US, Trump Defends Demonstrators,"*LA Times*, published April 18, 2020, accessed June 7, 2020, https://www.latimes.com/world-nation/story/ 2020-04-18/coronavirus-protests-texas-maryland-wisconsin-cuomo.

305 Seema Mehta, "As Coronavirus Restriction Protests Take Place Across the US, Trump Defends Demonstrators."

306 Stephanie Downs, "Jacksonville Beach Flooded with Visitors within Minutes of Reopening," *Pop Culture*, published April 18, 2020, accessed June 7, 2020, https://popculture.com/trending/news/jacksonville-beach-flooded- visitors-within-minutes-reopening.

307 Stephanie Downs, "Jacksonville Beach Flooded with Visitors within Minutes of Reopening."

308 Mark E. Czeislar et al., "Mental Health, Substance Use, and Suicidal Ideation During the COVID-19 Pandemic - United States, June 24-30, 2020," *Centers for Disease Control and Prevention: Morbidity and Mortality Weekly Report*, published August 14, 2020, accessed August 28, 2020, https://www.cdc.gov/mmwr/volumes/69/wr/mm6932a1.htm.

309 Jonathan Stevens, M.D., M.P.H., "Coping With Too Much Togetherness," *Psychology Today*, published April 13,

2020, accessed August 28, 2020,
https://www.psychologytoday.com/us/blog/mind-matters-menninger/202004/coping-too-much-togetherness.

[310] Center for Relationship and Sexual Wellness,
"Relationship Rescue Through the COVID-19 Pandemic,
Center for Relationship and Sexual Wellness, published April
13, 2020, accessed August 28, 2020,
https://relationshipandsexualwellness.com/blog/relationships-through-the-covid-19-pandemic.

[311] Iris Goldsztayn, "Why You Feel So Damn Tired
Working From Home," In Style, published April 8, 2020,
accessed June 24, 2020,
https://www.instyle.com/beauty/health-fitness/coronavirus-exhaustion-working-from-home.

[312] Rebecca Renner, "The Pandemic Is Giving People
Vivid, Unusual Dreams," National Geographic, published April
15, 2020, accessed June 24, 2020,
https://www.nationalgeographic.com/science/2020/04/coronavirus- pandemic-is-giving-people-vivid-unusual-dreams-here-is-why/.

[313] Paula Hancocks et al., "Recovered Coronavirus
Patients Are Testing Positive Again. Can You Get Reinfected?"
CNN Health, published April 18, 2020, accessed June 24, 2020,

https://www.cnn.com/2020/04/17/health/south-korea-coronavirus-retesting-positive-intl-hnk/index.html.

[314] Andrew Joseph, "Scientists Are Reporting Several Cases of Covid-19 Reinfection — but the Implications Are Complicated," *Stat News*, published August 28, 2020, accessed August 28, 2020, https://www.statnews.com/2020/08/28/covid-19-reinfection-implications/.

[315] BBC, "Coronavirus: Asian Nations Face Second Wave of Imported Cases, *BBC*, published March 19, 2020, accessed August 28, 2020, https://www.bbc.com/news/world-asia-51955931.

[316]Helen Regan et al., "Coronavirus News," *CNN*, published August 21, 2020, accessed August 28, 2020, https://www.cnn.com/world/live-news/coronavirus-pandemic-08-20-20-intl/h_4ddd94fd3e03d0b181664f94f9410ec4.

[317] The Hill Staff, "Selfless Acts: How Americans Are Helping Each Other Through the Coronavirus," *The Hill*, published March 24, 2020, accessed June 24, 2020, https://thehill.com/homenews/state-watch/489046-selfless-acts-how-americansa-are-helping-each-other-through-the-coronavirus.

318 Timothy Fanning, "'Win-Win:' Publix to Donate Extra Food, Milk It Buys From Struggling Farmers," *USA Today*, published April 23, 2020, accessed June 24, 2020, https://www.usatoday.com/story/money/ 2020/04/23/publix-support-florida-farmers-donate-produce-milk-food-banks/3016037001/.

319 Medea Giordano, "The Nonprofits and Companies Helping to Fight the Pandemic," *Wired*, published May 7, 2020, accessed June 24, 2020, https://www.wired.com/story/covid-19-charities-nonprofits-companies-helping/.

320 Meagan Flynn, "They Lived in a Factory for 28 Days to Make Millions of Pounds of Raw PPE Materials to Fight Coronavirus," *Washington Post*, published April 23, 2020, accessed June 24, 2020, https://www.washingtonpost.com/nation/2020/04/23/factory-masks-coronavirus-ppe/.

321 Katie Warren, "11 Mind-blowing Facts That Show Just How Wealthy Bill Gates Really Is," Business Insider, published May 14, 2019, accessed June 24, 2020, https://www.businessinsider.com/how-rich-is-bill-gates-net-worth- mind-blowing-facts-2019-5.

322 Rishi Iyengar, "MacKenzie Scott, Formerly Bezos, Says She Has Given Away $1.7 Billion of Her Wealth so Far," *CNN Business*, published July 28, 2020, accessed July 29, 2020, https://www.cnn.com/2020/07/28/tech/mackenzie-scott-bezos-donation/index.html.

323 Medea Giordano, "The Nonprofits and Companies Helping to Fight the Pandemic," *Wired*, published May 7, 2020, accessed June 24, 2020, https://www.wired.com/story/covid-19-charities-nonprofits-companies-helping/.

324 Judy Woodruff, "Asians Americans Report Rise in Racist Attacks Amid Pandemic, PBS, published April 1, 2020, accessed June 24, 2020, https://www.pbs.org/newshour/show/what-anti-asian-attacks-say-about-american-culture-during-crisis.

325 Terry Tang, "PBS 'Asian Americans' Explores Prejudice and Perseverance," *The Elwood City Ledger*, updated May 8, 2020, accessed June 24, 2020, https://www.ellwoodcityledger.com/ZZ/news/20200508/pbs-asian-americans-explores-prejudice-and-perseverance.

326 Cheryl Corley, "Some Stock Up on Guns and Ammunition During Coronavirus Crisis," *NPR*, published March 20, 2020, accessed June 24, 2020,

https://www.npr.org/2020/03/20/817369503/some-stock-up-on-guns-and- ammunition-during-coronavirus-crisis.

327 Matt Cortina, "Why Are Coloradans Stocking Up on Guns During the Pandemic?," *Boulder Weekly*, published April 9, 2020, accessed June 24, 2020, https://www.boulderweekly.com/news/taking-stock/.

328 Wikipedia, "List of Mass Shootings in the United States in 2020," *Wikipedia*, updated December 2, 2020, accessed December 3, 2020, https://en.wikipedia.org/wiki/List_of_mass_shootings_in_the_United_States_in_2020.

329 Ray Sanchez and Paula Newton, "Domestic Assault May Have Triggered Canadian Rampage That Left 22 Dead, Police Say," *CNN*, published April 24, 2020, accessed June 24, 2020, https://www.cnn.com/2020/04/24/americas/ nova-scotia-shooting-friday/index.html.

330 Lisa Lerer and Sidney Ember, "Examining Tara Reade's Sexual Assault Allegation Against Joe Biden," The New York Times, published May 22, 2020, accessed June 24, 2020, https://www.nytimes.com/2020/04/12/us/ politics/joe-biden-tara-reade-sexual-assault-complaint.html.

Repercussions from the Coronavirus - COVID-19 Pandemic of 2020

331 The art of living, accessed December7, 2020 https://sourcesofinsight.com/life-quotes/.

332 Robin Young, "Dr. Sanjay Gupta on the Battle Against Coronavirus: 'We Will Get Through It,'" *WBUR,* published May 21, 2020, accessed June 24, 2020, https://www.wbur.org/hereandnow/2020/05/21/dr-sanjay-gupta- coronavirus.

333 BBC, "Coronavirus: Countries Reject Chinese-made Equipment," *BBC News*, published March 30, 2020, accessed August 28, 2020, https://www.bbc.com/news/world-europe-52092395.

334 Sean Fleming, "Viet Nam Shows How You Can Contain COVID-19 with Limited Resources," *World Economic Forum,* published March 30, 2020, accessed June 24, 2020, https://www.weforum.org/agenda/2020/03/vietnam-contain-covid-19-limited-resources/.

335 James Griffiths, "Taiwan's Coronavirus Response Is Among the Best Globally," *CNN*, published April 5, 2020, accessed June 24, 2020,

https://www.cnn.com/2020/04/04/asia/taiwan-coronavirus-response-who-intl-hnk/index.html.

336 Tomas Chamorro-Premuzic, "Are Women Better at Managing the COVID-19 Pandemic?," *Forbes*, published April 10, 2020, accessed June 24, 2020, https://www.forbes.com/sites/tomaspremuzic/2020/04/10/are-female- leaders-better-at-managing-the-covid19-pandemic/#2035380828d4.

337 National Post Staff, "Don't Have Bread, Eat Crackers: Watch This Caribbean PM Chastise Citizens Who Are Not Social Distancing," *National Post*, published and aired April 9, 2020, accessed June 24, 2020, https://nationalpost.com/news/world/covid-19-social-distancing-sint-maarten-prime-minister.

338 Monika Evstatieva, "Elements of a Coronavirus Conspiracy Theory," *NPR*, published July 10, 2020, accessed August 14, 2020, https://www.npr.org/2020/07/10/889037310/anatomy-of-a-covid-19-conspiracy-theory.

339 Katherine Schaeffer, "25% in US See at Least Some Truth in Conspiracy Theory that COVID-19 Was Planned," *Pew Research Center*, published July 24, 2020, accessed August 14, 2020, https://www.pewresearch.org/fact-

tank/2020/07/24/a-look-at-the-americans-who-believe-there-is-some-truth-to-the-conspiracy-theory-that-covid-19-was-planned/.

340 Rachel Rettner, "COVID-19 Has Fueled More Than 2,000 Rumors and Conspiracy Theories, *Live Science*, published August 11, 2020, accessed August 14, 2020, https://www.livescience.com/covid-19-rumors-conspiracy-theories-infodemic.html.

341 Jane C. Hu, "No, 94% of Percent of COVID-19 Deaths Were Not Caused by Something Else," *Slate*, published September 1, 2020, accessed September 3, 2020, https://slate.com/technology/2020/09/94-percent-covid19-deaths-not-caused-by-something-else.html.

342The Conversation, "279,700 Deaths in the US so Far in This Pandemic Year," *The Conversation*, published October 14, 2020, accessed October 18, 2020, https://theconversation.com/279-700-extra-deaths-in-the-us-so-far-in-this-pandemic-year-147887.

343 Jamie Gangel et al., "'Play it down': Trump Admits to Concealing the True Threat of Coronavirus in New Woodward Book," *CNN Politics*, published September 9, 2020, accessed September 14, 2020,

https://www.cnn.com/2020/09/09/politics/bob-woodward-rage-book-trump-coronavirus/index.html.

344 Nick Valencia and Kristen Holmes, "Trump's HHS Alters CDC Documents for Political Reasons, Official Says,"CNN Politics, published September 12, 2020, accessed September 14, 2020, https://www.cnn.com/2020/09/12/politics/cdc-trump-science-reports/index.html.

345 Institute of Health Metrics and Evaluation, "New IMHE COVID-19 Forecasts See Nearly 300,000 Deaths by December 1," IMHE, published August 6, 2020, accessed September 16, 2020, http://www.healthdata.org/news-release/new-ihme-covid-19-forecasts-see-nearly-300000-deaths-december-1.

346 Christian Paz, "All the President's Lies About the Coronavirus," The Atlantic, published November 2, 2020, accessed November 4, 2020, https://www.theatlantic.com/politics/archive/2020/11/trumps-lies-about-coronavirus/608647/.

347 VOX Staff, "The Legacy of the Pandemic: 11 Ways It Will Change the Way We Live," VOX, published April 22, 2020, accessed June 24, 2020,

https://www.vox.com/the-
highlight/2020/4/16/21213635/coronavirus-covid-19-
pandemic-legacy-quarantine-state-of-mind-frugality.

348 Shannon Bond, "Twitter, Facebook, Remove Trump
Post Over False Claim About Children and COVID-19," *NPR*,
published August 5, 2020, accessed August 16, 2020,
https://www.npr.org/2020/08/05/899558311/facebook-
removes-trump-post-over-false-claim-about-children-and-
covid-19.

349 Molly Hensley et al., "The Truth Behind a Viral
Picture of a Reopening School Is Worse Than It Looked," *Buzz
Feed*, published August 5, 2020, accessed August 18,
https://flipboard.com/@Buzzfeed/the-truth-behind-a-viral-
picture-of-a-reopening-school-is-worse-than-it-looked/a-
elJgxTNyQFm8xliVlPzufQ%3Aa%3A80294823-
8055665ad6%2Fbuzzfeednews.com

350 Molly Hensley et al., "The Truth Behind a Viral
Picture of a Reopening School Is Worse Than It Looked."

351 BBC News, "Coronavirus: Denmark Lets Young
Children Return to School," *BBC News*, published April 15,
2020, accessed September 16, 2020,
https://www.bbc.com/news/world-europe-52291326.

352 Ed Yong, "Our Pandemic Summer," *The Atlantic*, published April 15, 2020, accessed June 24, 2020, https://www.theatlantic.com/health/archive/2020/04/pandemic-summer-coronavirus-reopening-back-normal/609940/.

353 Emma Reynolds, "Some Anti-vaxxers Are Changing Their Minds Because of the Coronavirus Pandemic," *CNN*, published April 20, 2020, accessed June 24, 2020, https://www.cnn.com/2020/04/20/health/anti-vaxxers-coronavirus-intl/index.html.

354 Jacqueline Howard, "A Herd Immunity Strategy to Fight the Pandemic Can Be 'Dangerous,' Experts Say. Here's Why." *CNN*, published October 17, 2020, accessed October 20, 2020, https://www.cnn.com/2020/09/01/health/herd-immunity-coronavirus-pandemic-explainer-wellness/index.html.

355 Lauren Mascarenhas et al., "ER Doctor Says 2 Million Americans Could Die in Effort to Achieve COVID-19 Herd Immunity," *CNN*, published August 31, 2020, accessed September 16, 2020, https://www.cnn.com/world/live-news/coronavirus-pandemic-08-31-20-intl/h_0b3e81bf22ad9cc7b9d1aaf21c38b046.

356 CNN Wire, "Fauci Says COVID-19 Vaccine Unlikely to Bring Sufficient Herd Immunity," *CNN Wire*, updated June 28, 2020, accessed July 19, 2020,

https://ktla.com/news/nationworld/fauci-says-covid-19-vaccine-unlikely-to-bring-sufficient-herd-immunity-with-many-americans-saying-they-wont-get-vaccinated/'.

357 Abdi Latif Dahir, "Instead of Coronavirus, the Hunger Will Kill Us. A Global Food Crisis Looms," CN New York Times, published April 23, 2020, accessed June 24, 2020, https://cn.nytimes.com/world/20200423/coronavirus-hunger-crisis/en-us/.

358 Ian Bogost, "The Supermarket after the Pandemic," The Atlantic, published April 17, 2020, accessed June 24, 2020, https://www.theatlantic.com/technology/archive/2020/04/how-youll-shop-for-groceries-after-the-pandemic/ 610135/.

359 Ian Bogost, "The Supermarket after the Pandemic".

360 Eric Rosen, "Will Travel Change after Coronavirus? Here's What Experts Have to Say," Travel and Leisure, published April 18, 2020, accessed June 24, 2020, https://www.travelandleisure.com/travel-tips/travel-trends/traveling-after-coronavirus.

361 Sully Barrett, "11% of CEOs Fear Their Business Won't Survive Coronavirus: YPO Survey," CNBC, published April 22, 2020, accessed June 24, 2020,

https://www.cnbc.com/2020/04/22/11percent-of-ceos-fear-their-business- wont-survive-coronavirus-ypo-survey.html.

362 VOX Staff, "The Legacy of the Pandemic: 11 Ways It Will Change the Way We Live."

363 Lindsey Ellefson, "CNN's Dr. Sanjay Gupta Calls Dr. Fauci's Low Profile a 'Loss for the Country,'" *The Wrap*, aired June 16, 2020, accessed September 17, 2020, https://www.thewrap.com/cnn-gupta-fauci/.

364 Joe Pinsker, "The Pandemic Has Created a Class of Super-Savers," *The Atlantic*, published September 3, 2020, accessed September 3, 2020, https://www.theatlantic.com/family/archive/2020/09/saving-money-pandemic/615949/.

365 Ann Bahney, "Evictions are halted: Here's what you need to know," *CNN Business*, published September 2, 2020, accessed September 3, 2020, https://www.cnn.com/2020/09/02/success/cdc-control-eviction-moratorium/index.html.

366 Aaron Cooper et al., "Many New Yorkers May Be Leaving. But Reports of the City's Demise Are Greatly Exaggerated," *CNN*, published August 24, 2020, accessed September 14, 2020,

https://www.cnn.com/2020/08/24/us/nyc-coronavirus-crime-leaving-new-york/index.html.

367 Derek Thompson, "Get Ready for the Great Urban Comeback, Visionary Responses to Catastrophes Have Changed City Life for the Better," *The Atlantic*, published October 2020, accessed September 5, 2020, https://www.theatlantic.com/magazine/archive/2020/10/how-disaster-shaped-the-modern-city/615484/.

368 Valerie Richardson, "Greta Thunberg Compares Coronavirus to Global Warming: 'We Need to Tackle Two Crises at Once,'" *Washington Times*, published April 22, 2020, accessed June 24, 2020, https://www.washingtontimes.com/news/2020/apr/22/greta-thunberg-compares-coronavirus-global-warming/.

369 Jessie Yeung, "The World Set a 2020 Deadline to Save Nature but Not a Single Target Was Met, UN Report Says," CNN World, published September 16, 2020 accessed September 18, 2020, https://www.cnn.com/2020/09/16/world/un-biodiversity-report-intl-hnk-scli-scn/index.html.

370 Rebecca Wright, "There's an Unlikely Beneficiary of the Coronavirus: The Planet," CNN, published March 17, 2020, accessed June 24, 2020,

https://www.cnn.com/2020/03/16/asia/china-pollution-coronavirus-hnk-intl/ index.html.

[371] Shayla Love, "You'll Probably Forget What It Was Like to Live Through a Pandemic," Vice, published April 21, 2020, accessed June 24, 2020, https://www.vice.com/en_us/article/5dmxvn/what-will-we-remember-from-the- coronavirus-covid19-pandemic.

[372] Shayla Love, "What Will We Remember from the Coronavirus Pandemic?"

[373] Derek Thompson, "Get Ready for the Great Urban Comeback, Visionary Responses to Catastrophes Have Changed City Life for the Better."

[374] Mahatma Gandhi, "Carefully watch your thoughts…," *AZ Quotes*, updated 2020, accessed September 17, 2020, https://www.azquotes.com/quote/453692#:~:text=Mahatma%20Gandhi.

About the Author

Dr. Patel's family's journey and her personal experiences from India to Africa to the United Kingdom transformed her into a global citizen. She came to live in America at the age of 26 years, at which time she embraced being an American. She has been passionate about the basic tenets of personal responsibility, respect and integrity of oneself and neighbor, community spirit and participation, a just and fair work environment, the institution of government for all people, and a final exit at the end of life, leaving behind a positive legacy.

As a licensed, practicing psychiatrist with over 25 years of experience working with both children and adults, her area of expertise focused on her patients' acceptance of their trauma and with her assistance and ability to enable them to heal and restore their well-being. She believes in strong relationships, be it with yourself, your partner, children, parents, or friends. Because of her training, she hopes to provide guidance about healthy male/female relationships and parenting issues.

She feels it is imperative for all Americans to recognize societal ills, take responsibility for healing themselves and change the destiny of American life for future generations.

Dr. Shila Patel, M.D.

Note from the Author

When I first started writing this book, I was mainly interested in exploring the ramifications of the #MeToo Movement and the impact of school shootings in the United States. These topics dominated the media in 2018. As time passed, I felt compelled to write about other societal issues. After finishing the book, it included so much information that I needed to divide the book into two parts: the first, exploring relationships as a couple or a family unit. The second, examining societal issues and the all-encompassing Covid-19 pandemic of 2020.

At the present time, I am contemplating a third book based on the fracture of American society beginning with the events of January 6th, 2021, the rioting and insurrection at the Capital Building in Washington D.C., and loss of freedom for women in what they can and cannot do with their own bodies. Multiple issues involving the vaccinated and the unvaccinated citizens of the US, ramifications for the children and the mental health of all involved, needs to be explored, analyzed, and understood. We are in the throes of a cultural collapse of our society. Self-destructive behavior, irrational thinking, and general mistrust of all authoritative figures have infiltrated every facet of our daily lives. It is only with an in-depth analysis and discussion of these issues that we can restore our beliefs in what it means to be an American living in the United States of America.

Word-of-mouth is crucial for any author to succeed. If you enjoyed reading Us Unhinged, please leave a review on the webpage or email at usunhinged@gmail.com. Your comments will be very much appreciated.

Thank you!

Dr. Shila Patel, M.D.

CPSIA information can be obtained
at www.ICGtesting.com
Printed in the USA
BVHW081216231121
622341BV00005B/37

9 781737 784951